THE PHILOSOPHERS' QUARREL

THE
PHILOSOPHERS'
QUARREL

*Rousseau, Hume,
and the Limits of Human
Understanding*

ROBERT ZARETSKY
JOHN T. SCOTT

YALE UNIVERSITY PRESS/NEW HAVEN & LONDON

Set in Fournier type by Integrated Publishing Solutions, Grand Rapids, Michigan.
Printed in the United States of America by Sheridan Books, Ann Arbor, Michigan.

Library of Congress Cataloging-in-Publication Data
Zaretsky, Robert, 1955–
The philosophers' quarrel : Rousseau, Hume, and the limits of human understanding /
Robert Zaretsky, John T. Scott.
p.   cm.
Includes bibliographical references (p.   ) and index.
ISBN 978-0-300-12193-3 (cloth : alk. paper)   1. Rousseau, Jean-Jacques, 1712–1778.
2. Hume, David, 1711–1776.   3. Enlightenment.   I. Scott, John T., 1963–.   II. Title.
B2137.Z37 2009
192—dc22
[B]   2008025224

A catalogue record for this book is available from the British Library.

This paper meets the requirements of
ANSI/NISO Z39.48-1992 (Permanence of Paper).

It contains 30 percent postconsumer waste (PCW) and is
certified by the Forest Stewardship Council (FSC).

10   9   8   7   6   5   4   3   2   1

For Julie and Adrienne

It is often revealing to ask of a philosopher,
"What is he afraid of?"
— Iris Murdoch

Contents

CONTENTS

Acknowledgments

Over the years we have profited from the patience, insights, and encouragement of numerous friends and colleagues: Michael Barnes, John Bernard, Mark Cambron, Malcolm Crook, Bob Duplessis, Sarah Fishman, Hildegard Glass, Dena Goodman, Patricia Hampl, Ryan Hanley, Christine Dunn Henderson, Christopher Kelly, John Lienhard, Alane Salierno Mason, Roger Masters, Michael Moore, Ourida Mostefai, Peter Potter, Willard Spiegelman, Walt Stone, Sandy Thatcher, Tzvetan Todorov, Mark Yellin, Karine Zbinden, and Judith Zinsser. We also thank John Antel, dean of the College of Liberal Arts and Social Sciences at the University of Houston, for his generous financial support. We would also like to thank our editor, Ileene Smith, for her enthusiasm and intelligent criticism; Dan Heaton, for his exceptional work editing our manuscript; and our agent, Marly Rusoff, for her support and encouragement. Finally, we would like to acknowledge the research assistance provided by John Warner.

Part of Chapter 8 appeared in different form as "Philosophy Leads to Sorrow: An Evening at the Drury Lane Theatre with Jean-Jacques Rousseau and

David Hume" in *Southwest Review* 91 (2006): 36 – 55; we thank the publisher for permission to adapt this material.

A particular debt of gratitude is owed to Ted Estess, the dean emeritus of the Honors College at the University of Houston. Beyond the simple fact that Ted brought us both into his faculty and provided the ground in which the seeds of this project germinated, he has selflessly given us his care, counsel, conversation, and, at critical moments, institutional support.

Finally, our love and gratitude go to our wives, Julie Zaretsky and Adrienne Scott. They have lived for several years under the shadow of this project: were it not for their love, encouragement, and patience, it would never have seen the light of day. We dedicate this book to them.

All translations are the authors' unless otherwise noted.

THE PHILOSOPHERS' QUARREL

An Enlightenment Quarrel

I have the feeling that philosophy leads to sorrow.
—Jean-Jacques Rousseau to Mme d'Épinay

Since reason is incapable of dispelling these clouds, nature herself suffices to
that purpose and cures me of this philosophical melancholy and delirium.
—David Hume, A Treatise of Human Nature

M arch 18, 1766, was meant to be the day for thanks and farewells between Europe's two most celebrated philosophers. Jean-Jacques Rousseau was set to leave London, with his companion Thérèse Le Vasseur, for Wootton Hall, an estate deep in north England. David Hume had arranged for this asylum, as he had most everything since he had accompanied Rousseau from France to England more than two months before, when Hume had first come to Rousseau's rescue. Though he had never before met the Swiss thinker and novelist, Hume had been moved by his plight: Rousseau's writings had been burned and his life threatened in his adopted France as well as his native Geneva. As a cosmopolitan freethinker in Calvinist Scotland and a Scottish Tory in Whiggish and xenophobic London, Hume had learned to sympathize with the persecuted. Learning of Rousseau's predicament, he had employed his considerable reputation and energy to resolve it.

Yet thanks, if not farewells, seemed the last thing on Rousseau's mind when he entered Hume's drawing room. Wearing his usual flowing Armenian caftan and tall fur cap, the Genevan turned on his host, blasting Hume for treating him like a child. Rousseau announced his discovery that the coach he and Thérèse were boarding the following day for Wootton Hall was offered under false pretenses. With Hume's acquiescence, Rousseau's patron and the owner of Wootton Hall, Richard Davenport, had paid for the chaise and, to spare the philosopher's abundant sensibilities and his meager pocketbook, had told the philosopher that a happy convergence of events meant that only a nominal fare would be charged.

This subterfuge, undertaken with the best of intentions, unleashed furies. While he might be poor, Rousseau told Hume that he preferred "to conform to his circumstances than live like a beggar on alms." Overwhelmed by the ferocity of his friend's attack, Hume, his round and fleshy face gone white, insisted upon his innocence — in vain. No less vain were his efforts to engage his friend in conversation. Rousseau gave curt replies, each time falling back into brooding silence.

This uneasy scene had lasted nearly an hour when, without warning, Rousseau leaped onto Hume's lap, threw his hands around his huge neck, and covered his face with tears and kisses. "Is it possible you can ever forgive me, my dear friend?" cried Rousseau. "After all the testimonies of affection I have received from you, I reward you at last with this folly and ill behavior. But I have notwithstanding a heart worthy of your friendship. I love you, I esteem you; and not an instance of your kindness is thrown away upon me."

Hume unraveled under this deluge of affection. As his friend clasped his neck, Hume too began to weep. Patting the folds of dark brown silk hanging limply along the man's back, Hume reassured Rousseau of his love and friendship. As Hume later confessed to a friend, "I think no scene of my life was ever more affecting."[1]

And perhaps no scene in Hume's life had ever been more drastically misunderstood. After Rousseau left for Wootton Hall the next day, he and Hume would never again see each other. Within a matter of weeks, their friendship dissolved into a passionate quarrel, played out in salvos of impassioned and recriminatory letters and pamphlets. The correspondence was quickly translated into French and English, becoming a subject of intense conversation and argument on both sides of the Channel. Europe's traditional aristocracy, and even more so the rising aristocracy of intelligence that formed the Continent's "Republic of Letters," were riveted by the feud, taking sides with a degree of conviction that the era's dynastic wars could not command. As Hume himself ruefully noted, the rise and fall of his friendship with Rousseau had made "so great a noise."

The sheer fascination with calamities partly explains the public fixation with the noisy row between Hume and Rousseau. Although of a different order of magnitude, just a decade earlier the 1755 Lisbon earthquake thus riveted the attention of Europeans. This was to be expected of a catastrophe that involved tidal waves, great fissures, raging fires, cinder-darkened skies, and vast carnage—all in a major capital of western Europe. Morbid curiosity was not the only reason for the unprecedented preoccupation with Lisbon, however. After all, there had always been earthquakes, but until Lisbon the tremors did not outrage human understanding. As Susan Neiman argues, earlier disasters—even a scant fifty years before, when an earthquake leveled Port Royal, Jamaica—failed to spark attention largely because they did not upset the moral or conceptual order of Western man. The European worldview was still rooted in a Christian understanding of Providence, whether citing God's mysterious ways or conceiving the order of the universe as having been set in motion by a clockmaker deity. But subsequent changes, especially in the intellectual terrain, made for a perfect philosophical storm after Lisbon. The event spurred a raft of essays, poems, pamphlets, and books, including an exchange between Rousseau and Voltaire and an appearance in *Candide*. All of these works raised questions concerning God's goodness and power, and, no less important, the fundamental intelligibility of the world and the human situation. As Neiman notes, the idea that the world and life "were not mysterious was a demand of reason embodied in natural religion as in other eighteenth century discoveries."[2]

Although it left no decaying bodies or demolished buildings in its wake, the Hume-Rousseau affair, like Lisbon, heaved critical questions to the surface of the intellectual world. Most particularly, the rift between these remarkable men posed the problem of understanding others and our own selves. Both Hume and Rousseau had devoted their lives to contributing to the great Enlightenment project of human understanding and, at the same time, challenging it. And yet not only did they come away with very different versions of what took place that evening at Hume's lodgings: it also became painfully clear that, from the outset, they never fully understood each other, or themselves.

The nature and response to the Hume-Rousseau affair, as with the aftermath of Lisbon, make sense only when set in the Enlightenment. Yet, as a theoretical concept and historical era, the Enlightenment has long meant different things to different scholars. For some the Enlightenment captures all that is good and great about the ideas and ideals of a liberal and liberating eighteenth century. Peter Gay memorably described the Enlightenment as the "recovery of nerve," led by heroic thinkers committed to the progress of humankind through the application of critical reason. For others, however, the Enlightenment exposes all that is wrong and tragic about the idols and ideologies of an illiberal and repressive West. From the Frankfurt theorists Theodor Adorno and Max Horkheimer to postmodern critics like Michel Foucault, the absolutist emphasis on reason by Enlightenment thinkers enabled rather than challenged the hierarchical and despotic character of society and politics in Old Regime Europe. The Enlightenment, for these critics, has been a nightmare of reason from which the West has never awakened.[3]

For yet others, the old notion of a single, pan-European Enlightenment reduces the complexity of its history—or, more accurately, its histories. A growing number of historians have argued that there were, in fact, several national Enlightenments, ranging from the French and German to the British and Scottish, distinguished from one another by various political, social, and cultural traits. Moreover, others have identified different Enlightenments within a single country. Robert Darnton has portrayed the difficult relationship between High and Low Enlightenments in eighteenth-century France, while, most recently, Jonathan Israel has claimed that a "radical Enlightenment" led by Benedict Spinoza and Pierre Bayle in the Dutch Republic preceded the better-known, less original High Enlightenment of Montesquieu and Voltaire.[4] In the end, there will almost certainly never be a unified field theory of the Enlightenment. But this is not a reason for disposing of the term: it is, in every sense of the phrase, easier to live with the Enlightenment than without it. As a social, philosophical, and political legacy for all who followed, as a heuristic concept for the scholars who study it, the Enlightenment is indispensible.

As with any historical caption, *the Age of Reason* hides as much as it reveals. Certainly, enlightened men and women of the eighteenth century began to question and ultimately reject the received truths of religion and faith, church, and traditional authorities. Dissatisfied with such constraints, they turned to critical reason to realize our potential as human beings. Historians have long noted that this generation of thinkers largely distrusted overly ambitious claims for reason that they associated with seventeenth-century systematic thinkers like Descartes and Leibniz. For this new and more skeptical generation, reason divorced from experience, doubt, and experiment was as useless as church dogma in making sense of our world and our own selves. Skeptics embraced the conviction that only scientific method could penetrate the secrets of nature and lead, as the English philosopher Francis Bacon wrote in *The New Atlantis,* to "the effecting of all things possible."[5]

Nevertheless, many leading figures of this movement insisted upon the great and good offices provided by scientific method and inductive reasoning. Despite doubts and hesitations, there was a widespread belief among the philosophes—the name given to the men and women, less original thinkers than brilliant pamphleteers and conversationalists, who identified with this intellectual movement—in the liberating power of reason. The declaration made by the Baron d'Holbach, who will play a critical role in our story, is telling:

> Despite all the efforts of tyranny, despite the violence and trickery of the priesthood, despite the vigilant efforts of all the enemies of mankind, the human race will attain enlightenment; nations will know their true interests; a multitude of rays, assembled, will form one day a boundless mass of light that will warm all hearts, that will illuminate all minds.[6]

Perhaps the most famous expression of this faith in reason is the Marquis de Condorcet's *Sketch for a Historical Picture of the Human Mind.* In this credo, Condorcet declares that human reason and established fact reveal "that nature has set no term to the perfection of human faculties; that the perfectibility of man is truly indefinite; and that the progress of this perfectibility, from now onwards independent of any power that might wish to halt it, has no other limit than the duration of the globe upon which nature has cast us."[7] Condorcet wrote these words while in hiding from the revolutionary Terror that would eventually claim his life—testimony to his faith in reason, and, tragically, to his blindness to reason's excesses in the course of the Revolution.

In this book we engage many of the historical and conceptual debates surrounding the Enlightenment, but we shall not try to answer them. The book is less about the Enlightenment than about a puzzling series of events that occurred within the Enlightenment. We tell the story of the brief and dramatic friendship between Hume and Rousseau, and point to the implications it may have for the Enlightenment's conception of human reason and understanding. In order to do so, we contextualize their thought within their own lives and the world they inhabited. We do so not on the assumption that their personalities and their time determined their thought, but in keeping with how they themselves saw philosophy: as a way of life and as a form of action in the world. The rise and fall of the friendship between Rousseau and Hume, then, was a particularly dramatic, and we think revealing, example of a collision between two individuals who struggled to understand themselves, each other, and the world they inhabited together.

It was in their attitudes toward reason, the Enlightenment's key article of faith, that Hume and Rousseau, opposites in so many other ways, became odd bedfellows. With calm and deliberation, the Scot blasted our deepest convictions concerning the reasonability of trusting in reason: though we pretend that reason rules our lives, he declared, habit and passion instead inevitably hold sway. Even for the happy few ruled by the "empire of philosophy," the reach of reason "is very weak and limited." Ultimately, reason was "the slave of our passions" — a state of affairs, paradoxically, Hume welcomed rather than regretted. As for Rousseau, reason did not even merit this reduced station. Not merely weaker than the passions, reason actually made moral, social, and individual matters worse. While Hume conceded that reason was strong enough to know its limitations, Rousseau identified reason as the disease for which it pretended to be the cure.

The two philosophers took very different consequences from their critiques of reason: Hume championed the progress of the sciences and arts (though with more modest expectations than those of his contemporaries), while Rousseau questioned progress, wondering whether it was just another word for moral decay and despair. Both men, nevertheless, were and remain our most important critics of reason. The grounds for their claims against reason are complex — neither man, we will see, was an irrationalist, much less a mystic. On the contrary, their critiques of reason are models of logic and lucidity. In this regard, their relevance for our own age is clear: religious fanatics and philosophical reactionaries hounded Hume and Rousseau throughout their lives. Both men, moreover, detested the hypocrisies and hubris of the political classes, just as they decried the ways in which greed and injustice were gussied up in noble sentiments.

No less important, the ways in which these two men lived their lives — and conducted their ill-fated friendship — pose the question of the relationship between ideas and life, thinking and living. Philosophy nowadays seems to be a profession, not a discipline. Academic philosophers write on the history of philosophy or work in analytic philosophy. But as for proposing a worldview — a coherent system by which we can understand the world and our place in it — and a reworking of our selves: this is no longer common.

Philosophy has too commonly become an occupation, where "doing" philosophy is no different from "doing" physics or psychology, literature or statistics. The contrarian historian of ancient philosophy Pierre Hadot worries that philosophy in our age has become the activity of bureaucrats, whose great task is to reproduce themselves: "to form other bureaucrats, rather than form man."[8] He has argued that ancient philosophy was not simply a theoretical discourse but also an art of living, a method for aligning our lives with our thought. Alexander Nehamas writes in a similar vein. The ancients, he declares, were onto critical matters that we have lost sight of in our age of hyperspecialization. "Theory and practice, discourse and life, affect one another," he writes, "and people become philosophers because they are able and willing to be the best human type and to live as well as a human being possibly can. What one believes and how one lives have a direct bearing on one another."[9] Our sensibilities are attuned to these worries about how philosophy seems to have fallen, for we are shocked when we learn that a philosopher can give aid and comfort to totalitarian regimes. In the end, we are shocked that philosophers are as thoughtless as the rest of us.

While the stance that philosophy is a way of life is usually associated with antiquity, this view remained alive and well during the Enlightenment. During the eighteenth century this view was, in a sense, resurrected as men and women came to expect great things of philosophers, with faith that they would make sense of our lives. Herein lies part of the tremendous appeal of Rousseau and Hume. The fascination that their lives, and not merely their thought, exercised on contemporaries carries across the centuries. We are historically bound and intellectually indebted to both men, and it may not be too naïve to believe that the unintended lessons of their work and lives, no less than the intended, still have something to teach us.

The Wild Philosopher

I'm cold, I'm sad, I can hardly piss.
—*Jean-Jacques Rousseau to Marc-Michel Rey*

T he peaks of the Swiss Jura were sheathed in snow, but the road bordering the eastern foothills was bare and hard. Among its travelers early on the morning of December 3, 1764, was a young Scot, James Boswell.

Boswell had set out from the town of Neuchâtel, cradled between the frozen sliver of lake that took its name from the city and the mountains rising behind it. As his horse's hooves echoed against the frozen ground of the high mountain valley called the Val de Travers, the twenty-four-year-old heir of an ancient Scottish family whistled a brisk French tune. Boswell was indifferent to the cold, however, for, as he wrote in his journal that evening, a "great object" crowded his mind.[1]

That "great object" was Jean-Jacques Rousseau.

Boswell had long nurtured ambitions for his anticipated meeting; while still a university student in Edinburgh, he had climbed with his friend William Temple to Arthur's Seat, the bluff overlooking the citadel, and shouted: "Voltaire! Rousseau! Immortal names!"[2] That Dr. Samuel Johnson considered Rousseau to be "a very bad man" amused more than bothered his young admirer. Prodding the irascible old political and religious conservative, Boswell asked Johnson whether Rousseau was as bad as Voltaire. His reply did not disappoint: "Why, Sir, it is difficult to settle the proportion of iniquity between them."[3]

Boswell had set out nearly two and a half years earlier on a grand tour of the Continent. A brilliant and obsessive reporter of the words of others, he had been advised by Dr. Johnson to keep a "fair and undisguised" account of his meetings and experiences. These pages, which served as the basis for his landmark *Life of Johnson*, provide equally rich material on the lives of many other literary figures of his day, including Rousseau, Hume, and Voltaire. Happily for us, Boswell's encounters with these men happened to occur just as our story was unfolding, and his descriptions provide an unparalleled firsthand introduction to the participants in the quarrel.

Boswell stopped for lunch at a village inn near Môtiers, the hamlet in which Rousseau lived. While pouring his wine, the innkeeper's daughter, Mlle Sandoz, regaled the visitor with tales of the local recluse. She spoke with the proprietary air of someone living near a natural wonder—a waterfall, say, or a volcano. "He's a very amiable man with a fine face. But he doesn't like to have people come and stare at him as if he were a man with two heads. Heavens! The curiosity of people is incredible." Pointing out the window to a mountain pass suspended above the village, the vivacious woman proudly described hiking with Rousseau and his companion Mlle Le Vasseur. An exceptional experience, Mlle Sandoz added, given his love of solitude: "He walks in such wild places for an entire day." As Boswell was settling his bill, she warned him that though many came to see Rousseau, few met him. "He's ill and doesn't wish to be disturbed." Still, Boswell remained resolute. After all, the reason for this journey was quite simply to "disturb" Rousseau.

When he first glimpsed Môtiers, a clump of low granite houses, Boswell began to hum with "a kind of pleasing trepidation." Môtiers was a village of about four hundred souls, many of whom were the sort of independent artisans, such as watchmakers and laceworkers, Rousseau had idealized in his writings. Distillers of absinthe formed another local guild, brewing the drink that by the following century would come to symbolize the corrosive core of urban life. Yet another shadow cast across this idyllic scene was the local asphalt mine, a harbinger of the industrial era anticipated and feared by Rousseau.

As he turned down the village's main street, Boswell passed a small Calvinist church whose spirit if not style recalled the austere church in his native Auchinleck. Suddenly uneasy, the young Scot took a room at the local inn, the

Maison de Village, in order to settle upon a method for meeting Rousseau. Sitting before the fire in the main room of the inn, he composed a letter of introduction. A few hours later, Boswell leaned back and pronounced his epistle "a masterpiece."

The letter, faithfully recopied by Boswell into his journal, presents the bare facts of his life and then becomes a paean to Rousseau's writings, which, he announced, melted his heart, elevated his soul, and fired his imagination. The feverish Scot went on to attribute to Rousseau a "perfect knowledge of all the principles of body and mind, of their movements, their sentiments; in short, of everything they can do, of everything they can acquire which truly affects man as man." Boswell therefore declared to Rousseau that he "was ready to stand the test of your penetration." With a flourish, he concluded his missive: "Open your door, then, Sir, to a man who dares to tell you that he deserves to enter it."

Boswell's urgency to meet Jean-Jacques Rousseau was not unusual. By the mid-1760s, Rousseau's life was no longer his own. The wandering philosopher, who so valued his independence, had become the cherished property of his readers. Even those who had not read him insisted on making his acquaintance. He complained endlessly about men and women who "traveled some thirty, forty, sixty, or even a hundred leagues to come and see, and to admire, the illustrious, the famous, the very famous, the great man, etc."[4] Môtiers risked becoming the Swiss Delphi. From the moment Rousseau moved there two and a half years earlier, fleeing Paris and the order for his arrest for subversive writings, the narrow path to the secluded village had been swollen with a constant traffic of pilgrims intent on visiting Europe's most public recluse.

While some made the difficult trip to Môtiers in order to meet the scourge of social and political institutions, most had another motivation. Today Rousseau is best known as a political theorist, as the author of the two *Discourses* and the *Social Contract*, but for his contemporaries he was first and foremost the creator of *Julie; or, the New Heloise*. This was clearly the case for Boswell, who underscored in his letter of introduction that he needed "the counsel of the author of *La Nouvelle Héloïse*."[5] Like Boswell, Rousseau's ardent readers believed he possessed a unique capacity of self-understanding. This capacity was above all revealed in the novel that romanticized the Alpine region where Rousseau now lived. The most popular book of the eighteenth century, *Julie* went through at least seventy editions by 1800. Rousseau's epistolary novel ended his life as he had known it and taught his readers how to begin anew their own lives.

This "novel that was not a novel," as Rousseau coyly described the book in the preface, recounts the ill-fated relationship of the lovers Saint-Preux and Julie. Kept apart by different social stations, they cultivate their romance through six volumes of correspondence, ultimately reuniting and regaining their virtue under the watchful eye of Julie's husband, the mysterious Wolmar. Against the backdrop of the Alps—a fittingly sublime stage for their impossible love—the lovers are naturalists of their inner worlds, describing their emotions and feelings in their letters with the care that Rousseau devoted to the flora of his many places of exile. The correspondence ends with Julie's death, a prolonged affair during which she confesses her undying love for Saint-Preux.

Remarkably, many of Rousseau's readers believed that the letters were authentic; that his characters truly lived and died as they had loved and suffered. The novel's seeming artlessness and its epistolary character gave it the veneer of authenticity and invited readers to feel an unprecedented degree of intimacy with the characters and, no less important, the supposed editor of the correspondence, Rousseau himself. The book created an avalanche of letters, from aristocratic and bourgeois readers alike, sharing their grief and delight. The Marquise de Polignac spoke for her generation when she described her reaction to Julie's death: "A sharp pain convulsed me. My heart was crushed. Julie dying was no longer an unknown person. I believed I was her sister."[6]

Rousseau's blurring of the line between reality and fiction helps explain the mad rush of afflicted readers to Môtiers. When he warned that this "book is not meant to circulate in society, and is suitable for very few readers," he cannily guaranteed what he ostensibly sought to prevent.[7] Only naïve and impressionable readers—that is to say, readers capable of forgetting themselves—could enter this world. The book had to be read far from the hall of mirrors we call society. This was a new way of reading not just a text but oneself, requiring the reader to unlearn her history and become innocent once again. Under the influence of Rousseau's love of mountains, travelers no longer avoided precipices or shut their eyes when crossing gorges. On the contrary, mountains became the goal, not the obstacle, of one's journey. These towering ruins lent themselves to majesty rather than despair; vertigo was proof of virtue. Encompassed by bristling peaks and blinding glaciers, readers would be restored to themselves. "I am in a beautiful, wild valley surrounded by immense mountains," Boswell wrote from Môtiers: "I am supremely happy."[8] Boswell was soon to learn that Rousseau, the guide to this world largely of his own making, could not say the same of himself.

Môtiers was not far from Geneva, Rousseau's native city. He had left that city some thirty-five years earlier, at sixteen years of age, never really to return. The great distances subsequently covered by the philosopher were no less physical peregrinations than journeys of the mind and the imagination. When Boswell visited him in late 1764, Rousseau had just started his account of these voyages in his autobiographical work the *Confessions,* a task that would occupy him throughout his stay in England.

Writing at the urging of his publisher, who anticipated strong sales, Rousseau transformed the traditional form of the memoir. He launched the autobiography as one of the supreme forms of literary genre fusion, incorporating self-analysis, self-justification, and self-celebration. Rousseau took as his model St. Augustine's *Confessions,* but he set the Bishop of Hippo on his head. Whereas Augustine's work used the story of his own conversion as proof of the need for divine assistance to overcome original sin, Rousseau offered the story of his life as proof that such aid was unnecessary since original sin did not exist. Instead, man is naturally good but is made evil by society. While Augustine appeals to God for the self-knowledge he cannot attain by himself, Rousseau proclaims at the beginning of his *Confessions:* "Here is the only portrait of a man, painted exactly according to nature and in all its truth, that exists and that will probably ever exist." He imagines himself standing at the last judgment before God and all of humankind, unveiling his innermost self as only he—Jean-Jacques Rousseau—is able to do, and daring anyone to say "I was better than that man."[9]

In his *Confessions,* Rousseau traced to his earliest experiences the knack for self-invention that allowed him to escape his dissatisfaction with the world. He explained that his imagination had been overheated from reading romantic novels, an inheritance from a mother who died giving him birth, and the ancient Greek and Roman authors he read with a father who would soon abandon his son to relatives and then artisans. The lovers and heroes that peopled his mind set too high a standard for reality. For the rest of Rousseau's life, his fellow men and women would invariably fall short of the ideals inspired by these writers. "In my youth," he recalled much later, "since I believed I found in the world the same people I had known in my books, I was always looking for what did not exist. In becoming more experienced, little by little I lost the hope of finding it."[10]

Among the people who disappointed the young Rousseau was his father, in whom the ancient moralists had failed to inspire the same love of virtue that burned in the son. Despite Rousseau's later depiction of Isaac Rousseau as a lover of Geneva, the elder Rousseau was in fact a truant patriot, whose absences included a six-year stay in Constantinople soon after Rousseau's elder brother, François, was born. Returning from the east, Isaac promptly fathered the future philosopher, lost his wife, and pursued his craft. The irascible watchmaker was almost as restless as his son, however, and after challenging a local patrician to a duel and then fleeing rather than stand trial, he fobbed off the ten-year-old Jean-Jacques onto relatives. Soon after, the boy was packed off with his cousin to the village of Bossey, at the foot of the French Alps, where they boarded with the local minister, M. Lambercier, and his sister. It was here that Rousseau discovered Eden, only to be banished from it soon after.[11]

Paradise regained was nature, which he found in the simplicity of life in the region surrounding Bossey. What he found in nature was himself—or, more precisely, the loss of self, a paradox that lies at the heart of Rousseau's thought. Running through the Alpine valleys and pastures, he shed the layers of social passions, pretenses, and concerns that, he believed, masked our original nature by settling like dust on a statue. These youthful experiences bordered on rapture in which the self and the world became a seamless unity. Late in life he told a visitor that when walking in the Alps he always let himself go to find himself. "If I slip in the mountains I just slide on my behind and I reach the bottom without the least harm. Such is the philosophy of children, and I've made it my own."[12]

But children devise philosophies only after they are thrust into adulthood. Two years after his arrival at Bossey, Rousseau fell from his state of innocence. One day Mlle Lambercier discovered that one of her combs had been broken and suspicion immediately fell upon Jean-Jacques. Despite his heartfelt denials, the Lamberciers, who had always been kind and considerate, held fast to their conviction that the child was lying. "Superior force itself had to yield in the end before the diabolical obstinacy of a child," Rousseau recalled, "for this was how my steadfastness was perceived."[13]

As with Augustine's celebrated account of stealing a neighbor's pears when he was a child, the seemingly trivial story of the broken comb assumes great significance in Rousseau's self-understanding. Though the bruises left by the caning healed, a deeper wound scarred Rousseau's world. The countryside itself now seemed to change. Dimmed and gloomy, "it had become as though covered with a veil, which obscured for us its beauties." Everything seemed the same, but in fact had become a lesser and sadder order of things. The transparency of childhood gave way to the uneasiness of adulthood. Try as he might, he had not been able to convey the truth of things to the Lamberciers: he was, he bitterly reflected, condemned by appearances. A half-century later, Rousseau still stands in horror at this moment. "While writing this I feel my pulse beat faster again; these moments will always be present to me if I live a hundred thousand years."[14] The child, in short, was flung from paradise. Like Augustine before him, Rousseau reenacts the biblical Fall in this story, but with a critical difference: he was innocent. As Rousseau's spiritual descendent William Wordsworth wrote, the world's trees, fields, and flowers "speak of something that is gone." Such a vision haunts Rousseau's writings and life.

The young Rousseau returned to Geneva soon after. The boy who had fancied himself as a lover or ancient patriot found himself cast, at his father's behest, in the far less romantic role of an engraver's apprentice. Toiling in a work-shop overseen by a short-tempered artisan, the author who would condemn the chains of society that destroy our natural freedom got his first taste of the cor-rupting effects of servitude.

Rousseau escaped his workaday life only on Sundays, when he would walk in the hills surrounding Geneva. For the son of a watchmaker, he was remark-ably indifferent to time. One day he found himself outside of the town walls when he heard the bugle and drums signaling that the gates would soon be closed. As the music rolled through the hills, he ran back toward the city. "I dou-bled my pace; I heard the drum beat, I ran up as fast as my legs could take me: I arrived out of breath, bathed in sweat: my heart was pounding . . . but it was too late." Throwing himself down on the riverbank as he watched the drawbridge rise, Rousseau made his fateful decision. He turned his back on his master and on Geneva, and set off for the castles in Spain his imagination had constructed.[15]

Jean-Jacques Rousseau thus became an exile, a condition he never escaped and a theme he would always pursue through his fiction and philosophy. He wandered across the Swiss border into the independent kingdom of Savoy, which included the Alpine region of what is now southeastern France. He had also crossed a re-ligious frontier as he now found himself among Catholics. To gain, if not heaven, a meal and a bed, he promptly converted to the Roman faith. His choice did not have great consequences for his religious convictions: Rousseau eventu-ally returned to Protestantism (though in a form scarcely recognizable to his fel-low Calvinists). Yet as he later wrote, this "epoch of life determined my charac-ter," if only because it led him to one of his most fateful encounters.[16]

The Catholic novitiate was directed to the town of Annecy, where, he was told, lived a charitable woman. Expecting a "very sullen devout old woman," he took his time, dawdling in the towns along the way, stopping to sing beneath the windows of promising houses, expecting the fair damsels of his mother's novels to appear. Finally arriving in the prosperous town that bordered a picturesque lake high in the mountains, he sought out his sponsor. It was Palm Sunday 1728 when he first saw her, an unexpectedly charming woman of twenty-eight. "Nothing escaped the rapid glance of the young proselyte," he later related, "for I became hers at that moment; certain that a religion preached by such mission-aries could not fail to lead to paradise." As for his sponsor, when she first set eyes on the thin, awkward Genevan nearly twelve years her junior, she exclaimed, "Ah! my child! You are very young to be roving around the country; it is truly a shame."[17]

And so did Louise de Warens, née Louise Eleanor de la Tour de Pil, antici-pate her dual role as the mother Jean-Jacques had never known and the lover he had yet to encounter. The woman had fled her unhappy marriage to a certain M. de Warens while still quite young and had thrown herself at the feet of the very Catholic King of Savoy. Moved by her predicament as well as her beauty, he granted her a pension. Freed from her husband, Mme de Warens promptly devoted herself to various projects. At times, they involved the saving and forming of lost souls like Rousseau, at other times ill-conceived schemes to raise money in order to supplement a pension that her forgetful monarch often neglected to pay.

Rousseau lived with Mme de Warens for a decade, but first he was sent by his religious sponsors to Turin to enter a hospice for new converts. He lasted no longer there than he had with the master engraver in Geneva. Still uncertain of his vocation, Rousseau found employment as a valet, an experience that further sharpened his taste for independence. Yet what most haunted him about working as a servant was not the injustice he experienced so much as the injustice he himself committed.

Setting the scene of his crime, Rousseau relates that he was employed in the household of Mme de Vercellis, whose "philosophic" death he witnessed: "She kept to her bed only for the last two days, and did not stop conversing peaceably with everyone. Finally, no longer speaking, and already in the throes of agony, she made a big fart. 'Good,' she said, 'a woman who farts is not dead.' These were the last words she pronounced." In the subsequent confusion after her heroic death, Rousseau stole a little pink and silver ribbon with the intention of giving it to another servant, Marion. When the ribbon was discovered, rather than confessing, Rousseau claimed that Marion had given the ribbon to him. Poor Marion's surprise and innocence were no match for the young Jean-Jacques's "diabolical audacity."[18] As Jean Starobinski notes, the story of the stolen ribbon is the mirror image of the tale of the broken comb: the victim at Bossey whose protestations of innocence are not believed when appearances are against him becomes the accuser whose lies are accepted because appearances— and prejudices—are on his side.[19] Admitting his crime for the first time in the *Confessions* more than thirty years later, writing far away in the cold north of England in the midst of his quarrel with Hume, Rousseau is still haunted by "cruel remembrance" of his act.

After a little more than a year in Turin, the young wanderer returned to Annecy and Mme de Warens. But Rousseau crossed the Alps bearing another love, a passion for Italian music that he would later famously champion over the French masters Rameau and Lully. Mme de Warens encouraged his desire to become a musician and had him enrolled in a seminary. There, too, Rousseau proved resistant to the tasks at hand: "I was distracted, a dreamer, I sighed; what could I do?" In the end, he did what he habitually did in such circumstances: he left after six months, ready to ply the trade of music teacher. In his lessons there were always two pupils, one of them himself. Rousseau tried his hand at playing the composer while away in Lausanne, under an assumed name and with humiliating results when, upon hearing one of his compositions, conducted by the imposter himself with amateurish brio, the audience burst into laughter.[20] Ancient patriot, knight errant, musical maestro: the young dreamer believed he could fill each role simply by imagining himself into it.

Mme de Warens and her young charge soon determined that since they already shared a passion for independence and freedom, they might as well also share a bed. The initiative seems to have been hers. According to Rousseau, one day his patroness explained to him that "to rescue me from the perils of my youth it was time to treat me as a man." Just past twenty, he settled down as the lover of the woman he referred to affectionately—and rather disconcertingly—as Maman.* Maman soon took a small house called Les Charmettes on the outskirts of Chambéry, the capital of Savoy, situated in the mountains north of Grenoble. For the next several years, with her encouragement and support, Rousseau immersed himself in reading—history, literature, philosophy, and science. His mind blossomed in the small garden behind the house, where he would spend his days devouring books. Sometimes, as he wandered through the estate's gardens, orchards, and vineyards, he would leave behind his books, only to rediscover them weeks later, rotting on the ground or "gnawed upon by ants and snails."[21] During this period, Rousseau also continued with his music, directing Mme de Warens's beloved evenings of musical entertainment, as well as composing his own works. Unlike his earlier efforts, these compositions, mostly operas and other vocal works, were the fruit of Rousseau's careful study of musical theory and practice. Continuing to teach music, he devised a new system of musical notation that used numbers instead of the traditional staffs and notes.

In later declaring in the *Confessions* that this "epoch of life determined my character," Rousseau seems to mean that his decade-long sojourn with Maman was a kind of extended childhood. This childhood was unlike that he had experienced as a child, and it also postponed his introduction into the corrupted and corrupting world of society and adulthood. "These long details about my earliest youth will have appeared very puerile and I am sorry about it: although born a man in certain respects, I was a child for a long time and I am still one in many others."[22] With Maman's strange brand of protection, Rousseau both nursed his ambitions as an artist, scientist, and man of letters and retained the childlike innocence that, he thought, enabled him in the end to reject the world he gained.

*Women who headed a house were, however, often called Maman in this period, and Rousseau is joined by Voltaire, among others, in calling his lover by this name.

As the horizons of his mind expanded, Rousseau began to chafe against the emotional and material constraints of the provincial world he inhabited. The financial situation at Les Charmettes was precarious; Rousseau was no better at balancing books than Mme de Warens, who increasingly looked to other men for financial and emotional support. Nearly thirty years old, unhappy over Maman's wandering eye, and eager to make his name and fortune, Rousseau decided to leave Les Charmettes for Paris. In 1742, with little more than his operas and system of musical notation, he left for the intellectual and artistic capital of Europe.

Just as St. Augustine burned to leave his native Carthage for Rome, so too had Rousseau gazed longingly toward Paris. These visions of Paris quickly proved illusory. Expecting a city as "broad as it was fair," he instead found himself traversing the foul Faubourg Saint-Marcel, a district lying at the eastern edge of the city, later immortalized by Balzac in *Père Goriot* as the "grimmest quarter of Paris." Though he subsequently encountered more elegant districts, young Rousseau's initial impression of Paris would never leave him.

His first stay proved short. He managed to introduce his system of musical notation to the august Academy of Sciences, but while the learned academicians politely claimed to find merit in his approach, they refused to find the money to subsidize it. Having scarcely settled in Paris, Rousseau was forced to cast about for employment and found a position as secretary to the French ambassador to Venice. He took full advantage of the embassy's boxes at the five opera and music houses in the city, and reveled in the *barcaroles* sung by the gondoliers plying the canals. Harmony did not long endure at the embassy, however, as Rousseau and the ambassador fell to quarreling. Recognizing his private secretary's talent, the Comte de Montaigu entrusted the embassy's business to Rousseau but insisted on treating him like a servant. Once again, Rousseau proved incapable of holding a position for long. Discharged from his post after scarcely a year, he decided to walk back to Paris. He crossed the high Alps and made his way toward Geneva, reluctantly agreeing to see his father in nearby Nyon. After lukewarm embraces and an awkward visit, the thirty-two-year-old Rousseau departed, never to see his father again.

Upon returning to Paris, Rousseau recommenced his musical career and composed an opera, *Les Muses galantes*. When he finally succeeded in having it performed, he was once again greeted with humiliation rather than applause. The opera was performed at the mansion of Alexandre Jean-Joseph Le Riche de la Pouplinière, who had made his fortune as a tax farmer, one of those hired by the monarch to "harvest" the many and crippling taxes levied on his subjects. Rousseau hoped for Pouplinière's support, but it was his misfortune that Jean-Philippe Rameau was among those in the audience. Rameau was not only the age's leading theorist and composer but also a notoriously difficult man who jealously guarded the tax farmer's patronage. After the piece was performed, Rameau accused Rousseau of plagiarizing the few worthy passages that he had heard and being all too responsible for the sorry remainder. Later Rousseau admitted the justness of Rameau's critique: "This work is so mediocre in its genre, and the genre is so bad, that one must recognize the power of habit and of prejudice in order to understand how it could ever have pleased me."[23]

During the next few years, the Genevan exile eked out an existence in the Parisian equivalent of Grub Street. While his musical compositions continued to be ignored, Rousseau spent much of his time strolling through the Luxembourg Gardens reciting Virgil's bucolic odes or frequenting such cafés as the Maugis and Procope. There he played chess as he would later write: by the intuition of the autodidact rather than the formulas of the formally tutored. (In fact, Rousseau was an excellent player, good enough to be a sparring partner for Philidor, considered the best player of his century.)[24] Perhaps more important, he used his time at the cafés to enrich his store of knowledge. Rousseau devoured the journals and periodicals available to those nursing a grog or a coffee, and absorbed the conversations of his fellow denizens of the city's literary underworld.

Among the most ambitious members of this demimonde was Denis Diderot, the man who first recognized Rousseau's genius. The two men, nearly the same age, had met shortly after the Genevan arrived in Paris, and they became inseparable. The estranged son of a master cutler from Langres, the provincial Diderot subsisted as the anonymous author of philosophical essays and erotic novels. Equally subversive in different ways, both kinds of literature were given the same label, *livres philosophiques* — less a bid to make pornography respectable than an ironic ruse by publishers trying to elude French censors.[25]

Rousseau and Diderot made a study in opposites. While the Genevan was pale and hesitant, Diderot was "thickset, with a build like a sedan-chair porter," as one contemporary declared. Moreover, Diderot was extremely physical: he would constantly gesticulate in conversation, give his interlocutors a sudden embrace to celebrate their consensus, and grasp their arms and legs to drive home a point. Catherine the Great of Russia, to whom Diderot paid a visit toward the end of his life and to whom he sold his vast library, complained: "I cannot get out of my conversations with him without having my thighs bruised black and blue."[26] With his flowing blond locks and expansive personality, Diderot mesmerized everyone else who came into his orbit, including the impressionable Rousseau.

The most significant difference between the two friends, however, revealed itself in the peculiarly gladiatorial manner of French conversation. Whether over the pocked tables of the cafés or the linen tablecloths of the salons, tedious talk was the one thing never tolerated in the Paris of the philosophes. While the

gregarious Diderot was energized by the unscripted and unpredictable dialogues
he immortalized in works such as *Rameau's Nephew*, Rousseau often felt ill at
ease in this world. It was hardly the place for a man convinced that he had "never,
on the spur of the moment, said or done anything worthwhile." He had a genius
for emotion, yet ideas came slowly. "It is as though my heart and my mind belonged to different people."[27]

If Rousseau's awkwardness in society at first hid his talents, they shone in
his tête-à-têtes with Diderot, as well as in their games of chess, which Rousseau
invariably won. To this strangely matched pair of friendly rivals gravitated Jean
le Rond d'Alembert. A few years their junior, d'Alembert was already known as
a brilliant mathematician and was soon to be elected to the Académie française.
D'Alembert was the illegitimate son of the Marquise de Tencin, the imperious
ruler of the most celebrated salon of the first half of the eighteenth century, but
all he inherited from his mother was his mind; she had abandoned her infant on
the steps of the church of Saint-Jean-le-Rond in Paris (the baptistery of Notre
Dame), from which he took his name. The boy's father soon retrieved him from
the church and placed him with the wife of a glazier (coincidentally named Mme
Rousseau), with whom d'Alembert lived until he was forty-seven years old. Like
Rousseau, d'Alembert was slight of build, but his quick wit and gifts as a mimic
quickly established him in the Parisian salons.[28]

This Bohemian trio plotted to take over Paris, and while none of the literary projects they devised together came to fruition, the wide-ranging intellectual
debates proved, as Leo Damrosch notes, "an indispensable stage in Rousseau's
apprenticeship as a writer and thinker."[29] What Rousseau himself most fondly
remembered were their weekly dinners at a tavern, the Panier Fleuri, in the rue
des Augustins, not far from his rooms on the rue Saint-Denis near the Opéra.
"These little weekly dinners must have pleased Diderot extremely," recalled
Rousseau, "for he, who missed almost all of his appointments, never missed one
of these."[30] For Rousseau, this period of common cause and struggle with Diderot and d'Alembert was "the glory and happiness of my life."[31]

When, in 1747, Diderot and d'Alembert assumed the editorial control of the
Encyclopédie, they shared their good fortune by offering Rousseau the opportunity to write the articles on music. Begun as a modest venture to translate
Ephraim Chambers's *Cyclopaedia*, the *Encyclopédie* soon broadened its goal: its
editors wished to collect the known knowledge of the world and to disseminate
it, in the words of Francis Bacon, for the "relief of man's estate." In keeping
with the Baconian admonition that scientific progress was necessarily a group
effort, the editors enlisted such leading figures as Voltaire and Montesquieu to
contribute a few articles to adorn the work and also employed the labors of such
lesser-known figures as Rousseau in the campaign of enlightenment.

Spurred on by a desire for glory—and by spite at the treatment he had received from Rameau—Rousseau wrote his assigned articles at a frenetic pace.[32] In just three months during the cold winter of 1749, he completed nearly four hundred in all, from "Accolade" to "Vuide." (He learned after he completed his assignment that none of the other contributors had bothered to heed the deadline.)[33] The fruits of his labor began to appear two years later with the publication of the first volume of the *Encyclopédie*, and subscribers to the venture, including Rousseau himself, received the subsequent volumes at irregular intervals over the next fourteen years until the last text volume appeared in 1765. (Volumes of illustrations continued to appear until 1772.)

The irregularity of the *Encyclopédie*'s publication was due, in part, to its semiclandestine nature. Factions within the Bourbon court were disturbed by the project's subversive character and kept close tabs on its editors. In the summer of 1749, as the monarchy was threatened with bankruptcy and sexual scandals, the decision was made to round up the usual suspects. Along with a motley collection of religious cranks, petty criminals, and pornographers, Diderot was sent to the massive prison of Vincennes. His imprisonment lasted only three months, and during his confinement he was allowed to stroll the fortress grounds and receive visitors. Rousseau made the most famous visit to his friend, perhaps because he recorded it himself. It was as dramatic a moment as these lovers of theater could wish. Upon entering Diderot's cell, Rousseau threw himself into his friend's arms "with my face pressed against his, speechless except for the tears and sobs that spoke on my behalf, for I was choked with tenderness and joy." When they finally disengaged, Diderot triumphantly turned to a priest who was visiting him: "Observe, Monsieur, how my friends love me."[34]

The most remarkable moment for Rousseau of Diderot's stay at Vincennes occurred not within the walls of the prison, however, but on the road leading to it. Vincennes was six miles east of the city. Unable to afford a carriage, Rousseau set out on foot to see his friend on what he recalled was an unusually hot day. Stopping to rest beneath a tree, he opened a copy of the *Mercure de France,* the magazine he had brought along for just such an eventuality. Scanning the pages, he happened upon the announcement of a prize competition by the Academy of Dijon, one of the institutions of learning established by Louis XIV to cultivate the sciences and arts. There he read the academy's fateful question: has the restoration of the sciences and arts tended to purify morals? "The moment I read these words I saw another universe and I became another man."[35]

Perhaps more accurately, this epiphany allowed Rousseau to rediscover the man he always was without realizing it. He pierced the veil of the vaunted civility and progress of his century and glimpsed a vision of "another universe." Instead of attaining truth through the deductive and methodical reasoning of his fellow philosophes, he had instead beheld a truer world largely invisible to the activities of reflection. Rather than the *esprit de géometrie*, such knowledge required the *esprit de finesse*. Recounting his epiphany a little more than a decade later, Rousseau therefore resorts to the language of religious vision to describe the experience. "If anything has ever resembled a sudden inspiration, it is the motion that was caused in me by that reading; suddenly I felt my mind dazzled by a thousand lights; crowds of lively ideas presented themselves at the same time with a strength and a confusion that threw me into an inexpressible perturbation . . .," and here, overcome with recalling this episode, Rousseau switches suddenly into the present tense: "I feel my head seized by a dizziness similar to drunkenness."[36] His whole life since that vision, he explains, has been devoted to trying to articulate what cannot be articulated, indicating what cannot be indicated, making seen what can be seen only through a different mode of vision. As Rousseau writes in the preface to *Emile:* "It will be believed that what is being read is less an educational treatise than a visionary's dreams about education. What is to be done about it? . . . I do not see as other men."[37]

Rousseau places this otherworldly event in summer, yet subsequent scholarship has established that it must have taken place in October, when the temperature barely ever reached sixty degrees. A slip perhaps, but Rousseau may have moved the events to the heat of summer in order to create a parallel to the story of Paul's conversion on the road to Damascus.[38] Regardless of the event's actual timing, though, Rousseau makes clear its effect. Overwhelmed by his vision, he staggered the rest of the way to Vincennes. Stumbling into Diderot's cell, Rousseau was in a "state of agitation bordering on delirium." When he learned the reason for this frenzy, Diderot urged him to give voice to his ideas and enter the competition. From that moment, Rousseau later concluded, "I was lost."[39]

If Rousseau the man was lost, the philosopher was found. Everything he wrote, he later maintained, sought to express the vision that befell him on the road to Vincennes.[40] The first fruit of that vision was the *Discourse on the Sciences and Arts*, whose contrarian position on the benefits of modern civilization won the academy's prize in 1750. Published anonymously the following year under the name "Citizen of Geneva," the discourse was an overnight success, earning Rousseau, whose authorship was quickly revealed, what he came to recognize as his unfortunate fame. "What an abyss of miseries the author would have avoided," he later wrote of himself, "if only this first written work had been received as it deserved to be!"[41]

Doubt the benefits of civilization? For eighteenth-century Europeans, one might as well doubt the benefits of monarchy (or twenty-first-century Westerners the benefits of democracy). The academy's question invited a positive reply—of course the sciences and arts purify morals—and the flurry of essays submitted to the competition almost all satisfied this expectation. Rousseau's entry stood out owing to its unexpected conclusion and paradoxical character, which adopted and then transformed the traditional religious and classical republican arguments against the corrosive effects of science on faith and patriotism. Yet Rousseau's essay presented a closely reasoned analysis of the causes and effects of the sciences and arts. Their advancement was accompanied by moral corruption in all times and places, he argued, no less consistently and universally than the sway of the moon over the ebb and flow of the tides. In short, Rousseau turned the tools of modern science against science itself. In an age when the sciences and especially arts are prized, talent and not character is honored, and the desire to advance the sciences and arts goes hand in hand with a passion for personal advancement. A fatal wedge is thereby driven between reality and appearance, and behind the veil of "civility" lie the cold calculation of self-interest and a pride that both fosters inequality and is nourished by it.[42]

The apparently perverse logic of the *Discourse* was heightened when its author's identity was revealed. How could an artist, a musician, if not very successful one, have composed this attack on the arts? More important, how could this philippic against Enlightenment come from a major contributor to the *Encyclopédie*, the first volume of which was published to great acclaim immediately after the publication of the *Discourse*? Rousseau himself acknowledges the paradox in the work itself: "I have seen these contradictions, and they have not rebuffed me." To his bemused critics, Rousseau explained that he had condemned not the sciences and arts in themselves but the corrupt motives that gave them birth and made them fashionable. Knowledge was good in itself, but it was not made for mankind. In the end, the citizen of Geneva sides with Plato: philosophy is not for the many, who are incapable of mastering its consequences, but for the few, who serve as "the preceptors of the human race."[43] As for the rest of humankind, the state should teach them how to be virtuous, not cultured.

Rousseau's *Discourse on the Sciences and Arts* made him an overnight celebrity. "It's catching on like wildfire," wrote Diderot; "there is no example of success like it."[44] His notoriety was only amplified by his participation shortly after the publication of his prize essay in the so-called Quarrel of the Bouffons, a pamphlet war over the relative merits of French and Italian music sparked by the successful presentation on August 1, 1752, of Pergolesi's *La serva padrona* by a traveling Italian troupe. A seemingly trifling matter of taste became a matter of national pride, and also political animosity, with the partisans of French music hunkering down in the "King's Corner" and the advocates of Italian music joining together in the "Queen's Corner." Long an enthusiast of the music he heard while serving as a lackey in Turin and then as secretary to the ambassador in

Venice, Rousseau championed the Italian side, along with most of the Encyclopedists. With his *Letter on French Music,* Rousseau tossed an especially incendi-
ary device in this war. His analysis of the relationship between language and
music in the *Letter* elevated the quarrel to a more philosophic level, but more notable were the conclusions he drew from this analysis: "The French do not at all
have a music and cannot have any, or . . . if they have any, it will be so much the
worse for them."[45] With this deliberate provocation, Rousseau succeeded in
drawing all of the critical fire toward himself.

By the time the *Letter on French Music* appeared in November 1753, the
struggling musician finally tasted success as a composer with his opera *Le Devin
du village*. First staged in the summer of 1753 at Fontainebleau before the king
and queen, Rousseau's opera proved to be one of the most popular of the eighteenth century and remained part of the repertory of the Paris Opéra until 1829.
The pastoral setting and simple melodic line of the work were in deliberate contrast to the complex staging and intricate harmonies of the dominant French
style. Louis XV, who was heard humming his favorite tune from the opera
for the rest of the day, was so taken with the work that he planned to offer the
composer a pension. To the horror of his friends, Rousseau slipped out of the
chateau the next morning rather than attend an audience with the sovereign,
sending word that, unwilling to compromise his independence, he would refuse
the pension. Although Rousseau's success as a musician added yet another paradox to his celebrity as the author of the *Discourse on the Sciences and Arts*, his emphasis in *Le Devin du village* on the simplicity of melody and action was a variation on the gap between reality and appearance, intention and action, that had
preoccupied him and that he hinted at in his *Discourse*.

Another competition sponsored by the Academy of Dijon, announced in
1754, gave Rousseau an opportunity to expand on the core problems of human
society and understanding that he had identified in his life and his thought. His
Discourse on the Origin and Foundations of Inequality Among Men stands as the
most far-reaching critique of civilization in Rousseau's own day and our own.

The academy had asked whether the inequality seen among us is authorized
by natural law, and Rousseau—recommending the question for slaves to discuss
before their masters—took the invitation to write an analysis of human nature
and development that concludes with a blistering attack on the reigning inequality. "The most useful and least advanced of all human knowledge appears to me
to be that of man," begins the *Discourse on Inequality*, "and I dare say that the inscription on the temple of Delphi alone contained a precept more important
and more difficult than all the thick volumes of the moralists." Yet the command
of the oracle to know oneself is far more problematic than previous philosophers had realized, according to Rousseau, for the very tool embraced for such

Maurice Quentin de la Tour (1704–88), portrait of Jean
Jacques Rousseau (1712–78), pastel on paper, 1753. © Musee
Antoine Lecuyer, Saint-Quentin, France / Giraudon / The
Bridgeman Art Library

knowledge—reason—was itself in question. "What is even crueler is that, as
all the progress of the human species continually moves it further away from its
primitive state, the more new knowledge we accumulate, the more we deprive
ourselves of the means of acquiring the most important knowledge of all; so that
it is, in a sense, by dint of studying man that we have made ourselves incapable
of knowing him."[46] Reason is unnatural, Rousseau insists, and the birth of reflection divorces us from our true nature. We come to see ourselves in the eyes of
others and thus learn to substitute appearances for reality, hiding from others
and ultimately from ourselves.

　　While meditating upon his subject, Rousseau plunged into the woods—
quite literally. Quitting Paris for the forested expanses of Saint Germain west of
Paris, Rousseau ruminated on the origins of the human predicament: "I sought,
I found the image of the first times whose history I proudly traced; I made a
clean sweep of the petty falsehoods of men, I dared to strip naked their nature,

to follow the progress of time and things that have disfigured it, and comparing the man of man with the natural man, to show them the genuine source of his miseries in his pretended perfection."[47] Through a kind of meditative self-analysis, Rousseau used his powers of reflection to peel away the layers that had accumulated through the influence of time and society so as to find the image of human nature within himself. There he would rediscover the "man of nature" obscured by the "man of man."[48]

In the *Discourse on Inequality,* Rousseau presents the image he found in the forest as a hypothetical history of mankind. He begins with a portrait of natural man as a solitary animal devoid of reason and speech, a being whose limited needs can be easily satisfied without depending upon anyone, whose soul is restricted to the sole sentiment of his own existence without any idea of the future, as near as it may be. Rousseau surrounds his description of this primal state with a fence of paradoxes meant to convince us that such a condition of undeveloped humanity is indeed possible, if not inevitable given his premises. On the subject of the mutual development of language and society, for example, he begs his reader to consider: "Which was most necessary, previously invented society for the institution of languages; or previously invented languages for the establishment of society?"[49] Man, for Rousseau, seems to be doomed to incomprehension both before society and within it. But this animal has possibilities. While initially indistinguishable from the other beasts, lying dormant in his soul is a faculty that will lead him and his fellows out of his original stupidity. This is "perfectibility," a word coined by Rousseau and a term the irony of which is immediately apparent: perfection is another word for corruption. Through his capacity for self-perfection, man becomes tyrant over himself and others.

Placing man in this garden and planting the seed of his corruption deep within him, Rousseau recasts the biblical story of the Fall. "People grew accustomed to assembling in front of the huts or around a large tree; song and dance, true children of love and leisure, became the amusement or rather the occupation of idle and assembled men and women. Each one began to look at the others and want to be looked at himself, and public esteem had a value. The one who sang or danced the best, the handsomest, the strongest, the most adroit, or the most eloquent became the most highly considered; and that was the first step toward inequality and, at the same time, toward vice."[50] All of the elements of the biblical story are here—pride, lust, the dawning knowledge of good and evil— everything, that is, except God and his commandment not to eat of the fruit. In Rousseau's version of the story, we are not at fault. He instead traces the corruption to an accident, the inevitable result of being cast into society. Man is naturally good, but society corrupts him: this is the revolutionary core of Rousseau's philosophy.[51]

Yet this stage of human history, Rousseau claims, is the best and happiest condition for mankind, a kind of "golden mean" between the stupidity of the natural state and the petulant activity of the civilized state: "All subsequent progress has been in appearance so many steps toward the perfection of the individual, and in fact toward the decrepitude of the species." In this early stage of history, we have become fully human, capable of experiencing the sweetest sentiments known to mankind of paternal and conjugal love and having attained nearly the full extent of development of which their faculties are capable. Only a terrible accident could lead to the further perfection of mankind. This was the discovery of the plow, and the moment when an individual, pointing to the furrowed earth, declares, "This is mine," and finds men simple enough to believe him.[52] This accident creates the inequalities that have since marked our history. The corruption leeches equally into master and slave, rich and poor, turning the former into tyrants and latter into flatterers. Now it was necessary to appear to be what one was not; being and seeming were divorced, and we become alienated from one another and from ourselves.

Rousseau's historical sketch culminates in contemporary European civilization, portrayed as a cauldron of inequality, corruption, and alienation. He ends the work with his caustic answer to the academy's question about whether existing inequalities are justified by natural law. His inquiry should make it sufficiently clear "what one ought to think in this regard of the sort of inequality that reigns among all civilized peoples" where children command men, imbeciles lead the wise, and "a handful of men [are] glutted with superfluities while the starving multitude lacks necessities."[53]

Having reached the end of Rousseau's story of original innocence and accidental corruption, which appeared in 1755, one very famous reader icily dissented. "I have received, Sir, your new book against the human race," wrote Voltaire: "One acquires the desire to walk on all fours when one reads your work. Nevertheless, since I lost the habit more than sixty years ago, I unfortunately feel that it is impossible for me to take it up again."[54] What, in other words, are we supposed to make of Rousseau's story? What relevance to us has natural man and a natural condition forever lost, if they even ever existed?

As in the *Discourse on the Sciences and Arts*, Rousseau anticipates the charge of self-contradiction. "What! Must we destroy societies, annihilate thine and mine, and go back to live in the forest with bears?" This was the sort of question, he wrote, that would come from his "adversaries" and, as in the earlier work, he again has a reply. If you can go back into the woods then do so. But as for men like himself, he says, who have been enlightened and therefore corrupted, this is not an option. What should they do? At the very least, we must not madly pur-

sue a poison others mistake for medicine. We may even seek remedies for the illness whose symptoms we now recognize.[55]

Increasingly ill at ease with the falseness of city life, Rousseau left Paris shortly
after the publication of the *Discourse on Inequality*. Along with his housekeeper
and mistress of ten years, Thérèse Le Vasseur, he took up residence in April 1756
at the Hermitage, a cottage in the forest of Montmorency north of Paris lent to
him by his friend Mme d'Épinay. There he began a personal reformation that
bordered on a spiritual quarantine, undertaking a kind of introspection possible
only in seclusion.[56] Intent on stripping from his soul the corruption of the city,
and the contagion of pride he had caught in his desire for celebrity, he grew increasingly reclusive, to the growing puzzlement of his friends and colleagues.

The Hermitage proved to be a productive setting for the self-exiled author.
Rousseau spent his days writing in the house's courtyard, which perhaps recalled
for him the happy days reading in Maman's garden at Les Charmettes. The pastoral retreat, along with a growing love for his host's sister-in-law, Sophie
d'Houdetot, inspired Rousseau's great novel *Julie; or, the New Heloise*, whose
heroine he modeled on Sophie and whose hero he drew after his own portrait.
The estranged wife of the Comte d'Houdetot was in her mid-twenties and, unhappily for Rousseau, faithful to her lover, the poet and Encyclopedist Jean-
François de Saint-Lambert, to whom she would remain devoted until he died in
her arms nearly fifty years later in a scene worthy of *Julie* itself. While Mme
d'Épinay grew jealous over Rousseau's unrequited love for Sophie, Rousseau grew
suspicious of his hostess's motives. In December 1757, following a series of accusatory letters, Rousseau left the Hermitage for a house in nearby Montmorency.

Rousseau soon began to quarrel with his former friends, the philosophes.
Rousseau unfairly suspected Diderot of conspiring with Mme d'Épinay in their
dispute, but he was most of all hurt by his friend's failure to visit him in his retreat. If Diderot was unusually prompt in their weekly dinners at the Panier
Fleuri, he now reverted to his usual ways, repeatedly leaving Rousseau waiting
all day for their appointed meetings at Saint Denis, four miles along the road to
Paris from Montmorency.[57] The deepest wound, however, came not from his
friend's neglect but from what Rousseau saw as his condemnation. In March 1757
Rousseau picked up a recently published play by Diderot, *The Natural Son*, and
was brought up short by a single line: "Only the wicked man lives alone."
Rousseau was convinced that he was the target of this aphorism, and the treas-
ured friendship began its rapid collapse. "Ingrate," he wrote to Diderot, "I have
never done you favors, but I loved you. . . . Show this to your wife, who is more
impartial than you are, and ask her whether, when my presence was soothing to

your afflicted heart, I counted my steps or paid attention to the weather when I went to Vincennes to comfort my friend."[58]

The final break between the Citizen of Geneva and his former companions resulted from what seemed, at first glance, to be the most benign of suggestions. In October 1757 the seventh volume of the *Encyclopédie* appeared with an article by d'Alembert on "Geneva." Buried in the entry was the plea for the Calvinist city to reconsider its prohibition of theater. Rousseau immediately concluded that d'Alembert's suggestion was an act of pandering to Voltaire, who lived just across the border from Geneva and would have appreciated a venue to stage his plays. This proved too much for the Citizen of Geneva, who replied by shooting off the *Letter to d'Alembert*, in which he publicly announced his break with Diderot. Rousseau's analysis of the theater in his *Letter* self-consciously reprises the argument in Plato's *Republic* for banishing the poets from the city. The theater might be a relative good for the corrupted inhabitants of Paris, at least keeping them off the streets and diverting them from their criminal behavior for a time, but the corrupting effects of the theater should be avoided in a virtuous republic. Instead, the Citizen of Geneva recommended patriotic festivals, where citizens and their families would join together in the open squares of the city to dance and sing, a kind of participatory theater in which they became, as Rousseau exclaimed, a spectacle to themselves.

In a concluding note to his *Letter*, Rousseau recalls such a festival from his youth. One summer evening the citizen militia, returning from their martial exercises, gathered in the square below the windows of his house. Joined by their women and children, they all began to dance in joyous unison. "Love your country, Jean-Jacques," he recalls his father saying to him as the two of them stood in the window watching the pageantry below. The irony, of course, is that Jean-Jacques and his father do not participate in this spontaneous theater but rather, framed by their window, observe the spectacle apart. Here, Rousseau again touches on his fate as an exile limited to the role of spectator of a community to which he no longer belongs.[59]

Imagining communities to which he would like to belong was Rousseau's specialty, and as his real friendships collapsed one after another he constructed better worlds out of prose. His words struck a chord with a readership that was unprecedented in both its magnitude and its fanatical attachment to the author. The creations of his mind and heart appeared in quick succession from January 1761 to May 1762, carrying Rousseau toward his fate with accelerating speed. Three great works were created in a mere four years, each very different from the next in content and style, each designed to affect the hearts and minds of his audience. The most successful was the first, his romantic novel, *Julie; or, the New Heloise*. Through this story of seduction and virtue, Rousseau created a readership that extended far beyond the drawing rooms and academies of Paris. Literally overnight—readers refused to sleep until finishing the final volume of the novel—Rousseau fully became the sage sought out by Boswell and legions of admirers.

Yet disaster soon followed success.

Writing again as the Citizen of Geneva—a title he reserved for works that would do honor to his fatherland, he explained, and therefore a title he would not use for a romantic novel—Rousseau extended the critical analysis of his *Discourses* in two equally bold works: *The Social Contract* and *Emile; or, On Education.*[60]

"Man is born free, and everywhere he is in chains." This peal of rhetorical thunder, which opens *The Social Contract,* stunned Europe. The proposed cure to the grim diagnosis of the two *Discourses* was hardly less astounding: Rousseau prescribed democracy. This represented a turning point in the history of political thought. Rousseau's apology for democracy is easy to overlook in an age where even dictators ape democratic practices, paying the compliment vice owes to virtue. Yet Rousseau's defense was perfectly subversive in the eighteenth century. Nearly all of the Genevan's fellow philosophes scorned the people (the *demos* in democracy) and believed that powerful and enlightened monarchs were essential to the betterment of humankind. Rousseau, however, proclaimed that the only legitimate form of rule is the self-rule of direct democracy. True laws can come only from the general will of the assembled people—a standard, Rousseau admits, that calls into question all existing legislation.

Reeling from the salvo of *The Social Contract,* an astonished public was hit barely a month later with *Emile.* If Rousseau's political treatise contemplates the project of reforming an entire society, his educational treatise-novel proposes the seemingly more modest undertaking of raising a single individual without letting him fall prey to the corruption of society. All very well and good, perhaps, were it not for the philosophical premise of his work. For the basis of Rousseau's argument in *Emile,* first glimpsed in the *Discourse on Inequality,* is the denial of the doctrine of original sin. "Everything is good as it leaves the hands of the Author of things; everything degenerates in the hands of man," he begins the work.[61] Even worse, aside from recommending that all religious instruction be postponed until adolescence, the spiritual teaching he does suggest, in a separate section of the book entitled the "Profession of Faith of the Savoyard Vicar," dismisses the need of revelation or miracles and denies the divinity of Christ.

Rousseau considered *Emile* his best and most important work—indeed, the most useful book written during the century.[62] Similarly, he viewed the "Profession of Faith" as uniquely useful to combating superstition and intolerance and to providing people with a faith that would sustain their virtue against the passions born of society and the doubts engendered by the philosophers. The authorities, however, did not see it that way. The institutions most vulnerable to

Rousseau's critiques finally struck back. Although the nervous philosopher had been assured by the head of censorship, Malesherbes, that his works could be published with unofficial permission, a force beyond the reach of the monarchy's bureaucracy did not adhere to the script. The Archbishop of Paris condemned *Emile,* and then, on June 9, 1762, an order for Rousseau's arrest was issued.

"Jean-Jacques Rousseau does not know how to hide," the condemned author insisted.[63] Informed about the philosopher's impending arrest, a group of his protectors, in a scene that was to be repeated numerous times over the next decade, gathered in the middle of the night to devise a strategy. After conferring, the Duc and Duchesse de Luxembourg, his friends and sometime hosts in Montmorency, and the Comtesse de Boufflers, who had urged him unsuccessfully to go to England, confronted Rousseau. If he did not know how to hide he could at least learn to run. The next morning, after breakfasting, Rousseau climbed into a borrowed cabriolet, a two-horse carriage with a folding top. As he left the grounds of the duc's estate, Rousseau passed the carriage bearing the officials coming to take him into custody. He headed for Paris, where passersby saluted the ill-concealed fugitive, then made his way east toward his native Geneva.[64]

The fugitive philosopher quickly learned, however, that Geneva was preparing to welcome its prodigal son by stoking an auto-da-fé with copies of his political treatise, whose democratic teaching the aristocratic elders correctly took as criticism of their rule. As a result, the Citizen of Geneva paused in the nearby town of Yverdon, at the home of his old friend Daniel Roguin, the man who had introduced him to Diderot twenty years earlier and whom Rousseau affectionately called Papa. Less than a month after the philosopher's arrival, however, nervous city elders, worried about the political fallout from neighboring Geneva, asked Rousseau to leave town. Seeking another refuge, he seized upon an offer by Roguin's daughter of a house in the village of Môtiers. Having first secured the consent of the patron and tormentor of Voltaire, King Frederick II of Prussia, who held nominal sway over the region, Rousseau set off from Yverdon on foot, arriving in Môtiers just days after his fiftieth birthday.

Such, then, was the itinerary of the wandering philosopher whom Boswell journeyed to meet two and a half years later in the cold winter month of December 1764.

With the brazen letter of self-introduction he wrote upon his arrival in Môtiers, Boswell had stumbled across the password to Rousseau's hermitage. Writing about the young Scotsman's letter to a friend a few days later, Rousseau explained: "In the first letter he wrote me he made a point of saying that he was a man *of singular merit.* I was curious to see the person who spoke in this way about himself, and I found that he was telling the truth."[65] Unable to resist Boswell's

George Willison (1741–97), portrait of James Boswell (1740–95), 1765. © Scottish National Portrait Gallery, Edinburgh / The Bridgeman Art Library

genial effrontery, Rousseau replied that he was ill and "in no state to receive visitors." Nevertheless, he continued, "I cannot deprive myself of Mr. Boswell's company, provided that out of consideration for my condition, he is willing to make it short." Though discomforted by the word *short*, Boswell gathered his courage, wits, and greatcoat, and launched himself out the door and down the street.[66]

When Thérèse Le Vasseur opened the door for the visitor, she confronted a sight that was rare in an austere mountain village. Ablaze in a bright scarlet coat and waistcoat, over which was thrown a greatcoat of green camlet lined with fox-skin fur, with matching fur collars and cuffs, a hat with solid gold lace nesting under his arm, stood Boswell. The gallant visitor was welcomed by Thérèse, whom he described — in contradiction to most other contemporary accounts of Rousseau's *gouvernante*, or housekeeper — as "a little, lively, neat French girl." She welcomed Boswell into the cottage and led him up a dark staircase, at the top of which the young Scot thought he would find Rousseau.[67]

Instead, Boswell found himself alone in the kitchen. As his eyes grew accustomed to the light, he had time to take in his surroundings. The room in which he stood was dominated by a large chimney, and served as a sort of vestibule where Rousseau received visitors. If Boswell had walked down the narrow hall, he would have passed three bedrooms. Rousseau had taken the largest and quietest one, a room overlooking the courtyard at the back of the house, which he turned into a combination sleeping quarters and study, calling it his "laboratory." He installed his gouvernante in a smaller but brighter bedroom, leaving the tiny third bedroom free.[68] Across the length of the south side of the shingled cottage ran a covered terrace with windows newly installed by the current occupant to take advantage of the view of the town's waterfall and the Jura range in the near distance.

After a few minutes, the philosopher emerged from his laboratory. Framed by the doorway, wearing a caftan he styled Armenian, stood Rousseau. He bowed, as did Boswell. These formalities may have allowed the Scot to confirm an earlier visitor's report on Rousseau's peculiar footwear: through star-shaped holes cut in the front of his wood-soled slippers there indeed wiggled several of the great man's toes.[69] Apart from his extraordinary attire, though, Rousseau appeared quite ordinary. Of middling height, slight build, and average appearance, he was unremarkable until the unmistakable fire of his passions set his face aglow. It was as though a lantern were suddenly lit, revealing Jean-Jacques, the author of the *Discourse on Inequality* or *Julie*.

The visitor hardly had time to contemplate Rousseau's appearance, however, for he was immediately invited to pace the floor of the room with the peripatetic philosopher. As the two men marched on the uneven floorboards, they quickly fell into conversation.

Rousseau quickly dealt with books and doctors: they were equally harmful, and he advised Boswell to avoid them both. The conversation soon shifted to Boswell's fellow Scot Lord Marischal George Keith, Rousseau's protector in his role as Frederick's appointed governor for the region until his retirement to Berlin in April 1763. Keith had taken particular care over the well-being of the philosopher, even contemplating taking Rousseau with him to Scotland to live in what he called a "philosophic ménage à trois" with none other than David Hume. "Each of us will contribute to the upkeep of the little republic according to his income, and each will tax himself," Keith had explained to Rousseau. "Food will be no great item, inasmuch as trout, salmon, seafood, and vegetables cost me nothing. David will pay for the roast beef because he eats it."[70] The project came to naught.

In the warmth of Rousseau's effusions over the man he fondly called his father, Boswell revealed that he carried with him a letter of introduction from Keith, whom he had met in Holland and accompanied to Berlin. He explained to Rousseau that he had not utilized this certain key of admittance, instead wanting to try and gain entrance unaided. Rousseau and Boswell then talked of politics, with the patriotic Boswell lamenting Scotland's union with England, a sentiment shared by Rousseau, whose love for lost causes and betrayed republics extended as far as the Highlands.

Boswell soon felt easy enough to be fully Boswell. He thumped Rousseau on the shoulder, as if they were old acquaintances, and at times even gripped the older man's arm to emphasize a point. Eventually, as the two men paced the length of the room, they turned to their favorite subject: themselves. Boswell expressed surprise at his host's forbidding reputation. "Sir," Rousseau replied, "you don't see before you the bear you have heard others tell of. I have no liking for the world, I live here in a world of fantasies, and I cannot tolerate the world as it is." Boswell parried: "But when you come across fantastical men, are they not to your liking?" The philosopher replied, "Why, Sir, they have not the same fantasies as myself."

After a few uneasy minutes as they continued to pace, Rousseau turned to Boswell: "I feel free to stroll here together without talking." Was this a peculiar proclamation of friendship? Or perhaps a polite invitation for his guest to leave? In either case, this particular freedom came at too great a price for the garrulous Boswell. Unable to hold his tongue any longer, he pressed Rousseau on whether he was equal to the description he provided of himself in his letter. When Rousseau said it was too soon to say, Boswell invited himself back the next day, causing his reclusive host to complain of being overwhelmed by visits from idlers. Opening the door to the room, he added that they had little better to do with their time than annoy those who only wished to be left in peace. Superbly deaf to the hint, Boswell assured Rousseau that he would remain in Môtiers in the hopes that he would again be allowed to call. He then flew back to the inn and into the arms of his journal. How magnificent, he wrote, "that I could support the character which I had given of myself to the author of whom I had thought so much." Suddenly, looking up from the writing tablet, Boswell exclaimed, "I have been with him!"

Over the next few days, time and again Boswell's raids on the cottage were repelled. Knocking at his door the very next morning after his first visit, he was sent away by Thérèse, who told him that the philosopher had gone out. Boswell gaily bowed and left, even though the bad weather and Rousseau's worse health meant that he was probably hiding in the adjacent barn, where he often took refuge from unwanted visitors.[71] That evening Boswell was again at the door. Flirting with Rousseau's protectress, who clearly admired his boldness, Boswell this time gained admittance, only to be regaled by Rousseau with a tale of a man who persists in his visits to a woman who wishes only to be left alone. When his importunate visitor failed to draw the lesson from the transparent allegory, Rousseau exploded, "*You* are irksome to me. It's my nature. I cannot help it. . . . Go away."

Boswell left, but not for long. The next day, the dogged Scot ignored Rousseau's plea for solitude and brightly "set conversation a-going" by introducing the subject of religion. "But tell me sincerely," he asked Rousseau, "are you a Christian?" "Yes," came the firm reply. Religion preoccupied Rousseau, though it was a topic on which his former Parisian friends found him altogether too serious and whose Catholic and Protestant foes found him not serious enough. "Rousseau is a Christian, as Jesus was a Jew," remarked Diderot, who probably knew what he was talking about.[72] Certainly, a philosopher who founded his system on the denial of original sin was a strange breed of Christian. Religion also preoccupied Boswell, who had reread and been deeply moved by the "Profession of Faith" while on his way to meet Rousseau. Like Rousseau a Calvinist by upbringing, Boswell took the state of his soul seriously, and genuinely repented his epic carousing, at least during his brief spells of reflection between sins. As Rousseau later wrote to a friend, he suspected that Boswell's tendency to alternate between great cheer and profound gloom was due largely to his unsettled religious views.[73] Sensitive to the caustic effects of reason on the old-fashioned virtues of religious belief and patriotism, Rousseau sympathized with Boswell.

Yet there clearly were limits to Rousseau's empathy. When Boswell suddenly asked Rousseau to serve as his confessor, the philosopher demurred: "I can be responsible only for myself." When Boswell persisted, his host groaned that he could not promise him anything: "I am in pain. I need a chamber pot every minute. . . . Be off!"

Boswell spent that evening jotting down talking points to keep the conversation going the next day in the face of Rousseau's hints and protestations. "Suicide. Hypochondria. A real malady: family madness. Self-destruction: your arguments not answered."

A little before noon the next day, Boswell arrived at Rousseau's door once again. A distracted Thérèse, telling him that Rousseau was sick, nevertheless showed him in. There, Boswell discovered why Rousseau had adopted his extravagant Armenian costume. "I am overcome with ailments, disappointments, and sorrow. I am using a probe." As Rousseau pointed to a catheter used to relieve a urinary obstruction, an embarrassed but still curious Boswell suddenly understood the reason for the flowing gown. While Rousseau had first contemplated a change of attire upon meeting an Armenian tailor in Paris, he finally had dared to adopt his eccentric costume after he moved to Môtiers. Securing the permission of the local pastor, who assured him that there would be no scandal even if he wore his dress to church, Rousseau donned the coat, caftan, fur cap, and belt. "*Salamaleki*" — "Peace be with you" in Arabic — was all Lord Keith had said to him when he presented himself so dressed, and Rousseau then resolved forever to wear his Armenian dress.[74]

For once even Boswell, having made his discovery, drew back in respect of the other. He left the poor man in peace — if only for that day. When Boswell returned for his appointed interview, he followed his list of prepared talking points, most of which characteristically concerned himself. Boswell wanted to know whether a man could retain his "singularity" while living among other men. Rousseau answered that he had done so himself. Then, perhaps inspired by Rousseau's garb, the lusty young Scot, who had solemnly sworn to his journal six weeks earlier to remain chaste until meeting the philosopher,[75] wondered whether he might satisfy his immense sexual appetites by taking thirty wives in the Oriental fashion. One should follow the customs of one's country, counseled a noncommittal Rousseau. Uncertain where the conversation would next go, Thérèse beat a hasty retreat. As there was so much more to discuss, the young Scot simply invited himself to dinner the following day. Rousseau acquiesced: his glacial regard was melting in the face of the relentlessly sunny man.

Boswell last saw Rousseau on December 15, 1765, once again dining at Rousseau's house. After fumbling about the kitchen pretending to help Thérèse make the soup, Boswell sat down with Rousseau and his gouvernante. He had been promised a "good, simple repast," and he carefully listed the seven courses in his journal, from an excellent soup through a *bouilli* of beef and veal to the concluding dessert of stoned pears and chestnuts, all served with the local wine. The conversation was spiced by Rousseau's blunt and often unorthodox declarations. His host lectured the young man when he asked if he could help himself to a second serving of pickled trout: "Is your arm long enough? A man does the honors of his house from a motive of vanity. He does not want it forgotten who is the master. I should like everyone to be his own master, and no one to play the part of host. Let each one ask for what he wants; if it is there to give, let him be given it; otherwise he must be satisfied without. Here you see true hospitality!" This was a decidedly odd form of hospitality. Boswell's every gesture, every habit, and every inclination became grist for Rousseau's cutting observations on man and society.

Planning on leaving the next day, Boswell apprised Rousseau of his travel plans, which included a visit to rebellious Corsica. Half in jest, he asked Rousseau to appoint him "Ambassador Extraordinary of Monsieur Rousseau to the Isle of Corsica"—a phantom nation for which the philosopher had recently been asked to write a constitution by the renowned patriot Paoli. "Perhaps you would rather be King of Corsica?" inquired Rousseau. The enemy of despotism then began to test the young man who, he himself said, thought of himself as "an ancient laird." The subject was cats: when Boswell said he didn't care for them, Rousseau pounced. Men who dislike cats were tyrannical: "They do not like cats because the cat is free and will never consent to become a slave. He will do nothing to your order, as the other animals do." "Nor a hen, either," Boswell objected. "A hen would obey your orders if you could make her understand them," the philosopher rejoined, "but a cat will understand you perfectly and not obey them." Rousseau seems to have been earnest with this theory of feline independence, for the frontispiece of *The Social Contract* features Lady Liberty accompanied by a cat.

In their parting conversation, Boswell tried to establish a lasting connection to the wild philosopher he had hunted down in the Alps. "Can I feel sure that I am held to you by a thread, even if of the finest? By a hair?" At that point, Boswell dramatically seized a hair on his head and threatened to pull it out. Staring at Boswell from below the mound of his fur cap, Rousseau reassured his fervent disciple: "Remember always that there are points at which our souls are bound." That Rousseau's declaration echoed, word for word, Saint-Preux's vow to Julie was not lost on the ecstatic young Scot.[76] Showing Boswell to the door, Thérèse told him, perhaps needlessly at this point, that Rousseau held him in high regard. After persuading Thérèse to let him write her and promising to send her a garnet necklace, he took his leave. The following morning, he slowly rode out of Môtiers, deep in thought, he wrote in his journal, about "how this day will appear to my mind some years hence."

The Great Scot

I am resolved to resist . . . any impulse towards writing, and I am
really so much ashamed of myself when I see my bulk on a shelf,
as well as when I see it in a glass, that I would fain prevent my
growing more corpulent either way.
— David Hume to David Mallet

D avid Hume would have been well placed to warn Rousseau about Boswell's mixture of brazen innocence and disarming geniality. The two men had first met in 1757, when Boswell, scarcely seventeen and already driven by the desire to meet the great thinkers of his age, arrived unannounced at the philosopher's door near High Street in Edinburgh. Talking his way past Hume's protective servant, Peggy Irvine, Boswell penetrated into the philosopher's rooms. The portly host welcomed the young bounder with such easygoing humor that Boswell later declared Hume to be "as affable a man I had ever met with."[1]

Settled in Hume's library, the two men chatted on subjects ranging from the nature of genius and styles of writing to the ways in which the ancients and moderns wrote history. What drew Boswell to the philosopher's door, however, was certainly less Hume's fame as the author of the popular *History of England* or the *Essays* than his infamy as a philosophical skeptic. Tormented by the terrors instilled by his Calvinist education, Boswell was perplexed by Hume's skepticism—another name, it seemed, for atheism. As in his later visits to Rousseau and Voltaire, foremost on the young Scot's mind in meeting Hume was the final disposition of his own soul. If they did speak of such matters, however, Boswell remained uncharacteristically silent in his journals. And yet he seems to refer to the subject by way of his pronounced silence about it: for after his visit, Boswell told himself that Hume was "a very proper person for a young man to cultivate an acquaintance with."[2]

The propriety of Hume's acquaintance was not, however, conceded by all of Boswell's contemporaries. Or even his friends. Although Boswell eventually reconciled Dr. Johnson to his fellow Scots, whom he had long despised, there would always be one resounding exception: David Hume. The good doctor "holds Mr. Hume in abhorrence and left a company one night upon his coming in," noted Boswell in a journal entry from 1762.[3] Attracted by Hume's good cheer, Boswell was acutely aware of the dangerous possibilities of the great Scot's thought.

The son of a Lowlands barrister and gentleman who died in 1713 when his child was barely two, David Hume entered the world "uncommonly wake-minded." While it was his beloved mother, Katherine Hume, who provided this testimony to young Davey's prodigious ways, her observation is certainly of a piece with her son's later career. As soon as he mastered reading, the boy was "seized" by the same passion for literature that had captured Rousseau, his junior by a year. His "ruling passion" was so great that, when packed off at the age of eleven to study law at the University of Edinburgh, he instead spent all of his time "secretly devouring" Cicero and Virgil.[4]

When he returned to the family estate of Ninewells in 1726, Hume had left the university with neither a law degree nor his Christian belief. The siren responsible for his spiritual deflowering was Calliope—the muse of philosophy. Once having read John Locke's study of the nature and limits of human understanding, Hume later told Boswell, he could never again follow any religion.[5] Having painlessly shed the gloomy Calvinism of his childhood, what the young man could not so easily shake were the disquieting effects of philosophy itself.

Resettled at home, the precocious fifteen-year-old declared his independence. He disdained his late father's career: the study of law appeared "nauseous" to him. Instead, he shut himself in the family library, where he read at his pleasure, "sometimes a philosopher, sometimes a poet." Being the second son of a genteel family who could expect only a meager income, Hume claimed that such a course of study made eminent sense, for both philosophers and poets seek "peace of mind, in a liberty and independency on fortune, and contempt of riches, power and glory."[6]

Yet peace of mind was the last thing Hume found. Like Rousseau on the road to Vincennes, Hume had a philosophical rapture of sorts, in his case when he was scarcely eighteen. He compared this glimpse of a "new scene of thought" with the experiences of those French mystics whose "rapturous admirations might discompose the fabric of the nerves and brain." This vision, he said, "transported me beyond measure, and made me, with an ardor natural to young men, throw up every other pleasure or business to apply entirely to it." The congenial youth plunged into a nearly monastic life of study in order to explore this vista of ideas. In his self-imposed isolation Hume ushered in a nervous depression. He was soon unable "to follow any train of thought, by one continued stretch of view," while his energy "seemed in a moment to be extinguished." Once confident and easygoing, he had become, he said, "very uneasy to myself." Despite the different regimens prescribed by doctors—from infusions of claret and bitters to long horse rides—Hume remained weakened for the next few years by what one specialist diagnosed as the "Disease of the Learned." He eventually found salvation not in medical quackery but in the exercise of his own reason. More precisely—and paradoxically—Hume concluded, reason alone could not pull him out of this philosophical bog. His fragile emotional health, he realized, resulted from exclusive devotion to work and idleness. It stood to reason that reason was not enough. He concluded that he had "to seek out a more active life" that would banish the melancholy disposition into which he had fallen.[7]

Hume soon "roused" himself up. He blithely noted in "My Own Life" shortly before he died that his health had been, during this period, "a little broken."[8] Unlike Rousseau, Hume was far from prolix about his own mental and personal history, as evidenced by the contrast between the sheer length of Rousseau's *Confessions* and other autobiographical writings (more than one thousand tight pages in the standard French edition of his works) and Hume's "My Own Life" (a mere seven or eight pages). As a consequence, we have less direct evidence about the effects of Hume's early crisis and, in general, about Hume's internal and external life than we do for Rousseau. Hume's great struggle appears to have left few marks apart from a thoroughly changed physiognomy. From a lanky youth of six foot, Hume changed into a robust man whose great appetite created an equally great belly that he carried for the rest of his life and which, he joked, could not, like gray hair, be "disguised with powder and pomation."[9] An-

other scar perhaps left by the disease of the learned was a vacant stare that un-
nerved friends and strangers alike, and which was to play so unfortunate a role
in the collapse of his friendship with Rousseau. Still, although Hume's account
of his depression suggests that the experience had left him with no more than a
vast gut and a blank gaze, uneasiness over the finality of the cure runs like an
underground stream through his philosophy.

Shortly before his death, Hume still recalled the dangers of a life devoted exclu-
sively to intensive and solitary study. "Relaxation for amusement you may use
(or not) as you fancy," he warned his young nephew David Home in 1775, "but
that for health is absolutely necessary." To Hume's taste there was nò better
place for such relaxation, for health or not, than France. The modern French,
like the ancient Athenians, had mastered all the arts and sciences, Hume pronounced in one of his essays, but they had also "perfected that art, the most useful and agreeable of any, *l'Art de Vivre*, the art of society and conversation."[10] In
1734 France welcomed the young philosopher, scarcely recovered from his depression and determined to combine amusement with work.

Crossing the Channel, Hume went straight to Paris, where he called on family and friends. Short of money and durable connections, however, he was
forced to reverse the usual path of worldly and ambitious pilgrims by quitting
the capital for the provinces. A year's stay in Rheims in the heart of the Cham-
pagne region helped him polish his French, but finding even that provincial city
too expensive, Hume next moved to La Flèche, a town in the Loire Valley. His
choice was not arbitrary. A sleepy backwater, the town did not tax his lean purse.
Equally important, La Flèche was home to a Jesuit college whose library ad-
mirably served Hume's purposes. Over the college hovered the spirit of its most
famous graduate, René Descartes, who had left the school more than a century
earlier, resolved to throw off the useless learning he had acquired there through
the unorthodox method of locking himself up in a warm room, only to emerge
with the Archimedean point of modern philosophy: "I think, therefore I am."
For the next two years, Hume made his life in this small town nestled in the heart
of vineyards, where he read, wrote, and occasionally chatted with the locals and
the Jesuit fathers. All in all, it was an idyll that contained little drama or adven-
ture but was the setting for the composition of one of the most unsettling works
in the history of Western thought, the *Treatise of Human Nature*.

Like Rousseau's writings, which embraced the scientific approach and critical spirit of modern philosophy only then to turn them back against philosophy
and its fruits, Hume's *Treatise* reflects the enlightened spirit of the principles of
science yet veers in directions that seemed perverse to the faithful in the congre-

gation of philosophers, as well as subversive to the faithful in the choir of the religious.

On the one hand, Hume's book reflects the confident spirit of the Enlightenment. In the introduction he rehearses the usual modern philosophic tropes: he finds the foundation of existing philosophic systems "weak"; he complains of the "present imperfect condition of the sciences"; instead of progress in learning, disputes reign among the learned. Then, like Descartes, Locke, and others before him, Hume resolves to put science on a firmer footing by acquainting us with the "extent and force of human understanding." By taking careful inventory of our minds and reviewing the list of ideas delivered by experience, we will be able to make progress precisely because we will understand the sources and—no less important—the limits of human understanding. Paradoxically, by recognizing the limits of human understanding the horizon for the advancement of knowledge will be limitless. "Here then is the only expedient, from which we can hope for success in our philosophical researches," he explains at the outset of the *Treatise:* "to leave the tedious lingering method, which we have hitherto followed, and instead of taking now and then a castle or village on the frontier, to march up directly to the capital or center of these sciences, to human nature itself; which being once masters of, we may every where else hope for an easy victory."[11] Flush from his anticipated victory, Hume says he will prosecute the war by turning his sights and his method of "experimental philosophy" to moral and political subjects. His ambition is nothing less than to be the Newton of the mental and moral universe.

Hume's march on the capital of the sciences, however, resulted in a conquest that may have seemed more like a Pyrrhic victory to his fellow warriors in the cause of Enlightenment. After he had successfully stormed the citadel of human nature, Hume's readers discovered what had so unsettled the young philosopher. Far from finding the commanding force of reason, they instead discovered that reason was severely constrained in its power. What we thought we understood about the world through reason turned out to be illusory. More unsettling still, what we thought we understood about ourselves, our very "selves," was wrong.

Hume illustrated these disturbing conclusions by considering a parlor game. "Here is a billiard-ball lying on a table," he announces, "and another ball moving towards it with rapidity. They strike; and the ball, which was formerly at rest, now acquires a motion. This is as perfect an instance of the relation of cause and effect as any which we know, either by sensation or reflection. Let us therefore examine it."[12]

This commonplace example of the predictable motion of billiard balls then swerves in an uncommon direction. No matter how far we lean over the table, how closely or carefully we fix our eyes on the balls, we will not have the "impression" of cause. Following Locke's empiricism, which holds that all knowledge derives from sense experience, Hume leads us into an impasse that his predecessor seems to have overlooked. There is nothing, he observes, in the sensory world that constitutes the cause of the moving billiard balls. We never have the "impression" of a cause for the good reason that cause is not material. We never see, hear, or touch a cause; instead, we have only a series of contingent impressions. Hume asks us to break the images of billiard balls flitting before our eyes into a succession of separate frames, like the figures a child draws in the edges of his notebook before flipping the pages to entertain himself with this crude animation. On the first page, we see one ball moving toward a second ball; on the second, the moment of contact; and on the third, the second ball moving in turn. Yet nowhere on any of these pages, and certainly not in the space between them, is there a "sensible interval." No matter how much we ruffle the pages or hold them to the light, cause is absent—and there is no point in seeking it.

If cause is not to be found in the sensible world, why do we speak about it as if it *did* exist? Hume replies that experience is, well, the *cause* of our unfounded but essential belief in cause. Every causal act carries the idea of contiguity—namely, a temporal link between two events that seem invariably to follow one another. Experience tells us that when struck by a moving billiard ball, the second ball will move at a certain speed and in a particular direction: "After the discovery of the constant conjunction of any two or more objects, we always draw an inference from one object to another." Hume concludes that our abiding faith in cause and effect is not shaped by reason; rather, it arises from an all too human source: habit. The imperative of the laws of nature, of supposedly necessary connections like cause and effect, "exists in the mind, not in objects."[13] Without the unthinking habit into which experience tricks us, we could not function in the world. Having reduced the moving picture of our experience into the separate frames of which it is composed, and realized that one image does not necessarily lead to the next, we nevertheless have no choice but to flip the pages and watch the show.

"Tis in vain to rack ourselves with *farther* thought and reflection," Hume advises us with the assurance of someone who has been to the edge of the abyss and back: "We can go no *farther* in considering this particular subject."[14] Yet he does go farther, underscoring the fine mess in which reason finds itself with regard to the very object we thought we understood best: ourselves. The difficulty in the admonition inscribed on the Temple of Delphi, embraced by philosophers ever since Socrates, had always seemed to reside in the subject's arduous task of self-knowledge, not in first locating the self. "Know thyself"? Well, if I do not yet know *who* I am, I at least know *that* I am, standing somewhere in there, minding the operations of my mind. Yet Hume questions the very assumption that there is a "self" to know.

Hume's skeptical analysis does not lead to the destination we recognize as our own selves, but instead ushers us into a hall of mirrors from which there is no exit. "For my part, when I enter most intimately into what I call myself, I always stumble on some particular perception or other, of heat or cold, light or shade, love or hatred, pain or pleasure. I never can catch myself at any time without a perception, and never can observe any thing but the perception." To insist that we can glimpse our selves in the buff, stripped of particular perceptions or emotions, is as nonsensical as asking our shadows to stand still while we step back better to observe them. Hume's world reveals that everything we thought to be solid and constant in regard to ourselves constitutes little more than evanescent stages with phony characters. Indeed, Hume compares the mind to a kind of theater "where several perceptions successively make their appearance; pass, repass, glide away, and mingle in an infinite variety of postures and situations."[15]

Just who or what is viewing this ghostly Kabuki play is a question Hume does not address. Instead, he invokes his earlier answer to the conundrum of causation: our mind, not nature, assures the continuity of our selves. Thanks to the resemblance of various experiences in our lives, we come to believe in the existence of a single mind and a unified self. Identity is little more than a "quality" that we attach to sundry perceptions "because of the union of their ideas in the imagination, when we reflect upon them."[16] Yet this union no more exists in the external and objective world than does causation. Both are happy conceits of human nature.

Such, then, was the "new scene of thought" that had appeared in the theater of Hume's young mind, both elevating his ambition and plunging him into depression. While Hume's radical skepticism would eventually unsettle academic and religious establishments, for the moment it disturbed only its young practitioner. This unease pervades the passage at the end of book one of the *Treatise*, where Hume contemplates the wreckage he has wrought of our everyday assumptions. "This sudden view of my danger strikes me with melancholy; and as 'tis usual for that passion, above all others, to indulge itself, I cannot forbear feeding my despair with all the desponding reflections, which the present subject furnishes me with in such abundance." Tinged with personal confession, Hume's description of the isolation of melancholy is also evocative of his analysis three decades later of what he saw as the philosophical delirium into which Rousseau's own reflections on the self—and himself—had led him: "I am first affrighted and confounded with that forlorn solitude, in which I am placed in my philosophy, and fancy myself some strange uncouth monster, who not being able to mingle and unite in society, has been expelled [from] all human commerce, and left utterly abandoned and disconsolate."[17]

If Hume flirted with the potentially debilitating introspection more characteristic of Rousseau, and if he anticipated the Romantic sensibility more usually associated with his future friend, he nonetheless steps back from the precipice to which reason has led him. And his cure for this philosophical melancholy is as stunning as the unexpected cause of the disease, in part owing to its faux-naïveté. Although reason cannot dispel the clouds of skeptical doubt, nature can and nature does. "Most fortunately it happens, that since reason is incapable of dispelling these clouds, nature herself suffices to that purpose, and cures me of this philosophical melancholy and delirium." With a shrug of his great shoulders, Hume abandons his unsettling reflections: "I dine, I play a game of backgammon, I converse, and am merry with my friends; and when after three or four hours' amusement, I would return to these speculations, they appear so cold, and strained, and ridiculous, that I cannot find in my heart to enter into them any farther."[18]

Reason thus is not made the handmaiden to faith, according to the medieval scholastics, nor does it become faith's master, as affirmed the philosophes. Instead, it is made subservient to nature. And faithful to his analysis, Hume does what nature demands. He leaves the dark theater whose images move in strobe-lit procession, rubs his eyes to accustom them to the daylight, and steps into everyday life. What Nietzsche later said of the Greeks applies to Hume: he is superficial because of his profundity.

Massive manuscript in hand, Hume bade farewell to France in the summer of 1737 and left for London. After a difficult search that lasted a year, he finally engaged a publisher, and his work appeared in February 1739. After presenting copies to his London friends, he headed northward to a home he had not seen in five years to await his anticipated fame.

"Never literary attempt was more unfortunate. . . . It fell dead-born from the press, without reaching such distinction, as even to excite a murmur among the zealots."[19] Such, according to Hume, was the welcome given to his Treatise. Rarely in the history of philosophy has so seminal a work been so indifferently welcomed. The general silence that greeted the Treatise's publication taught Hume the limits of philosophical indifference: "How happens it that we philosophers cannot as heartily despise the world as it despises us?"[20]

Yet he persevered. Perhaps recalling his own remark in the beginning of the Treatise that philosophical works were written in language too "abstruse" for most readers, the young philosopher concluded that his book's failure "had proceeded more from the manner than the matter."[21] How could he not have such suspicions when even his friend and elder cousin, the jurist and philosopher Lord Kames, accepted Hume's *Treatise* with trepidation: "I'll do any thing to oblige you. But you must sit by and try to beat your book into my head."[22] A decade later, Hume would recast the philosophy of the *Treatise* into the more accessible *Enquiries*, but in preparation for that task the ambitious young man reassessed the strategy he employed for satisfying his yearning for literary fame.

Hume's literary success came from refashioning his own role as an author. Rather than struggling to explain the admittedly abstruse conclusions of his reasoning to an abstract and unknown audience, Hume began by thinking of the reader himself. Or herself. Intent on gently bringing both gentlemen and gentlewomen to philosophy, Hume adopted a more popular style for his thought. In a fashion, then, Hume anticipated Rousseau's own decision to write a novel, but whereas the author of *Julie* hoped to inspire his readers to resist the corruptions of the city and citified philosophy, the future diplomat conceived his new authorial role as a kind of ambassadorship from the realm of philosophy to a wide readership.

Hume's self-appointment as emissary between the "learned" and the "conversable" worlds was announced in his *Essays, Moral and Political,* the first installment of which appeared in 1741. "I cannot but consider myself as a kind of resident or ambassador from the dominions of learning to those of conversation," he explained, "and shall think it my constant duty to promote a good correspondence betwixt these two states, which have so great a dependence upon each other." The division of the world between these two parts has been a great defect of the age, Hume complained. Without recourse to the literary, historical, and philosophical subjects explored in the world of learning, what is left for residents of the world of conversation but trifling subjects? On the other hand, the world of learning has suffered "by being shut up in colleges and cells, and secluded from the world and good company. . . . Even philosophy went to wrack by this moping recluse method of study." Here we see traces of Hume's own experience as a youth. Philosophy, he declared, must seek out the experience to be found in common life and conversation.[23]

Hume's ambassadorial communications took the form of essays. Originated in the late sixteenth century by Michel de Montaigne, imported to Great Britain and adapted by Francis Bacon, then popularized by Addison and Steele in the early eighteenth century, the essay allowed its practitioner to sketch a subject, developing his thoughts in a seemingly casual and even conversational manner. This proved an ideal medium for Hume. He was soon writing on a wide array of subjects, ranging from politics and economics to love and marriage, supplying the drawing rooms and clubs of Britain with a steady stream of talking points for thoughtful conversation. Commencing his ambassadorship with fifteen essays in the first edition of 1741, Hume nearly doubled his offerings in the next edition, published the following year, and then added as many again in 1752. By midcentury he had written a sufficient number of essays to fill three volumes.

The essays allowed Hume to pursue by other means his war against the philosophical assumptions of his age. Rather than treating philosophy as an abstract system of thought, he embraced the classical notion of philosophy as a way of life. Thus in a remarkable four essay series on the various philosophical approaches he himself had surveyed in his youth — "The Epicurean," "The Stoic," "The Platonist," and, finally, "The Sceptic" — Hume explained how these philosophical schools represent different human character types who are drawn to the competing philosophies as ways of life no less than as ways of thought. While showing sympathy for each of the sects insofar as they appeal to the various facets of our nature, Hume gives the last word to the "Sceptic." Yet the last word is hardly simple. Instead, it sounds a note of caution about the reach of skepticism, an admonition born of Hume's own painful experience with the caustic effects of doubt. "The empire of philosophy extends over a few; and with regard to these too, her authority is very weak and limited." While philosophy is ever eager to force life to obey its dictates, it must instead be made to serve life. "To reduce life to exact rule and method, is commonly a painful, oft a fruitless occupation: And is it not also a proof, that we overvalue the prize for which we contend?"[24] The wise no less than the ignorant are at the mercy of human nature.

Hume brought the same commonsensical tone to essays on political subjects. Politics can indeed be a science, he declared, but it is an incremental and modest science founded upon the hard-earned historical experience with politics, ever cognizant of the inevitably flawed and nicked timber of humanity. The "first principles" of government are neither the social contracts nor abstract ideas brewed in the philosopher's kitchen but rather the practical staples of everyday life: opinion and self-interest. Of course, opinions can be fanciful and self-interest is often myopic, but proper political institutions and enlightened statesmanship can educate opinion and extend the view of interest. "Men must, therefore, endeavor to palliate what they cannot cure," Hume counseled, and they must be led "to consult their own real and permanent interests" by making them see the long-term benefits of obeying law and doing justice.[25]

While skeptical of reason's reach in politics no less than in philosophy, Hume championed the progress in the sciences and arts that Rousseau condemned. Indeed, the essayist may have had the Citizen of Geneva's *Discourse on the Sciences and Arts* in mind when he wrote "Of Refinement in the Arts," which he included in the 1752 edition of the *Essays*, published a year after the appearance of the discourse that made Rousseau famous.[26] While Rousseau wrung his hands over the enervating effect of the arts on our minds and bodies and feared the incompatibility of liberty and the arts, Hume was reassured by the march of human ingenuity. Evidence abounds that industry and art are good not just for our physical and moral constitutions but also for freedom: such activities, history reveals, most often create free government. As a result, while the false "civility" of the cities appalled Rousseau, it cheered Hume. "The more these refined arts advance, the more sociable men become." Aware of the dangers posed by excessive luxury, Hume nonetheless clung to stubborn moderation against drastic responses. Spartan cures are much worse than the Athenian disease. Far better luxury when accompanied by industry than the sloth that reigns among uncultivated individuals and societies. The true statesman must take men as they are, not as they ought to be: "He cannot cure every vice by substituting virtue in its place. Very often he can only cure one vice by another."[27] These sentiments, heir to Mandeville's infamous claim that private vice makes public benefit, and ancestor to Madison's argument in the *Federalist* that "ambition must be made to counteract ambition" in a properly balanced political machine, are far from Rousseau's nostalgic account of an ancient world rich in selfless virtue.

In the *Essays* and his other writings, Hume reveals himself to be skeptical of the prodigies of human nature to which Rousseau appealed as evidence for the puny soul of modern man, the "bourgeois." For Rousseau, history demonstrates how much we have changed, to the point that we no longer believe the stories of virtuous and great-souled men of ancient times. "Base souls do not believe in great men," he would admonish the incredulous reader of the *Social Contract*.[28] Indeed, Hume viewed such stories with just that skeptical attitude. "It is universally acknowledged that there is a great uniformity among the actions of men, in all nations and ages, and that human nature remains still the same, in its principles and operations," Hume maintains, suggesting that this human understanding got by experience serves a critical purpose. "Should a traveler, returning from a far country, bring us an account of men, wholly different from any with whom we were acquainted; men who were entirely divested of avarice, ambition, or revenge; who knew no pleasure but friendship, generosity, and public spirit; we should immediately, from these circumstances, detect the falsehood, and prove him a liar, with the same certainty as if he had stuffed his narration with stories of centaurs and dragons, miracles and prodigies."[29]

What must Hume have thought, then, a few years after he had made this claim, of Rousseau's *Discourse on Inequality*, with its description of human nature through a portrait of a solitary man living in the state of nature, without speech or reason, curiosity or pride? While Hume left no record of his specific impression of Rousseau's *Discourse*, we can safely assume that, for him, it shared the "extravagance" of his future friend's work as a whole. For Hume, Rousseau's solitary and natural man and selfless citizen are chimerical beings, belied by historical testimony. For Rousseau, Hume is guilty of the same sin he alleges against all previous philosophers: they have falsely assumed that human nature does not change, and have failed to look beneath the artificial accretions of society. In short, for Rousseau, the philosophers "spoke about savage man and they described civil man."[30] Hume, of course, was happy to be just such a civil man.

In 1751, with the success of the *Essays* having guaranteed Hume's fame and financial security, he moved from the family estate at Ninewells to Edinburgh. Tellingly, in moving from country to town, Hume reversed Rousseau's own course of a few years later, when, in the face of his own success, he repaired from Paris to the relative isolation of the country. For Hume, as for Rousseau's perplexed friends, a city such as Edinburgh was "the true scene for a man of letters."[31]

Edinburgh had not always been so true a scene. The Scottish capital and university town had been transformed over the first half of the eighteenth century from a sleepy and dank backwater into a lively—though still dank—intellectual center, the home of what came to be called the Scottish Enlightenment. Although the third-largest city of Britain, after London and Bristol, boasting a population of more than fifty thousand, the renaissance of the northern outpost was an unlikely success story. Bolted to England by the 1707 Act of Union and ridden roughshod by an inquisitorial Presbyterian Church, known as the Kirk, Scotland seemed bound for historical irrelevance. Yet a combination of industrious Glaswegian merchants and ambitious intellectuals gave the country a new vitality. Strong-willed and independent-minded men like the philosophers Francis Hutcheson and Lord Kames created a liberal and innovative intellectual climate in which the likes of David Hume, Thomas Reid, Adam Ferguson, and Adam Smith were able to breathe and flourish.

Clubs and societies provided an important structure for this burgeoning class of intellectuals, and the easily sociable Hume took full advantage of the attractions afforded by the city.* He was an assiduous attendee of the Poker Club, which assembled every Friday at Fortune's Tavern, where Hume shared his final political views and sipped his last cup of wine just eight months before his death. Another club, of shorter pedigree but greater note, was the Select Society. Founded in 1754 by Hume's friend the portraitist Allan Ramsay, who was to play an unanticipated role in the fall of Hume's friendship with Rousseau, the Select's

---

*Paradoxically, because the sociable Hume spent so much time with his wide circle of friends, especially after he moved to Edinburgh, we have far fewer letters and other materials by which to trace his life than we do for Rousseau, who maintained a voluminous correspondence from his various places of solitude and exile.

fame grew as quickly as did the list of those waiting to join the original fifteen members. Indeed, the Select was a victim of its own success, swelling to more than a hundred members before it was disbanded in 1763, the same year Hume left Edinburgh for Paris. "Young and old, noble and ignoble, witty and dull, laity and clergy . . . are ambitious of a place amongst us," Hume proudly observed to Ramsay in 1755, shortly after the society's founding. The club had grown to be a matter of "national concern," he added, pronouncing that "the House of Commons was less the object of general curiosity at London than the Select Society at Edinburgh"[32]

Hume was right to crow: rarely have so many remarkable minds sat together on so regular a basis (every Wednesday) in so dim a space (the university's Advocates' Library). Joining Hume at the weekly meetings was his elder cousin, the overbearing Lord Kames, as well as a younger cousin, the nationalist poet and dramatist John Home, with whom Hume carried on a lifelong debate over the correct spelling of their common last name. (Hume had the last word by stipulating in his will that Home could receive his bequeathed case of claret only if he signed his name with a *u*.) Also in attendance were a group of philosophers who would come to be seen as luminaries in the Scottish Enlightenment inspired in part by Hume, including Lord Monboddo, Adam Ferguson, and, closest to Hume, Adam Smith, who commuted from Glasgow, having moved there in the early 1750s to take the chair of moral philosophy.

In addition to discussing such subjects as morals, jurisprudence, political economy, and other topics of philosophical import, the members must have first debated Rousseau's ideas, which were then gaining prominence. For example, the eccentric Lord Monboddo had written a six-volume work on the origins of language, the argument of which in certain respects paralleled Rousseau's own paradoxical position on the subject. After hearing Dr. Johnson ridicule Monboddo's theories and asking whether Rousseau, too, did not "talk such nonsense," Boswell received a characteristically lapidary pronouncement: "True, Sir, but Rousseau *knows* he is talking nonsense, and laughs at the world for staring at him. . . . But I am *afraid*, (chuckling and laughing), Monboddo does *not* know he is talking nonsense."[33] As for Hume, while he dismissed his fellow Scot's work, he appreciated the "diverting oddities" of the jurist's behavior at the meetings.[34] Likewise, the young Adam Ferguson wrote the popular and vaguely Rousseauian *Essay on the History of Civil Society*, published in 1767, shortly after Hume's quarrel with Rousseau and against his advice. Finally, almost twenty years before he published *The Wealth of Nations*, Adam Smith first came to prominence as the author of *The Theory of Moral Sentiments*, published in 1759. Smith's theory joined an analysis of human nature that drew largely on Hume with an account of sympathy that is as much indebted to Hume's hints on the

subject as it is, arguably, decisively influenced by Rousseau. Smith's own appreciation of Rousseau's thought is indicated by the fact that he was among the first
and most sympathetic reviewers of the *Discourse on Inequality,* publishing an account of the Genevan's work in the *Edinburgh Review* in 1756. For all his appreciation for Rousseau's critique of society (witness his discussion in book five of
The Wealth of Nations of how to ameliorate the debasing characteristics of the
division of labor), Smith joined Hume in seeing in the division of the self the
root of morality and civil society, and the spur to progress, while Rousseau
lamented it as our fall from paradise.[35]

At the same time that Rousseau was plunging into the woods to examine the
foundations of society through a hypothetical history of the human species,
Hume was for much the same reasons immersing himself in the much more
mundane task of archival research for his own history. Hume's new literary ambition happily coincided with his appointment, in 1752, as Keeper of the Advocates' Library at the University of Edinburgh. A "genteel office, though of small
revenue," the position was significant for its access to a collection of more than
thirty thousand volumes.[36] Such access was invaluable in a time before the opening of the British Museum, when important historical documents were in private
collections.

Hume's *History of England* secured the foothold on fame he gained with the
Essays. It also secured his fortune: he earned some £3,200 for the work in an age
when a man could consider himself well-to-do on £80 per year.[37] Hume began at
the end of his story, with the first volume, published in 1754, covering the reign
of the first Stuarts and climaxing with the "tragic death" of Charles. The judi-
cious tone of Hume's analysis was initially greeted with an uncertain reception
in a political climate still charged with clashes between Whigs and Tories, each
with their own partisan reading of the events the historian related. "I was, I own,
sanguine in my expectations of the success of this work. I thought that I was the
only historian, that had at once neglected present power, interest, and authority,
and the cry of popular prejudices; and as the subject was suited to every capacity, I expected proportional applause," Hume later wrote; "But miserable was
my disappointment: I was assailed by one cry of reproach, disapprobation, and
even detestation; English, Scotch, and Irish, Whig and Tory, churchman and
sectary, freethinker and religionist, patriot and courtier, united in their rage
against the man, who had presumed to shed a generous tear for the fate of
Charles I."[38] Over the next eight years, Hume made his way more or less back-
ward through history. He completed his task in 1762, ending with the invasion
of Julius Caesar and thus realizing the incredible feat of sixteen hundred years
of history written in less than a decade.

As a historian, Hume offered the same ambassadorial services he had earlier provided in the *Essays*. He described this role in an essay "Of the Study of History," where he addressed a female readership: "There is nothing which I would recommend more earnestly to my female readers than the study of history, as an occupation, of all others, the best suited both to their sex and education, much more instructive than their ordinary books of amusement." The paternalistic tone of this essay, which he eliminated from subsequent editions, obscures a critical point: historical perspective not only readjusts a woman's understanding of public affairs but does so for men as well. As for the ancient Roman historians Tacitus and Sallust, history writing was a tool for cultivating virtue by strengthening the reader's desire to excel among his peers. Historians were "the true friends of virtue."[39] Unlike novelists, metaphysicians, or priests, historians were rooted in the world of experience, training themselves and their readers to distinguish between the credible and incredible, the probable and improbable. Invention and fancy—the siren calls of extravagance—were thus resisted.

Hume aimed his work at the same middle-class readership that fed on Richardson's novels as well as Rousseau's six-part *Julie*, which was published as Hume's six-volume history neared completion.[40] Indeed, as many tears may have been shed over Hume's rendering of Charles I's final moments before his execution as over the (much longer) death of Rousseau's Julie. For Hume the reasons were clear: "I did indeed endeavor to paint the King's catastrophe (which was singular and dismal) in as pathetic a manner as I could; and to engage me, needed I any other motive, than my interest as a writer, who desires to please and interest his readers?"[41] And there is evidence that Hume's higher goal as a professor of virtue also was met on occasion. Louis XVI reread the passage on Charles's death on the eve of his own singular and dismal beheading by the French revolutionaries.[42] Perhaps Hume's account contributed to the fortitude with which Louis met his end. And James Boswell, a less resolute apprentice in virtue, reported to his journal in 1763 that he had spent the day reading the *History*, which, he wrote, "enlarged my views, filled me with great ideas, and rendered me happy."[43]

Despite having finally fully attained the literary fame he longed for, Hume was growing unhappy in Edinburgh. Despite its reputation for being a "new Athens" of the North, Edinburgh still revealed the influence of its more Spartan past in the form of determined Presbyterians, known as the High-Flyers, who continued to preach hellfire and brimstone. This group of stern men, spiritual kin of Rousseau's Calvinist persecutors in Geneva, was convinced that the good people of Edinburgh were the "Heirs of Wrath." Looking with suspicion at the capital

Louis Carrogis (1717–1806), portrait of David Hume (1711–76), pencil, chalk, and watercolor. © Scottish National Portrait Gallery, Edinburgh / The Bridgeman Art Library

from their rural Lowland and remote Highland parishes, the High-Flyers detected worrisome implications for morality and religion in the new philosophy invading their native shores.

A number of Hume's friends and members of the Select were themselves ordained in the Church of Scotland. Several of them, including the philosopher's cousin John Home, were ordained ministers who pursued secular careers, while Hume's good friend the literary scholar Hugh Blair won renown through the sermons he delivered from the pulpit of the High Church at Saint Giles, Edinburgh's largest and most prestigious church. Yet they were moderates who were convinced that reason and faith could coexist. At least to a point. The liberty to discuss any topic at the Select Society admitted two exceptions: subjects that "regarded revealed religion or which might give occasion to vent any principles of Jacobitism."[44] These urbane ministers nonetheless did not represent the silent Scotland, still attached to the harsh and unbending ways of the traditional Kirk. These were the faithful descendants of the Edinburgh officials who, scarcely fifty years before, had sentenced to death Thomas Aikenhead, an eighteen-year-old student accused of blasphemous remarks against the Christian faith. While the youth's body, strung up at "Galowlee betwixt Leith and Edinburgh," no longer cast as long and chilling a shadow on the city's denizens as it had at the turn of the century, the war between faith and reason had not yet ended.[45]

David Hume's writings proved to be one battlefield on which this war was waged. The clergy's running skirmishes with the philosopher had erupted into outright hostilities when Hume, in 1748, published *An Enquiry Concerning Human Understanding*. A substantial reworking of the first part of the *Treatise*, which he said corrected "some negligences in his former reasoning and more in the expression,"[46] the *Enquiry* contained material Hume had prudently omitted from the earlier work. The suspicion of the faithful about the philosopher's sins of omission in the *Treatise* were therefore confirmed by the sin of commission with the inclusion of the chapter "On Miracles."

In his discussion of miracles, Hume made the simple claim there that we must always give greater weight to any event that seems the lesser miracle: "One should only believe in an improbable event if the alternative was to believe in an even less probable event."[47] History shows that claims on behalf of miracles—spurred as they were by superstition, desire, peer pressure, ignorance, or hypocrisy—have always been less probable than the basis for rejecting those claims. "Where a supposition is so contrary to common sense, any positive evidence of it ought never be regarded," Hume told his fellow doubter Edward Gibbon: "Men run with great avidity to give their evidence in favor of what flatters their passions, and their national prejudices."[48]

Intent on preventing "demented men from doing harm to others," the High-Flyers went on the offensive, eventually attempting to pass a resolution before the General Assembly of the Church of Scotland demanding that the church condemn with "the utmost abhorrence . . . those impious and infidel principles which are subversive of all religion natural and revealed and have such pernicious influence on life and morals."[49] Though not named, Hume was clearly the demented infidel most on their minds. As he wrote in a jocular though uneasy tone to Ramsay: "They did not propose to burn me, because they cannot. But they intend to give me over to Satan, which they think they have the power of doing."[50] They had, however, demonstrated the power to frustrate Hume's candidacy for a chair in ethics at the University of Edinburgh in 1744, and once again checked him in 1752 when his name was put forward to replace Adam Smith as he vacated his chair at Glasgow. "I should prefer David Hume to any man for a colleague," wrote Smith, "but I am afraid the public would not be of my opinion."[51]

The philosopher's antagonists—whose leader, the Reverend George Anderson, Hume referred to as the "godly, spiteful, pious, splenetic, charitable, unrelenting, meek, persecuting, Christian, inhuman, peace-making, furious Anderson"— were outnumbered by friends and admirers. Yet the dogged persistence of religious controversy had leached even into Hume's friendships with moderates like Hugh Blair. Their disputes left Hume so "tired" and Blair so "angry" that the two friends agreed never again to discuss religion.[52] The habitual gloom of Edinburgh began to descend like the fog over Hume, made uneasy by a growing sense of inner exile.

Hume's professional woes chafed his deepening ambivalence: he was uncertain whether he had reached a crossroads or quite simply the end of the road.

By the early 1760s his writings enjoyed an audience exceeded in size only by Rousseau's, and Boswell was justified in claiming that Hume was "Britain's greatest writer."[53] Yet having attained the summit, where does one next go? Not only were his great philosophical works behind him, but so too were the popular essays and historical writings. Even those works not yet in print—like the corrosive *Dialogues Concerning Natural Religion*, which Smith and his other friends prevailed upon him to keep to himself until his death—had already been written. With a self-deprecating touch, he told his old Scottish acquaintance David Mallet that he was "resolved to resist, as a temptation of the devil, any impulse towards writing, and I am really so much ashamed of myself when I see my bulk on a shelf, as well as when I see it in a glass, that I would fain prevent my growing more corpulent either way."[54]

Hume was certainly sincere in his claim that he had reached the end of his writing life, but his bantering tone failed to disguise a deeper ambivalence. Alarmingly, the mist of melancholy—the paralyzing "cloud" he first knew as a youth—seemed to be gathering again on the horizon. Unlike Rousseau, Hume had little appetite for self-analysis, or at least he did not involve those around him in the activity. Yet, tellingly, he confided to a friend that he was slipping toward "a total indifference towards everything in human life."[55] To another correspondent he owned that he had become a "recluse and ascetic, who retains no ambition, who has lost his relish for pleasure."[56] "I never had much ambition, I mean, for power and dignities; and I am heartily cured of the little I had," he wrote his brother in early 1761: "I believe a fireside and a book, the best things in the world for my age and disposition."[57] Claiming to be content, Hume was in actuality spent.

Hume was ready to move on, but where and to what end? "I have been accustomed to meet with nothing but insults and indignities from my native country," he confided to his friend Gilbert Elliot in late March 1764. Then, with a mocking air of self-importance, Hume quoted the epitaph of the Roman general Scipio Africanus: *Ingrata patria, ne ossa quidem habebis*—"Ungrateful country, you will not even have my bones."[58] Yet when he made this aside, Hume already knew that another country—the same country that had welcomed him at the end of his first, youthful bout of melancholy—was keen to have him, bones and all, in order to express its gratitude.

CHAPTER FOUR

The Lord of Ferney

*Ah, the scoundrel! Ah! The monster! I shall
have to have him beaten to death.*
— *Voltaire*

Having successfully bound his soul to Rousseau, even if by a hair, Boswell set out from Môtiers on the morning of December 16, 1764, following *la bise*, the icy wind that swept southward through the Jura. His next stop was Ferney, Voltaire's estate on the outskirts of Geneva. Fortunately, the voluble Scot did not mention Voltaire's name during his stay with Rousseau. By then he knew that they were not just immortal thinkers but also mortal enemies.

When Rousseau fled Paris in 1762 for Môtiers, he became a neighbor of sorts to Voltaire, another exile who had recently settled nearby in the seigniorial splendor of Ferney. The two men never enjoyed particularly warm ties.[1] Their first contact occurred when Voltaire, at the height of literary fame in 1745, received a fan letter from Rousseau declaring that he had been working for fifteen years to merit the great man's attention and earn his patronage.[2] Given the thankless task of shortening Voltaire's libretto for Rameau's opera *La Princesse de Navarre*, the self-taught musician struggled for several weeks; in the end his labor went unrecognized and unremunerated. From this inauspicious beginning, relations only worsened. When, in his prizewinning *Discourse on the Arts and Sciences*, Rousseau accused "famed Arouet" of prostituting his literary talents, he reminded his readers of Voltaire's given name rather than his nom de plume, thus indirectly accusing him of hypocrisy. And Rousseau's *Discourse on Inequality* hardly improved relations, as Voltaire's acid reply, in which he thanked the author for the copy of his "new book against the human race," had made clear.

By the end of the 1750s, however, mutual diffidence had given way to enmity, spurred by the controversy over Rousseau's *Letter to d'Alembert*. Voltaire believed that Rousseau's animus toward the establishment of a theater in Geneva was directed at him, referring to the work as the "Letter on the Subject of the Theater at Ferney."[3] Rousseau was more than willing to confirm Voltaire's belief. Convinced that Voltaire was at the root of both his and Geneva's misfortune, Rousseau could not restrain himself. "The wretch has ruined my country. I would hate him more if I despised him less," he raged to a mutual acquaintance: "His talents only serve, like his wealth, to nourish the depravity of his heart."[4] Then, finally, in a notorious letter to Voltaire in June 1760, Rousseau declared with brutal simplicity: "I hate you."[5]

The feeling was mutual. While Voltaire was above responding to such a letter, he was not above regaling his many correspondents with a display of magnanimous pity for poor Jean-Jacques mixed with vicious innuendoes. But Voltaire could not stop there. The man for whom no enemy however small was beneath notice then penned *Four Letters on the Nouvelle Héloïse* under the pseudonym the Marquis de Ximénès, characterizing Rousseau's novel as "stupid, bourgeois, impudent," and, perhaps worst of all, "boring."[6] The philosophes were shocked by the brutality of the attack, leveled as much at the author as his work, and when d'Alembert protested, Voltaire shot back: "The philosophes are disunited. The little troupe devours one another while the wolves come to devour it. I am angriest with your Jean-Jacques. The arch-fool, who might have amounted to something if he had allowed himself be guided by you, has decided to stand apart; he writes against the theater after having written a bad play; he writes against France, which nourishes him; he finds four or five rotten planks of Diogenes' barrel and climbs inside to bark."[7]

Voltaire was contemptuous of the barking philosopher, but also clearly worried over his bite. Yet after the condemnation of *Emile* and the *Social Contract*, even Voltaire seemed to commiserate with the plight of his fellow exile, restricting his attacks to the semipublic realm of his letters. Yet at the very moment Boswell traveled the hundred miles or so that divided the two great men, events were unfolding that would turn Voltaire into Rousseau's irreconcilable enemy, determined to chase him from his mountain refuge and hound him even as far as England.

Voltaire had settled at Ferney in 1758. Though located in France, his estate was a short ride from Geneva; should the authorities knock at the front door, Voltaire was well placed to slip out the back door and across the border. Approaching seventy, Voltaire could look back upon a life that justified such caution. Born into a bourgeois Parisian family during the reign of Louis XIV—a period he would brilliantly narrate in *The Age of Louis XIV*—the young François-Marie Arouet excelled at the renowned Jesuit school Louis le Grand. As with Hume, Diderot, and so many of his peers in the Republic of Letters, he rebelled against the career in law for which he was groomed. Tensions grew so great between father and son that Arouet the elder threatened the younger with a lettre de cachet, the vehicle by which state or parental authorities in France could imprison an individual without charge or legal recourse.

Young Arouet managed to avoid the Bastille, but he became an intimate of the prison soon after he launched himself in society. During the Regency, the period stretching from Louis XIV's death in 1715 to Louis XV's ascension in 1723, Voltaire was *embastillé*—the prison's infamy had spawned a verb—for writing erotic poems at the expense of the regent, Philippe duc de Bourbon, whom the author congratulated as a "new Lot" for his incestuous affair with his daughter.[8] Freed after nearly a year, the poet adopted his pen name (an approximate anagram of Arouet le J[eune]) and quickly won literary fame as Voltaire.

Given his taste for rebellion, the ambitious writer did not remain a stranger to prison and exile. Only a few years later, while enjoying the great success of his tragedy *Oedipe* and of the epic poem he had begun in the Bastille, the *Henriade*, which celebrated the reign of Henri IV—and by implication condemned the religious fanaticism that Henri sought to tame—Voltaire was again hustled back to the Bastille, but not for his poetry this time.

At a gathering in Paris, the Chevalier de Rohan had encountered the bright, ambitious, and bourgeois Voltaire. The aristocrat smirked, "Arouet? Voltaire? Just what is your name?" Insulted by a man with nothing other than birth to recommend him, Voltaire shot back: "Whatever it may be, at least I bring it honor." Shortly after, several of Rohan's servants roughed up Voltaire. Watching the mugging from his carriage window, Rohan called out: "Don't hit his head: it may still have some use."[9]

Voltaire's appeals for justice went unheard: his aristocratic friends closed ranks behind Rohan, and his eyes opened to the reality of his world. When he began sword lessons in order to challenge the chevalier to a duel, Voltaire explained himself with the same wit that had led to his predicament: "I have constantly sought to restore not my honor, but the chevalier's, which has proved too difficult."[10] Rohan's family was not amused and had Voltaire trundled off once again to the Bastille. The frustrated duelist secured his release only upon promising to leave France for an extended period. His choice of exile was England.[11] Once there, true to Rohan's taunt, Voltaire revealed that his head still had some use—fittingly, to call into question the society that bred and coddled men like Rohan: a world of arbitrary and irresponsible power, hidebound traditions, and unjustified social distinctions.

Voltaire's English sojourn, begun in 1727, lasted nearly three years, time enough to meet a number of famous Englishmen, including Alexander Pope and Jonathan Swift. Voltaire was too late, though, to meet the most famous Englishman of all, Isaac Newton, who had died shortly before his arrival. Lost in the crowd that surged into Westminster Abbey for the funeral of the author of the *Principia Mathematica*, Voltaire was thunderstruck. Even in death, Newton's impact on the Frenchman was immense. Having come from a nation where the aristocracy and clergy held a monopoly on power and privilege, Voltaire marveled at a society where a scientist was buried with the honors of a king.[12]

Voltaire recollects his wonder in the *Philosophical Letters*, first titled *English Letters* and begun during his exile in London. The "letters" vibrate even today with the excitement of a man who had crossed the Channel yet seemed to have landed in a New World. As Voltaire wrote (in English) to a friend in 1728, "I think and write like a free Englishman."[13] A series of frequently idealized set scenes, the letters lightly move between France and England, Old World and New, past and future. The common theme is the need to free reason from the chains of religious and political tyranny. Hence his claim that rather than persecuted and hounded—the fate Voltaire, with some exaggeration, claimed France had reserved for Descartes—Newton's great fortune was not only to have been "born in a free country, but in an age when . . . reason alone was cultivated."[14] Along with his repeated invocations of Francis Bacon and John Locke, Voltaire's references to Newton in his *Philosophical Letters* prepared the ground for the eventual canonization by the editors of the *Encyclopédie* of this trinity of English thinkers.

Voltaire's praise for the way the English practiced religion as well as business was an implicit but sharp slap at France. In the hurly-burly of the London Exchange, Voltaire observed, religious faith counted for little: "Only those who go bankrupt earn the epithet 'infidel.'" Only when these businessmen return home at the end of the day do they take up the religious practices they had left at their doors that same morning. The moral? "Were there just one religion in England, despotism might arise; were there two, people would be cutting one another's throats; but as there are dozens, they are all happy and live in peace."[15] The underlying contrast was with France, where despotism and religious warfare had coexisted for centuries.

Paris proscribed the book in 1732, declaring that it presented "the greatest danger for religion and public order," thus illustrating the validity of the book's thesis.[16] (Hume and Pope, the one excoriated for his skepticism and the other excluded from public posts for his Roman Catholicism, must have smiled at fellow Britons who preened themselves on Voltaire's exaggerated account of their religious toleration.) The most delicious irony, though, attended the ritual shredding and burning of the proscribed work outside the Palais de Justice: the government official in charge of the auto-da-fé wanted to read the book himself, so he carefully tucked away the offending copy and tossed a different book to the flames.[17]

Fleeing Paris, Voltaire had to savor these ironies on the run. Though he could not know it at the time, he was launching himself into a long life of exile, tracing the same arc as Rousseau and Hume, as well as of his greatest fictional creation, Candide. For the next two decades, Voltaire largely depended upon the kindness of others, especially on Émilie du Châtelet. This extraordinary woman was not just his lover and protector, having set up home at Cirey, her amiable husband's chateau in the Lorraine, but also Voltaire's mathematics and physics teacher. During their time at Cirey, Châtelet translated Newton's *Principia* into French—the version is still in print today—while Voltaire published a popularization of the Englishman's work, the *Elements of the Philosophy of Newton*. Their days were devoted to research and writing amid a jumble of laboratory instruments, books, and manuscripts. According to one visitor, the two of them were "plunged in gaiety, one writing verse in his corner, the other triangles in hers."[18]

Voltaire's writings of this period are animated by the same concerns found in the *Henriade* and *Philosophical Letters*—hatred of religious fanaticism and faith in the progress in the sciences and arts—but the more mature writer had learned to buffer his criticism. This was the period of his greatest and most popular dramatic works, beginning with *Zaïre*, the so-called Christian tragedy of 1732, in which he treated religious difference under the guise of a love story, and followed by plays with similar concerns, including *Alzire* and *Mahomet; or, On Fanaticism*.[19] During this same period he turned his attention to history as well, beginning with the *History of Charles XII*, published in 1731. His examination of the spectacular rise and fall of the young Swedish warrior king inaugurated a new kind of historical writing. In contrast with chronicles commissioned by monarchs more interested in shoring up their legitimacy than getting the facts straight, Voltaire's work concluded with a lengthy diatribe against the royal in-

justices and depredations that litter the course of history.[20] He applied his critical tools closer to home in the great *Age of Louis XIV* (1751), a work that emphasized the "age"—its literary and scientific accomplishments—more than
the monarch who lent his name to it. Hume, for one, owed a great debt to the
kind of historical writing Voltaire practiced.

Eventually, Voltaire's continued success in so many genres could no longer
be ignored. The fifty-year-old author was therefore elected in 1746 to the
Académie française, an honor that followed on the heels of his appointment
by Louis XV as historiographer of France, and then as gentleman of the bedchamber. The former enfant terrible had established himself as the leading man
of letters in France, and even a member of the establishment itself—an accom-
plishment Voltaire viewed with the ambivalence of someone who both envied
and scorned the well born.

As he passed fifty years of age, then, Voltaire seemed to have reached the
pinnacle of fame and the heights of personal happiness. But a series of catastro-
phes, personal and philosophical, then struck. First, there was the death of Émilie
de Châtelet. Even after their relationship as lovers ended, the intimate friendship
between these two remarkable individuals continued until 1749. By then, Châtelet
had taken a new and feckless lover, the soldier and poet Saint Lambert. At the age
of forty-two, she became pregnant and gave birth to an infant who survived
barely two weeks. Yet the child outlived the unfortunate mother, who died of
puerperal fever. While Voltaire buried the dead, Saint Lambert became the lover
of Rousseau's own great love, Sophie d'Houdetot. Voltaire was shattered and
never fully recovered.

Bereft of Châtelet's steadying influence, Voltaire moved to Prussia in 1750 at
the invitation of Frederick the Great. Like many of the philosophes, Voltaire admired enlightened despots, though not without some nervous ambiguity, in part
because he saw such kings and queens as the necessary patrons of the project of
enlightenment. For their part, Frederick and his brethren saw the philosophes
as possible agents of their own economic and political progress and were also
keen for the publicity that patronage brought. The young and ruthless Prussian
monarch had wooed Voltaire for a number of years to adorn his court in Berlin
and Potsdam. Which one needed the other more is difficult to say: Frederick to
serve as Voltaire's guarantor of his freedom, or Voltaire to be Frederick's guarantor of his intellectual pretensions. Like Diderot, who remarked of his own
frustrating visit to the court of Catherine the Great of Russia that he had not
until then seen a tiger in the flesh, Voltaire soon learned that enlightened despots
are better admired from afar.[21] As Frederick warned him, "I like people who are
quiet and peaceful, who do not display tragic passions in their conduct."[22]

In the end, Voltaire proved as allergic to a quiet life as Frederick did to limits on his will and rule. Friction between the two men grew so great by 1753 that Voltaire, who had hurriedly written to a friend that "the orange has been pressed, and I must now think of saving the rind," tried stealing out of the kingdom.[23] Learning of Voltaire's flight, Frederick reacted with sovereign rage: he had the writer imprisoned in Frankfort. Managing to escape his jailers a few weeks later, Voltaire succeeded in blackening the king's reputation and burnishing his own, while Frederick in his turn thought his fugitive man of letters "the most treacherous rascal in the universe."[24] As Voltaire's friends and foes alike knew, there was much truth to this declaration.

Had Voltaire died before turning sixty, Paul Valéry remarked, he would be forgotten today. And well he might have been. The heartbroken fifty-seven-year-old who barely escaped Frederick's suffocating embrace was an old man by the standards of his day. Moreover, he had always been somewhat sickly. Sparing his delicate digestion by consuming little more than tea and clear broth, he had been "dying" for decades. Yet Voltaire now risked outliving his literary reputation. The *Henriade* lay thirty years behind, more revered than read. While the Comédie française continued to perform his dramatic works, Voltaire would never again know the success of *Zaïre* or *Alzire*. Indeed, even these works were calcifying, impressive fossils from an earlier age. True, his importation of English science and philosophy through the *Philosophical Letters* had helped transform continental thought, and he was honored as the patriarch of the philosophes who were just beginning their labor on the *Encyclopédie*. But being a patriarch is an old man's job, and Voltaire seemed more a figurehead of the Enlightenment than its captain. Most important, the intellectual terrain was shifting dramatically. At the very moment Voltaire's star was waning, Rousseau shot to celebrity with his first *Discourse*, which attacked the sciences and arts whose progress Voltaire had dedicated his life to furthering.

At this critical juncture, however, Voltaire became the "Voltaire" we know today. Working first from his mansion Les Délices in Geneva, where he moved in 1755 after fleeing Frederick, and then at Ferney, he launched a new career as a public intellectual. Though the term *intellectual* would not be coined for another century, Voltaire has often and rightly been cast as the ancestor of Victor Hugo, Émile Zola, and Albert Camus: thinkers who, in their battle against the arbitrary actions of the state and church, fought for reason, truth, and justice. In the words of his younger contemporary Condorcet, the old philosophe was to be "found beginning the fight or determining the victory" wherever reason and humanity were hanging in the balance.[25]

The occasion for his new vocation was the Calas Affair. In October 1761 Jean Calas, a merchant in the city of Toulouse, was charged with the murder of one of his sons, found hanging lifelessly from a rafter in the father's cloth shop.

In the era's roiling brew of religious fanaticism, the Catholic authorities of the city's *parlement* accused the Protestant Calas of killing his son to prevent his conversion to Catholicism. Condemned to death, the elder Calas was tortured, broken on the wheel, and, following a two-hour "pause" for confession, which the bloodied and maimed Calas refused to provide, strangled to death. With the family's property confiscated, Calas's wife was reduced to poverty, the two daughters were packed off to Catholic convents, and another son fled to Geneva. The case seemed closed.

And closed it would have stayed were it not for Voltaire, who learned about Calas's fate from visitors to his estate a few weeks later. At first tempted to dismiss the trial as an internal affair between two bands of fanatics, he soon realized the challenge it posed to the values of the Enlightenment. "My tragedies are not so tragic" as Calas's death, he concluded.[26] Was there a better illustration of Voltaire's battle cry, "*Écrasez l'infâme*"? The "infamy" that had to be crushed — religious intolerance married to absolute political power — had reared its awful head in Toulouse, and Voltaire decided to confront it. Launching an investigation, Voltaire quickly discovered that there had been a fatal miscarriage of justice. As he implored his friend d'Alembert: "Shout everywhere, I beg you, for the Calas and against fanaticism, for it is *l'infâme* that has caused their misery."[27]

From his bedchamber at Ferney, Voltaire singlehandedly forced this affair onto center stage of the Republic of Letters, and onto the docket of the French state. He wrote countless letters to government ministers — even drawing the king's mistress, Madame de Pompadour, into the case — publicized the affair in English newspapers, and composed a small, sparkling work called *Treatise on Toleration*, which was published in 1763. Finally, Voltaire's efforts were rewarded: a Paris court annulled the judgment against Calas in 1765, and Louis XV provided a grant to the family.

Among Voltaire's most precious possessions was a copy of Carmontelle's engraving of the Calas family, gathered to hear the verdict clearing the name of their murdered father and husband. This print can be glimpsed hanging above Voltaire's bed in Jean Huber's painting *La Levée de Voltaire*. In this small and striking canvas, Huber, the Swiss artist whose paintings documented Voltaire's life at Ferney, conveys the drama of this seemingly mismatched contest between one man and the vast bureaucratic machinery of state and church. Still in bedclothes and nightcap, a vigorous Voltaire stands on one leg by his bed, pulling red breeches over his other leg. He is busy dictating a letter, one of several thousand he dictated to Jean-Louis Wagnière, the last, most competent, and most faithful in a long line of exhausted secretaries, who is seated at a desk in the lower right-hand corner of the painting. From this bedroom in a distant corner of France, Voltaire exhorted, explained, and excoriated, creating a one-man public relations firm that rallied enlightened Europeans to the values of the era Voltaire had done so much to shape.

Voltaire's moral ascendancy in the wake of the Calas Affair partly explained the constant stream of visitors to Ferney. Unlike Rousseau, who drew so many visitors because he wished to be left alone, Voltaire courted and embraced them. He happily referred to himself as the "innkeeper of Europe," estimating toward the end of his life that he had entertained as many as five hundred Englishmen and Scots alone.[28] Voltaire invested great amounts of money, time, and attention on cultivating his garden; with just slight exaggeration he declared that, apart from lumberjack, there wasn't a job he had not done on his estate.[29] His favorite role, however, was theatrical impresario. He had a small theater built in the chateau that could seat three hundred people to watch his many tragedies. Writer and director, Voltaire often also starred in his productions. He especially enjoyed the role of Lusignan, the ill-starred father of Zaïre. His performances left some visitors untouched; one guest mocked his host's "tall gaunt figure with a sword of corresponding dimensions constantly getting between his legs" while he strutted tragically across the small stage. Yet his performances brought tears to the eyes of many others—including Voltaire himself, often overcome by his own eloquence. As one tourist justifiably exclaimed, "It would be scandalous to go home without having seen Voltaire."[30]

James Boswell, for once, would not risk *this* scandal. Having departed Rousseau's cottage in Môtiers a week earlier, Boswell finally arrived in Geneva on Christmas Eve 1764. Scarcely pausing to unpack his bags, he immediately hired a coach and appeared at Voltaire's door unannounced. Liveried footmen showed Boswell to the drawing room while his letter was taken up to their lord. Biding his time, the visitor studied the crowd he had joined. Like a rococo ancestor of reality shows, Ferney on most days housed more than fifty family members, sycophants, hangers-on, servants, and visitors. Running the household, when not starring in one of the master's tragedies, was Voltaire's niece and mistress Mme Denis, described by one English visitor as a "well-painted, fat, and middle-aged French lady."[31] Other denizens were a destitute grand-niece of the playwright Corneille (along with her husband and children); a defrocked Jesuit, Père Adam, who when not playing chess with Voltaire served as his foil for anti-Catholic jibes; and Wagnière, whose office was below a trapdoor in Voltaire's bedroom.

To Boswell's great disappointment, Voltaire sent word that he was very ill and "abed"—not at all unusual for a man who, as Boswell noted, "is in opposition to our sun, for he rises in the evening." Unimpressed by the motley gathering in whose midst he found himself, Boswell grew impatient. He had not trav-

Jean Huber (1721 – 86), *The Levée of Voltaire at Ferney*, oil on canvas, after 1759. © Musée de la Ville de Paris, Musée Carnavalet / Lauros / Giraudon / The Bridgeman Art Library

eled across the snowbound Jura in order to gossip with provincial gentry. At that moment, though, he was pulled from his reflections by Voltaire's sudden arrival. The grand old man looked just like his portrait: a skeletal frame enclosed in a stylish slate blue nightgown, and a raptorlike head crowned by a large, rather dirty three-knotted wig that had long since passed out of fashion. Beneath the ornate hairpiece, Voltaire's deeply set blue eyes shined while his thin lips were pulled across a toothless mouth.

"He was not in spirits, nor I either," the Scot later wrote in his journal about their first meeting. Yet Voltaire, even when ill, was incapable of being dull. When the guest had asked him whether he still spoke English, the "monarch of French literature" replied that he did not: "To speak English one must place the tongue between the teeth, and I have lost my teeth." Glancing at Père Adam, he gleefully declared, "There, Sir, is a young man, a scholar who is learning your language, a broken soldier of the Company of Jesus."[32] With a theatrical flourish, Voltaire then turned to his other guests and soon returned to his bedchamber while Boswell and the others were invited to dine.

Boswell returned to Geneva and attended Christmas services, all the while plotting another visit to Ferney. In a letter to Mme Denis, Boswell baldly asked to spend a night at Ferney. The reason was simple: just as the sun, in the person of Voltaire, was rising at Ferney, it was setting over Geneva, whose gates swung shut before dark. Consequently, Boswell noted, he was prevented from making a full acquaintance with Voltaire—or, for that matter, from paying court to his admirable niece. He could, if need be, lodge in the coldest garret of the chateau. Or, indeed, sleep on two chairs set up in the bedchamber of the comely maid he had glimpsed earlier that day. "I beg you may let me know if the favor which I ask is granted, that I may bring a nightcap with me." The Scot's effrontery again carried the day: Voltaire's curiosity was piqued. Predictably for someone whose life was spent juggling pseudonyms, Voltaire replied (in English) under the guise of his niece. "We have few beds, but you will not sleep on two chairs. My uncle, though very sick, hath guessed at your merit. I know it more, because I have seen you longer"[33]

Nightcap in hand, an exuberant Scot set out two days later for his appointed stay at Ferney. When "the magician" appeared at about seven that evening, he immediately sat at the chessboard, calling, "Fetch Père Adam," and the old Jesuit came running for his appointed match. As the guests gathered, Boswell positioned himself next to Voltaire to "put him in tune." Never tiring of trying to make his host speak English, Boswell drew out Voltaire by getting him to debate the merits of Shakespeare ("a buffoon at Bartholomew Fair"), his friend Dr. Johnson ("a superstitious dog"), and English government ("You are the slaves of laws. The French are the slaves of men"). Voltaire even warbled tunes learned decades earlier in London, performed with such bold flights of mimicry and humor, vaudevillian bearing and toothless articulation, that Boswell repeatedly exclaimed to himself, "Upon my soul this is astonishing!"

While the other guests retired to dine, Boswell remained glued to his host's side in the drawing room. Intent on picking up with Voltaire where he had left off with Rousseau, the Scot dragged an enormous Bible over to his host in order to dispute the Scriptures. "For a certain portion of time there was a fair opposition between Voltaire and Boswell," he boasted to his journal, adding less confidently: "The daring bursts of his ridicule confounded my understanding." Having resembled "an orator of ancient Rome" just moments before, Voltaire suddenly turned into one of his tragic heroines: overwhelmed by dizziness, he dramatically swooned into a chair.

As he prepared to quit Ferney the next day, Boswell thanked his host. "When I came to see you, I thought to see a very great, but a very bad, man," he told Voltaire. A bemused Voltaire, perhaps relieved that his obstinate and quirky visitor was leaving, replied, "You are very sincere." Then as he did with Rousseau, Boswell requested permission to write him in English. Voltaire agreed; the men parted. A few months later, Boswell did write, returning to his great obsession: the ultimate fate of our souls. The sigh from Ferney was audible: while "young scholars and priests know all of that perfectly," Voltaire confessed that he was himself "but a very ignorant fellow." Despite Boswell's subsequent efforts to continue the conversation about his soul's ultimate disposition, Voltaire never again replied.[34]

"I have been with Monsieur Voltaire," Boswell wrote Rousseau on New Year's Eve as he prepared to leave Geneva for Italy: "His conversation is the most brilliant I have ever heard. I had a conversation alone with him lasting an hour. It was a very serious conversation. He spoke to me of his natural religion in a way that struck me. In spite of all that has happened, you would have loved him that evening."[35]

Boswell could not have been more mistaken. As the young Scot wrote these lines, open warfare was breaking out between the two men. The casus belli was the book Voltaire was reading at the very moment Boswell had showed up at his door. This was Rousseau's *Letters Written from the Mountain*, his impassioned defense of his besieged *Social Contract* and attack on the usurpation of democratic authority in his native Geneva. The book had just been published and was already casting a spark into the dry tinder of partisan politics in Geneva. Reading the book the same night that Boswell was seeking permission to visit from Mme Denis, Voltaire bounded from his bed and shouted, "Ah, the scoundrel! Ah! The monster! I shall have to have him beaten to death. . . . Yes, I'll have him beaten to death between his *gouvernante*'s knees."[36]

What drove Voltaire to such fury? He could easily overlook the book's withering critique of the autocratic Small Council and its effective assumption of power from the more democratic General Council. Likewise, having praised the "Profession of Faith of the Savoyard Vicar" in *Emile* as the only good thing

Rousseau ever wrote, Voltaire had no real quarrel with Rousseau's defense of natural religion and attack on intolerance in that work. The source of Voltaire's rage was neither philosophical nor political but personal. In a passage of the *Letters* in which he is defending his views on toleration, Rousseau sarcastically asks why Voltaire's Genevan friends had not imbibed the spirit of toleration ceaselessly preached by their leader, citing Voltaire's *Oath of the Fifty* as proof of his hypocritical stand.[37] What Rousseau had committed in Voltaire's eyes was the one unpardonable crime in the Republic of Letters: he had revealed Voltaire as the author of a work he had published anonymously.

Voltaire's violent reaction can be understood only when we recall that many of the Enlightenment's most important works were published anonymously. Along with scandalous works like Helvétius's materialist tract *De l'esprit*, La Mettrie's *Man, a Machine*, and Diderot's erotic *Indiscreet Jewels* and philosophical *Letter on the Blind*, even Montesquieu's *Persian Letters* was published anonymously. The ubiquity of anonymity resulted from the system of censorship in France, where censors and authors played a careful game of cat and mouse. This game included a whole series of diversionary tactics. Works printed in France bore the imprint of false publishers in Amsterdam, London, or other locales where censorship was less rigorous and where French law could not reach. In turn, books bearing the name of French publishers were produced just across the border, and authorities looked the other way when trunks filled with forbidden merchandise made their way across the mountains from border towns like Neuchâtel (a precarious trip that Rousseau himself took as a young man while smuggling a box of music taken by his teacher from the cathedral). The censors, moreover, were largely complicit, harrumphing that they were shocked— shocked!—by such transgressions when their spies supplied them with irrefutable evidence of authorship.[38] The great master of this game was Voltaire, who juggled many pseudonyms over the course of more than half a century and who published most of his major works, from the *Philosophical Letters* to *Candide*, anonymously. Whether pseudonymous or anonymous, Voltaire's vast brood of skeptical and irreligious writings was thrown into the world without acknowledged paternity. Voltaire kept up the elaborate game even with fellow philosophes like d'Alembert and Diderot, wary of openly acknowledging blood ties to these miscreant offspring.

Of all of his irreligious progeny, however, Voltaire was perhaps least anxious to acknowledge the *Sermon des cinquante*, or *Oath of the Fifty*. In this little work published in 1762, Voltaire portrays a group of fifty pious and reasonable individuals gathered together in secret to pray to the one true God of nature. Indeed, what other god would be worthy of our love and respect? After a savagely funny catalogue of the abominations and absurdities concerning the Jews of the

Old Testament along with the contradictions and misinterpretations of the New Testament, Voltaire offered the simple and reasonable faith of the deist. Instead of cutting one another's throats over dogmatic differences, he asked, could we not accept that we all share the same morality and must share with one another this same small planet?

The *Oath of the Fifty*, however, did not share the same fate as Voltaire's other anonymous works. To the horror of his fellow authors, Rousseau refused to play this game of literary charades. The practice of publishing works anonymously created irresponsible authors, he argued, writers who did not have to consider the good of their readers or accept the consequences of their works. With the initial exception of his early prize essay, Rousseau himself published all of his writings under his own name. His insistence on avowing ownership of one's works ushered in a new understanding of the relationship among author, work, and reader, yet also carried tremendous peril not just for himself but for others as well.[39]

When he named Voltaire in his *Letters*, Rousseau thus transformed the lord of Ferney into the most implacable of enemies. On the same Christmas Day that he had written to invite Boswell to bring his nightcap to Ferney, Voltaire was busily copying thirteen offensive passages from Rousseau's *Letters Written from the Mountain*, a list of irreligious excerpts he then sent to Jean-Robert Tronchin. Author of *Letters Written from the Countryside*, an anti-Rousseauian tract that had originally provoked Rousseau's response, Tronchin naturally welcomed Voltaire's assistance. The aid was timely. Tronchin was a member of Geneva's Small Council, the aristocratic ruling body whose political legitimacy Rousseau attacked in his *Letters*.

Voltaire's letter to Tronchin was a tactical move in a broader strategy. A slim brochure of eight pages, bearing the title of the *Sentiment of Citizens*, appeared the following day in Geneva. Miraculously, it cited the very same thirteen offending passages from the *Letters Written from the Mountain* that Voltaire had copied in his Christmas letter to Tronchin. For good measure, the anonymous author of the pamphlet added a couple of spectacular revelations. Jean-Jacques Rousseau, according to the pamphlet, was a charlatan who "drags with him, from village to village, from mountain to mountain, the wretched woman whose mother he killed and whose children he exposed at the gates of an asylum, rejecting a charitable person who wanted to take care of them, abjuring all natural feelings even as he casts off those of honor and religion."[40]

Voltaire had conflated appalling truths and equally appalling falsehoods. While Rousseau was indeed guilty of the serial abandonment of the five children Thérèse had borne him, Thérèse's mother, who was alive and well, would have been surprised to read about her death at Rousseau's hands. Yet Voltaire did not

pause over such niceties. Hume later remarked that no enemy was below Voltaire's
notice. In the case of Rousseau, however, the enemy embodied all that Voltaire
feared and hated.

Voltaire had already been increasingly agitated by the danger he thought the
Citizen of Geneva posed to the accomplishments of the Enlightenment, as evident in the letter he wrote d'Alembert worrying about the unity of the philosophes and pointing to "your Jean-Jacques" in particular as a divisive influence.
When Rousseau broke from his fellow philosophes, he began referring to them
as a "sect," a charge of fanaticism that the philosophes, and above all Voltaire,
were hurling against the established religion.[41] "Ardent missionaries of atheism
and very imperious dogmatists," Rousseau later wrote in the *Reveries*, "there is
no way that they would, without anger, put up with anyone daring to think other
than they did about any point whatever."[42] For Voltaire, then, Rousseau was no
better than Charles Palissot, whose plays, including *Les Philosophes* of 1760,
mocked the Encyclopedists (most of all Rousseau) and who relentlessly attacked
the *Encyclopédie* and the other works of the philosophes: "At the front of certain
philosophical productions," Palissot wrote, "one may observe a tone of authority and assurance that until now only the pulpit has exercised."[43] Tellingly, then,
the *l'affaire du Sentiment des citoyens* followed close on the heels of *l'affaire Calas:*
both events revealed Voltaire's attachment to the Enlightenment and degree to
which he would go to protect it. "Me, a persecutor of a man of letters!" Voltaire
waxed indignant over the suggestion that he was harassing Rousseau, citing his
role in the Calas Affair as proof positive of his innocence.

Yet other less selfless motives may also have been in play. Aware that Rousseau was leading his legions of readers toward a new world bathed in the light of
Romanticism, Voltaire was as perplexed as he was repelled. Born while Racine
still lived and while his tragedies reigned on the French stage, Voltaire was
steeped in the classical values that privileged clarity, balance, and moderation.
"The secret of the arts," he declared, "is to correct nature."[44] Rousseau turned
this classical credo on its head, insisting that the secret of the arts is to return nature to all of its purity. Not surprisingly, the unbound sensibility of Rousseau's
writings disgusted Voltaire. "Never has a whore preached more, and never has a
valet, seducer of girls, been more philosophic" was his withering assessment of
Julie; he dismissed all of *Emile*, with the exception of "The Profession of Faith,"
as pernicious nonsense; and he termed the *Social Contract* Rousseau's *Unsocial
Contract.* Yet as Voltaire dismissed Rousseau's works, his own creative fires seemed
spent, and he must have resented the meteoric rise of a writer who seemed des-
tined to displace his own works and eclipse his own reputation.

The *Sentiment of the Citizens* was only the opening broadside of a two-year
campaign to blacken Rousseau's reputation. The warfare included several more

scurrilous pamphlets but was mainly epistolary in nature, with Voltaire launching numerous letters across Europe to claim his innocence and, more important,
argue for Rousseau's guilt. In a letter written while Boswell was nervously await-
ing their second meeting, Voltaire rehearsed a refrain that he would frequently
repeat: Rousseau "is neither a philosopher nor an honest man; if he had been, he
would have rendered great service to the good cause."[45] His network of sympathetic correspondents was soon humming with activity. Voltaire's doctor, the
renowned Théodore Tronchin, wrote of Jean-Jacques to Mme Necker, the mother
of the future apostle of Rousseau, Mme de Staël: "He is a monster whose mask
will not fool anyone."[46] Not to be outdone, Voltaire had also written to Charles
Bordes, Rousseau's former close friend turned one of his most inveterate critics:
"Ah, Sir, you see how Jean-Jacques resembles a philosopher like a monkey resembles a man. It seems to me that his books and he have been recognized beneath the mask."[47] Accustomed to literary brawls, the Republic of Letters was
nevertheless stunned by Voltaire's vitriol. Once again, d'Alembert tried to me-
diate: Rousseau's great powers, he told Voltaire, resulted from an "inflamed
mind [which] must neither be cured nor abused."[48] He might have said the same
thing about Voltaire. The consequences of Voltaire's response were immediate
and far-reaching, and quickened the logic of events that would drive Rousseau
into the arms of Hume.

CHAPTER FIVE

Le Bon David

*Allow me in friendship also to tell you, I think I see you at
present upon the very brink of a precipice.*
— *Gilbert Elliot to David Hume*

I have hitherto been a wanderer on the face of the earth, without any abiding city."[1] By the early 1760s both Rousseau and Voltaire had acquired experience enough as exiles to have uttered this lament. Yet it was David Hume who wrote these words little more than a month after the Citizen of Geneva fled from Paris and Voltaire was settling down in Ferney. While his predicament was not nearly as dire as those of his fugitive counterparts, both of whom risked losing their freedom and health, Hume could nevertheless sympathize with their plight. The Scottish philosopher had always felt a stranger abroad and had become a stranger at home owing to the relentless harassment of his orthodox adversaries. Having just retired from the life of writing after completing his *History of England*, Hume realized he did not know how — or indeed *where*—to spend his retirement. Yet Paris, the very cause of Rousseau's plight, would soon offer itself as the cure for Hume's own predicament.

The French had long pegged Hume not as a philosopher but as a philosophical historian. As in Britain, it was the *History of England* that secured Hume's reputation. The Abbé Prévost, author of the tragic romance *Manon Lescaut* and translator of Samuel Richardson's epistolary novel *Clarissa* (a model for Rousseau's *Julie*), rendered the first volumes of the *History* into French in the early 1760s. The work was an instant success, and Scots traveling through Paris reported on their good fortune to share the same nationality with the man dubbed the British Tacitus. Voltaire himself declared Hume's work as "perhaps the best written in any language," a remarkable concession by the author of *The Age of Louis XIV.* And here, if nowhere else, Elie Fréron, the avowed enemy of Voltaire and the Encyclopedists, found common ground concerning Hume: "What distinguishes him above all is the love of truth that consistently leads him; always a philosopher, never an enthusiast, he praises and blames equally those who seem to him in effect worthy of praise or reproach."[2]

Taking her place in the increasingly crowded company of Gallic admirers was Marie-Charlotte Hippolyte de Campet de Saujon, Comtesse de Boufflers. The estranged wife of an indifferent aristocrat, the comtesse stood at the very center of Parisian social and intellectual circles as the cherished mistress of the Prince de Conti. As for the prince, he had been the trusted favorite of his cousin King Louis XV until he ran afoul of Madame de Pompadour, the sovereign's mistress and political confidante, and retreated to his Paris residence, the Temple. In addition to presiding over a kind of court in exile, the prince entertained artists and men of letters, including Abbé Prévost, who served as his chaplain, and literary thorns in the royal side of his cousin such as Beaumarchais and Rousseau.

Standing at the prince's side was "the idol of the Temple," as Boufflers was called with a mixture of envy and irony. From the beginning of their relationship in 1751, when she was twenty-six, until the prince's death in 1776, the comtesse welcomed the guests and moderated the tone and direction of the weekly salons and other entertainments at the Temple. An accomplished writer and conversationalist, Boufflers suffered from her very prominence. The era's most imperious salonnière, Madame du Deffand, noted that Boufflers did well, despite the limited resources nature granted her, and demanded a high ethical standard—though "this lofty morality is not perfectly in accord with her conduct."[3] Deffand's intimate friend, the forty-eight-year-old Englishman Horace Walpole, who will play a crucial role in our story, also came to praise, then bury, the comtesse. She is "very sensible and has a measured eloquence that is just and pleasing," he conceded, "but all is spoiled by an unrelaxed attention to applause. You would think she was always sitting for her picture."[4] Yet such cattiness fails to explain Boufflers's intellectual attraction to Hume, or the demanding and thankless role she was to play in his friendship with Rousseau.

In early 1761 Boufflers addressed a long and adoring letter—in English— to the author of the *History of England,* declaring her admiration for a work too "sublime" for words. Despite her profession of speechlessness, the comtesse found words enough to cover several pages. Hume's writing "enlightens the soul and fills the heart with sentiments of humanity and benevolence," she wrote. "It enlightens the mind by showing that true happiness is closely united with virtue and discovers, by the same light, what is the end, the sole end, of every reasonable being." The history had to be the work of "some celestial being, free from human passions, who, for the sake of mankind, has deigned to write the history of these latter times." Perhaps most revealingly, she echoed a line from Hume's *History:* "Men's views of things are the result of their understanding alone: their conduct is regulated by their understanding, their temper, and their passions."[5] Boufflers was surely aware that this observation both underscored and undermined her portrayal of Hume as nearly divine. Did Boufflers anticipate how greatly her missive would upset the passions of her correspondent?

The letter overwhelmed Hume, who was without sentimental attachment or clear idea of his future. He replied gratefully, thanking Boufflers for such praise. Recalling his youthful sojourn in France, Hume hinted that he would again like to cross the Channel, revisit the country, and, of course, pay his respects to her. But he asked her indulgence: his "imperfectly learned" French had since fallen into complete disuse. Indeed, Hume continued in self-deprecating fashion, he himself had grown creaky: "I have rusted amid books and study [and] have been little engaged in the active, and not much in the pleasurable scenes of life."[6]

As long as the Seven Years' War followed its spasmodically bloody course, however, a trip across the Channel was impossible. Hume may well have been relieved: like Rousseau, he was more at ease cultivating his imagination than cultivating actual relationships with women. He perhaps felt even more the pull of his fireplace when Boufflers sent a second letter, offering him an open-ended invitation to stay at her Paris townhouse. In his response, the diffident Hume bemoaned the seemingly distant prospect of peace between their two nations. Then, piling conditional upon conditional—*if* peace were reached, *if* he had the time, and *if* he had the occasion for such a voyage—he nevertheless turned down the invitation, insisting that it would cause too much trouble for his host.

Clearly, Hume did not know his woman.

When peace finally broke out between France and England in February

1763, Boufflers decided that as the mountain would not come to her, she would go to the mountain. That spring, she made plans to visit England with the hope of meeting the author responsible for emotions that were, as she had written in her first letter, "too painful in their continuance."[7] Upon her arrival in London in early May, the local press reported on the activities of "Madame Blewflower." Walpole gave a great party for his guest at his country retreat, the pseudo-Gothic castle called Strawberry Hill, where she met London's elite, including the recently appointed ambassador to France, Lord Hertford. Either indifferent to or ignorant of Dr. Johnson's opinion of Hume, Boufflers also called on the literary critic and lexicographer at his London apartment. After a convivial tea, Johnson officiously accompanied her back to her carriage, wonderfully oblivious to the crowd of gawking onlookers struck by the sight of this charming and slight woman on the arm of the huge, lurching, and pockmarked scholar, garbed in ragged suit and breeches, with battered shoes that now served him as slippers, and a "little shriveled wig" sticking on the top of his head.[8]

Johnson's bête noire, however, was nowhere to be seen. Boufflers's "celestial being" had, in fact, retreated to Scotland in advance of her arrival. And there he stubbornly remained. "You cannot in decency, neglect the opportunity of gratifying this flattering curiosity, perhaps passion, of the most amiable of god's creation," wrote Lord Elibank, who had accompanied the comtesse on her Channel crossing.[9] By way of reply, Hume burrowed even more deeply into his Edinburgh lodgings. Finally, steeling himself to write the comtesse in early July, more than two months after her arrival in England, Hume declared that though he wished dearly to travel to London and meet his admirer, the "reasons which detain me in this country are so powerful, that I must lay aside for the present so flattering a project."[10] No doubt aware that additional explanation would further illuminate the feeble character of his excuses, Hume did not bother to elaborate on these "powerful" reasons. In the end, reticence, uncertainty, and insecurity seem to have overpowered the philosopher's reason and determined him to remain in Edinburgh.

When Boufflers finally returned to France in late July, then, she did so without having attained the goal for her visit: meeting Hume. But a veteran of court intrigue and salon diplomacy, she was not prepared to surrender.

If pleading letters from his insistent admirer could not overcome his inertia, an unexpected invitation he received in July 1763 from Lord Hertford to accompany the British embassy to Paris as his private secretary ultimately moved Hume.

The Scot was far from an obvious choice for this role as emissary, in part because he *was* a Scot. British politics was stirred by anti-Scottish sentiment sur-

rounding the controversial rise and fall of the young king's favorite and former
tutor, John Stuart, Earl of Bute. Hume's sole qualification apart from his self-
appointed role as ambassador between the learned and conversable worlds was
his service more than a decade and a half earlier as secretary to a military mis-
sion to Vienna and Turin during the War of Austrian Succession. And Hume had
hardly distinguished himself on that occasion. "You must know, that you neither
bow nor kneel to Emperors and Empresses, but curtsey," Hume wrote in his
journal of meeting the Empress Maria Theresa. "So that after we had a little conversation with her Imperial Majesty, we were to walk backwards, through a very
long room, curtsying all the way. And there was great danger of our falling foul
of each other, as well as tumbling topsy-turvy." Seeing the difficult straits in
which the philosopher found himself, the empress allowed his party to leave
without the customary courtesy. "We esteemed ourselves very much obliged to
her for this attention," Hume confessed, "especially my companions, who were
desperately afraid of my falling on them and crushing them."[11]

Hertford's offer was even odder because he had never met Hume and does
not appear to have read his books. A man of property and propriety, Francis Seymour Conway, Earl of Hertford, was more dedicated to adding to his family—he
had just fathered his thirteenth child in 1763—than to adding to his knowledge
of philosophy or literature. A man of neither great wit nor imagination, Hertford was best known for his piety, a trait that could hardly attract him to the notorious skeptic.

Who, then, planted the idea in his lordship's ear? Influential friends may
have suggested how enthusiastically France would welcome the historian's appointment. Yet a more intriguing possibility is Boufflers, who found herself
Hertford's fellow houseguest at Strawberry Hill. Learning that he had just been
named ambassador to France, is it conceivable that the comtesse would *not* have
sung Hume's praises? Boufflers seems to suggest this herself when she later told
Hume that the "reception which was given to me in England is so flattering that
I dare not speak of it, for fear that what I would say would be attributed to vanity rather than gratitude."[12]

Boufflers's chance meeting with Hertford, then, may have allowed her to as-
semble the system of pulleys and ropes that would haul the Scottish mountain to
Paris. Yet Hume still could not overcome his diffidence, and he refused Hertford's offer. Agreeing to serve when Hertford inexplicably renewed his offer,
Hume still confessed to Adam Smith that he was hardly at peace with himself
and the future: "I repine at my loss of ease and leisure and retirement and independence, and it is not without a sigh I look backwards nor without reluctance
that I cast my eye forwards."[13] In the welter of doubt and fears, Hume tried to fix
his sights on the promise of Paris, telling yet another friend, Alexander Carlyle,

that he was going "to a place of the world which I have always admired the most; and it is not easy to imagine a reception better than I have reason to expect. What then can be wanting to my happiness?"[14]

What indeed? Despite the hesitations he expressed to friends, Hume grasped the dangers he ran if he remained in Great Britain. In a letter to Boufflers just days before his departure, he explained that the prospect of Paris roused him "from a state of indolence and sloth which I falsely dignified with the name of philosophy." In the end, Hume recalled the lesson of his youthful battle with the melancholy born of reflection: "It is better for a man to keep in the midst of society."[15]

Hume must have held on to that lesson as if it were a buoy during his crossing of the English Channel. Adverse winds forced Hertford's party to land in Boulogne rather than Calais. The philosopher-diplomat soon found himself in a carriage bound for Paris, reaching the city on October 18, 1763, after a three-day journey. Once there, he took up residence in a private apartment at the British embassy, located in the Hôtel de Brancas, a stately pile on the rue de l'Université in the Latin Quarter whose windows looked north onto the Seine.

Just as Hume failed to be in London to welcome Boufflers two years earlier, so too was Boufflers absent upon Hume's arrival. A case of measles—not cold feet—prevented her from meeting him in town. Though recovering, she had to remain in seclusion and was prevented, she wrote Hume, "from giving you proof of my esteem and regard, and doing myself the honor of being the first in the Kingdom who pays what is due to so illustrious a man."[16] Replying to her before he had fully unpacked, Hume could not help but reveal his ambivalence about meeting this formidable woman. He reminded the comtesse (again) that he was no longer the man he had been on his first visit to France: "A more quiet manner of sliding through life would perhaps suit better my habits and turn of mind."[17]

Quiet, it turned out, was a rare commodity in Paris. Like a Rabelaisian character whose swelling gut bursts his belts and suspenders, the city had over the centuries spilled over a succession of defensive walls. In the ancient heart of the city, the medieval stamp remained fast: it was an urban landscape where the sewers were open and gardens were closed. The narrow streets more closely resembled canyons, with dense tenements rising on both sides, forcing out light and pushing pedestrians into the muck- and dung-filled streets, where they engaged in deadly pas-de-deux with carts, carriages, and horses. Though a native son, Voltaire cursed the city as "dark, hideous, closed in as in the age of the most frightful barbarism."[18] For once he and Rousseau concurred: "Adieu, then, Paris, celebrated city, city of noise, smoke, and mud," Rousseau wrote in *Emile*.[19] In short, Paris had not yet undergone the urban horticulture undertaken by Baron Haussmann a century later, transforming the medieval brier through massive pruning and replanting into the rational grid of broad boulevards and monumental squares we know today. In the mid-eighteenth century, the City of Lights remained an unusually dim place to serve as the Enlightenment's headquarters.

Along with the congested heart of the city, there were the (then) outlying neighborhoods of the Faubourg Saint-Germain and Faubourg Saint-Honoré, facing each other across the Seine. These were the quarters most frequented by Hume, where the Parisian aristocracy built their great *hôtels*, or mansions. Unlike Rousseau, who was shocked by the squalor and immensity of the city when he first visited, Hume seems to have been perfectly indifferent to the sights. His letters are almost entirely bereft of impressions of the streets and crowds, perhaps because as a foreign dignitary, he rarely went out on foot, instead traveling by carriage from the British embassy to his various destinations. "I have not absolutely leisure to look about me," he wrote breathlessly to his friend the lawyer Alexander Wedderburn; "what between business and company, what between receiving and returning civilities, between the commerce of the great and the learned, it is scarce possible for me to think of an absent friend."[20]

There were not idle excuses: hardly had he arrived before Hume became the most sought after commodity in city and court alike. Hume reported that he was "mortified" by the scant attention paid to him by Louis XV when he was presented at court, unaware that Louis was equally indifferent to all visitors, but the rest of the royal family compensated for the king's phlegm. Lined up to greet Hume was what remained of the future of the Bourbon dynasty: the ten-year-old Duc de Berry (the future Louis XVI), the eight-year-old Comte de Provence (who would regain the throne in 1815 as Louis XVIII), and finally the toddler Comte d'Artois (who, as Charles X, lost the throne once and for all for the Bourbons in 1830). The two older princes welcomed Hume with polish and presence, reciting speeches of praise that focused on his historical writing, including such passages as the historian's account of the exemplary death of Charles I, a macabre rehearsal of sorts for the eldest. The older boys were followed by Artois, who stepped forward but could scarcely pronounce anything beyond the word *histoire*.[21]

"Mr. Hume is fashion itself here, although his French is almost as unintelligible as his English," reported an envious Horace Walpole back to England.[22] Hume's charm admittedly worked in mysterious ways: his physical awkwardness and halting French made him an improbable success among *le tout Paris*. In an acid-etched vignette, Rousseau's former confidante Mme d'Épinay portrayed Hume at an impromptu turn at theater. Assigned the unlikely role of a sultan, Hume was placed between two coquettish women, designated as his slaves, and given the task of winning their love. Alas, the urbane and eloquent essayist found himself dreadfully short of words. According to Mme d'Épinay, Hume stared at the women, "smote the pit of his stomach and his knees several times, and could find nothing to say but, 'Well, young ladies; well, there you are, then! Well, there you are! There you are, then?'" Mercifully, after fifteen minutes of this piteous performance, Hume was banished from subsequent games, to everyone's relief, especially his own.[23]*

Yet even such theatrical flops failed to dim Hume's luster. Attending a masquerade ball in the spring of 1764, Hume arrived unmasked. A disguised woman immediately accosted him, gaily warning that he was running the risk of being overwhelmed by admirers. The lady's prediction was fulfilled as Hume was besieged by "caresses, civilities, and panegyrics."[24] Hume's intimates at home thought their friend's success perfectly reasonable. As Andrew Stuart reported to William Mure, amid this mild hysteria their mutual friend had preserved "his own natural style and simplicity of manners; and deigns to be cheerful and jolly, as if no such things had happened to him."[25]

Naturally, the "rusting" man of letters reveled in the attention. With a mixture of joy and irony, Hume reported his escapades to his Edinburgh circle. "I can only say that I eat nothing but ambrosia, drink nothing but nectar, breathe nothing but incense, and tread on nothing but flowers," he wrote William Robertson.[26] Having narrated the events at the masquerade ball to Blair, he then invited his Presbyterian friend to share the account with a mutual friend, the minister John Jardine. With a sense of humor as mischievous as Hume's, Jardine knowingly rose to the bait: "I clearly perceive, though you don't seem to have the least apprehension of it yourself, that you are in great danger of being seduced to the commission of the sin of uncleanliness. . . . Believe me, all those fine ladies of wit and beauty are all devils." Jardine then concluded with a mock peroration: "I beseech you consider seriously what dishonor it will reflect on your character as an apostle sent from the purest church on earth to convert the idolatrous papists, if it shall hereafter appear that you have been carrying on a criminal correspondence with French succubas."[27]

Within weeks of his arrival, Hume had conquered not only the court and aristocratic society but, more important for the philosopher, the citizens of that state within a state, the Republic of Letters. Paris was the capital of the cosmopolitan league of philosophers, artists, and thinkers that stretched across Europe, and even to America, and the salon was the most important place of assembly for its citizens. The display of erudition and wit, the dignity of the life of the mind,

---

*Rousseau would have sympathized, having described in *Emile* a similar predicament that rings of autobiographical authenticity: "Do you want to see an embarrassed person? Put a man between two women with whom he has secret relations, and then observe what a foolish figure he cuts" (trans. and ed. Allan Bloom [New York: Basic, 1979]).

the delight in a common moral and intellectual purpose all held sway in these well-appointed salons. By the time Hume reached the city, inveterate salon trawlers like the writer Jean-François Marmontel, whose company the Scot enjoyed, could find their fill of urbane conversation every day of the week. In fact, by midcentury, the salons began to displace the academy and university as the city's centers of learning.[28]

This world must have reminded Hume of the Select Society back home, but there was at least one great difference between Edinburgh and Paris: while the Scottish clubs were entirely masculine, the salons were thoroughly feminine. Ironically, eighteenth-century French women benefited from what they were thought to lack: a robust ego that reveled in competition and glory.[29] Considered less selfish and egotistical, more attentive and modest than men, women were "naturally" endowed to understand the complexities of public debate and conversation. By their self-effacing and tactful art of governance, the salonnières helped secure the republican ethos of this society of letters. Here, regardless of birth or social distinction, one could claim citizenship by accepting the protocols of polite conversation and, of course, by presenting the requisite credentials of intelligence and wit. The salonnières governed the tone and direction of philosophical and literary discourse in polite society. Through their choice of guests to their choice of topics, these women, most though not all of aristocratic birth, wielded a remarkable degree of influence, indeed power, in a world ever more sensitive to enlightened opinion. Madame de Staël, who witnessed this world firsthand as the daughter of Suzanne Necker, a leading salonnière of pre-revolutionary Paris, claimed, with only slight exaggeration, that the cultivation of ideas over the century had "been entirely directed by conversation."[30]

Of course, there were dissenters from this heroic view of the salons, including Madame de Staël's favorite writer, Rousseau. "But what do you think one actually learns from such charming conversation?" Rousseau has Saint-Preux write his beloved from Paris in *Julie:* "One learns to plead artfully the cause of the lie, to unsettle with as much philosophy all the principles of virtue, to color one's passions and prejudices with subtle sophisms, and to lend to error a certain stylish turn in keeping with the maxims of the day. It is not necessary to know people's character, but only their interests, to make a fair guess about what they will say on every subject."[31] For his part, however, Hume delighted in this world. So much so, in fact, that he idealizes the female and male citizens of the Republic of Letters: they are "living in entire or almost entire harmony among themselves, and [are] quite irreproachable in their morals."[32] Having just arrived, Hume could not be expected to know the conflicts and rivalries that cut across this "harmonious" world.

Hume happily made his way from one salon to another, like a great bumble-

bee ponderously moving from flower to flower. The most established of the
grandes salonnières was the Marquise du Deffand, whose salon attracted a largely
aristocratic crowd leavened by such men of letters as Montesquieu and Voltaire.
Born near the end of the previous century and blind from middle age, Marie du
Deffand compensated for her handicap with acute psychological insight, expressed with cynical flair and surgical precision. Her merciless wit was already
pronounced in her youth: having listened to the Cardinal de Polignac's account
of the miracle of Saint Denis, who, beheaded by the Vandals, cradled his head in
his arms and walked two miles, she replied, "Oh monsieur, it is only the first step
that counts!"[33] Though Deffand's cynicism had grown corrosive, Hume's personality defied even her blighted view of humanity. The Scot, she wrote to
Voltaire, was "gay, simple, and good." Deffand's rival, Mme Geoffrin, agreed.
Known as much for her humble origins as a servant's daughter and her good nature as was Deffand for her aristocratic manners and ill temper, Geoffrin welcomed Hume to her Wednesday soirées for men of letters, playfully calling him
her "fat wag" and "fat rascal." Upon Hume's departure from France, she lamented, "I wish that I could forget you, but I cannot."[34]

What Hume could least forget, however, was the salon of Julie de Lespinasse, Deffand's former protégée. Lespinasse had been dismissed from her mistress's household a year before Hume's arrival when Deffand discovered that her
apprentice threatened to displace her, receiving guests on her own an hour before the appointed time. The old woman's resentment toward her young rival
was increased by the fact that Lespinasse took with her one of her most cherished regulars, Jean le Rond d'Alembert, who became not only the center of her
salon but her lifelong companion (though she was probably not the sexually ambiguous man's lover). By orchestrating her guests with effortless ability, Lespinasse embodied the talents of the successful salonnière. She matched her guests so
well, explained Marmontel, that "they found themselves in harmony like the
strings of an instrument played by an able hand [and] she seemed to know which
sound the string she had touched would make; I would say that she knew our
minds and our characters so well that, to put them in play, she had only to say a
word."[35] Though not as lyrical, Hume shared his friend's esteem for Lespinasse,
announcing that she was "really one of the most sensible women in Paris."[36]

Lespinasse's salon was firmly established by the time Hume arrived in Paris,
and d'Alembert, Diderot, Marmontel, and other regular congregants quickly
befriended him. Emblematic of his warm welcome was one widely circulated
anecdote. One afternoon, as Hume joined their company, d'Alembert loudly
announced, *Et verbum caro factum est:* "And the word was made flesh." The
good-natured joke took an unusual turn when a smitten woman repeated the
phrase but, wittingly or not, substituted *carum* for *caro,* thus turning "flesh" into

"beloved." In recounting this anecdote to Blair, Hume added that, when told of her mistake, the good lady "would not allow it to be one."[37] Beloved by Julie de Lespinasse and her philosophes, the great Scot, far from London and Edinburgh, finally felt at home. After his return to England, Hume would turn to this group of intimates for counsel and assistance in his quarrel with their former friend Rousseau.

The fault line between Rousseau and the philosophes would become evident to Hume at another nerve center of the Enlightenment, the salon of Paul-Henri Thiry, Baron d'Holbach. It was also there that Hume glimpsed what separated him from the most radical philosophes—and what, in certain respects, united him with Rousseau. Possessed of a considerable fortune and great charm, Holbach surrounded himself with a coterie of philosophes who attended his weekly dinners for more than three decades. Holbach was a tireless supporter of the Enlightenment project and a dogged foe of religion. His *Christianity Unveiled* had recently created an uproar that would soon be exceeded by his *System of Nature*, one of the most relentlessly materialist tracts of the century. His salon was unique in several regards. Unlike the female-centered salons of the Marquise du Deffand or Julie de Lespinasse, the baron himself presided over his gatherings, and the host also encouraged conversation much more audacious than was permitted in other salons.[38] One notorious exchange involved Hume himself. Invited to dinner shortly after his arrival, Hume announced that he did not believe in atheists since he had never in fact met one. Holbach leaped at the remark: "Look around you!" Noting that eighteen people were sitting around the table, the baron laughed: "I can show you fifteen atheists right off. The other three haven't made up their minds."[39]

Hume seems to have been as bothered as he was amused by Holbach's provocative exercise in arithmetic.[40] The evident discomfort of Hume, reported by Diderot, may have been due to Holbach's simple audacity: one did not speak so bluntly at Lespinasse's, much less at the Select Society. Yet Hume, long accused of atheism, may also have been more consistently skeptical than his tablemates. The young Edward Gibbon, certainly no friend of the church, recalled with distaste the "intolerant zeal" of those philosophes who "laughed at the skepticism of Hume, preached the tenets of atheism with the bigotry of dogmatists, and damned all believers with ridicule and contempt."[41] For Hume, the claims of atheism (in the literal sense of denying the existence of a deity, as opposed to the more general usage of the time of someone who denied the particular providence of the deity), were as nonsensical as were proofs of God's existence concocted by his deist friends in Scotland. In Hume's eyes, the three fence-sitters at Holbach's table were the only reasonable men in the room. Ever since the *Treatise*, Hume had argued that this was precisely the point to skepticism. If human understanding is as frail a faculty as Hume revealed, few if any positive claims about the world, much less what lies behind it, can be justified. After all, if we cannot provide a cogent and reasonable argument for our belief that tomorrow will follow today—a belief based uniquely on experience that provides no guarantee for future events—we are utterly incapable of making rational claims for the necessity of a being whose existence falls outside the pale of common life.

Holbach had missed the subtlety of Hume's remark: he had never met an atheist for the simple reason that our "instincts and propensities of nature" lead most of us toward belief in a supernatural being.[42] We are as unlikely, in the end, to meet a consistent atheist as we are a consistent skeptic. As Hume argued in his *Natural History of Religion*, religion issues "from a concern with regard to the events of life, and from the incessant hopes and fears, which actuate the human mind."[43] Most of humankind could no more live without belief in deities than without belief in causality. Yet while Hume hailed the obstinacy of nature, which overwhelms the arguments of the skeptic and allows us to live in the world, he was far more, well, *skeptical* about the persistence of religious belief, which more often than not conflicted with our ability to pursue our lives in peace. In the end, for Hume mitigated skepticism was the only consistent philosophical stance. Such an approach "may be of advantage to mankind" insofar as it is "best adapted to the narrow capacity of human understanding." Rather than delving into matters too great for our comprehension, which inevitably leads to zealotry and intolerance, we do better by confining our reason "to common life, and to such subjects as fall under daily practice and experience."[44] Hume and Rousseau both battled against the religious enthusiasm born of vain certainty, although Rousseau was more solicitous of the salutary effects of properly tempered religious belief than was Hume. They both also lamented the rationalist enthusiasm of the philosophes, but whereas Rousseau turned against what he termed the *parti philosophique* of Diderot, d'Alembert, Holbach, and others, Hume ultimately turned to that same coterie, whatever the misgivings rooted in his skepticism.

Recovered from her bout of measles, the Comtesse de Boufflers finally encountered Hume at the end of 1763 and quickly ushered him into her brilliant world. No doubt the two friends also regularly saw one another in salon and aristocratic society during the winter of 1763–64. It is likely, for example, that Boufflers was among the nearly three hundred English and French guests for a sermon given by the novelist Laurence Sterne at the Hôtel de Bracas in March 1764.[45] The absence of any correspondence between the two during this period, however, makes it impossible to know how the two correspondents managed the transition to flesh and blood encounters.

Carmontelle (Louis Carrogis) (1717–1806), portrait of *Marie-Charlotte Hippolyte de Campet de Saujon* (1725–1800), Countess of Boufflers-Rouverel, watercolor on paper, 1760. © Musée Conde, Chantilly, France / Giraudon / The Bridgeman Art Library

In July 1764 diplomatic duty delivered an unenthusiastic Hume to the French court at the royal chateau in Compiègne, favored by French kings ever since the Merovingian dynasty for its hunting. While Louis XV and his retinue pounded through the royal woods beyond the chateau, Hume retreated to his habitual ways of reading and reflection. This idyllic existence would normally have delighted the philosopher, but he instead restlessly wandered the gardens and woods. The reason became clear when, on July 6, he sat down at his bureau and took out his stationery. Even though the two friends had apparently struck an agreement, just before Hume left Paris, that Boufflers would write first, he began to compose a letter. Offering a transparent alibi—conveying a message from a mutual friend—Hume gallantly added that, were it not for that obligation, "I could have held out two or three days longer at the least." He bantered in the same vein for the remainder of the letter, but his need to reach out to Boufflers was clear, despite his claim that "I make advantage of the ten leagues of interval that lie between us, and feel already some progress in the noble resolution I have formed of forgetting you entirely before the end of the summer."[46]

Upon receiving Hume's letter, Boufflers replied immediately, confessing with great relief that her resolve to forget Hume was as weak as his to forget her; that she had wished to forget Hume for the simple and paradoxical reason that he was so memorable; and that she worried over a future without him when he returned to his native country: she would be abandoned in Paris, she declared, with little more than "distaste for the majority of people with whom I must live." Comparing herself to a frail bush whose roots have spread too far, thus exposing her to injury, Boufflers concludes by informing her "*cher maître*" that she will hasten to "stop loving him so as to avoid the shame" of being forgotten before she can forget.[47]

Winged from Paris, Boufflers's epistle hit its mark. Realizing that his earlier jesting would now seem callow, yet still unwilling to accept Boufflers's challenge, Hume shifted into the most formal of styles. No other letter, Hume allowed, had "conveyed more satisfaction than did that [with] which you favored me." Sliding into the first person plural, he declared, as though addressing a session of the Select, "What pleasure to receive testimonies and assurances of good will from a person we highly value, and whose sentiments are of such importance to us!" Having thanked her for giving him "matter for the most agreeable musing," Hume then revealed that he was jealous of Conti, especially as, having arrived "at a time of life when I can less expect to please, I must be more subject to inroads of suspicion." As a result, it would be "the height of folly to lay myself at the mercy of a person whose situation seems calculated to inspire doubt, and who, being so little at her own disposal, could not be able, even if willing, to seek such remedies as might appease that tormenting sentiment."[48]

Boufflers let Hume stew for several days in silence. When she finally wrote, she took him to task for doubting her sincerity and constancy. Why allow imaginary obstacles to stand in their way, she wondered, especially as very real obstacles already existed? In a strikingly candid passage, Boufflers reminded Hume of her obligations to the prince. Though they had not been lovers since 1757, the comtesse remained committed to him as his most intimate friend and adviser. As a result, her attachment to Hume would necessarily give way at times to "duties imposed upon me by an older relationship I will always recognize. These duties are sacred and, should the occasion arrive, would entail on my part great sacrifice." And yet neither the occasion, nor even the person of the prince, seemed to threaten such self-renunciation anytime soon. Besides, her "sacred" duties were hardly a full-time occupation—she had, she wrote, "space in my heart for other sentiments." Free to dispose of her time mostly as she wished, Boufflers offered that time to Hume. Reassuring him that her life was already filled with good health, good humor, a taste for reading and study, and even "a bit of philosophy," Boufflers concluded, "Were I to add our deepened friendship to my other sources of happiness . . . I cannot conceive how I could ever complain of my destiny."[49]

As it turned out, Boufflers would have no reason for complaint: by the end of the summer, Hume's infatuation was as public as most private affairs were in that small world. "They say that Hume is madly in love with Mme de Boufflers,"[50] Mme de Verdelin reported from Paris to Rousseau's retreat at Môtiers. Hume gave touching proof of Verdelin's report: in one letter to Boufflers, he ended by kissing her hands "with the greatest devotion and most sincere affection." Then, in a striking confession, he added impulsively: "Among other obligations, which I owe you, without number, you have saved me from a total indifference towards every thing in human life. I was falling very fast into that state of mind, and it is perhaps worse than even the inquietudes of the most unfortunate passion: how much, then, is it inferior to the sweetness of your commerce and friendship!"[51]

Poor Hume! The quality of his sentiments was not sufficient; the comtesse also demanded quantity. Boufflers replied sharply: "Your letter arrived this morning, but do you think that it has made me happy? I wrote eight pages to you, yet you reply in just two!" This "celestial being" was now revealed to be a mere mortal—worse, a mortal *man*. On the topic of men, Boufflers was merciless. She told Hume that his sex "like to be mistreated; they are avid for severity, all the while indifferent to kindness." Most men, she long ago had concluded, had "servile souls." Hume had seemed different, but the comtesse warned, if "I have been mistaken, my affection and all that supports it will soon be destroyed." While she hoped that she would not have to treat Hume as she would other men, Boufflers concluded with a dramatic flourish: "I cannot help but say that I had long awaited your letter, awaited it with impatience, and am not at all satisfied by it. We shall see the excuses you will present!"[52]

Hume reveled in the role Boufflers had cast him. Swearing that it was not his intention to convey indifference, he declared that he was so attached to her that were she to cut him to pieces, he would, "like those pertinacious animals of my country . . . expire still attached to you, and you will in vain attempt to get free." While her authority over him was unquestioned, there was one exception: he would never let her end their friendship. Hume begged her to adopt the following reasoning: "This poor fellow is resolved never to leave me: let me take compassion on him; and endeavor to render our intercourse as agreeable to him and as little burdensome to myself as possible."[53]

When Hume, back in Paris, welcomed his friend Gilbert Elliot a few days later, Elliot was troubled. Not having seen Hume since he had left for Paris the preceding year, Elliot was struck by his preoccupation with Boufflers. Elliot, who had recently served as Lord of the Admiralty, kept his concerns to himself, instead concentrating on the stated purpose to his visit: arranging for French tutors to his two sons during their planned stay in Paris. No sooner had he left Paris for Brussels, however, than Elliot wrote to Hume: "Allow me in friendship also to tell you, I think I see you at present upon the very brink of a precipice. . . . Love the French as much as you will, many of the individuals are surely the proper objects of affection, but above all continue to be an Englishman. You know better than any body, that the active powers of our mind are much too limited to be usefully employed in any pursuit more general than the service of that portion of mankind we call our country."[54]

Hume's emotional upheaval served as evidence for his own critique of human reason. The traditional Western conception of human liberty, stretching from ancient Greece through Renaissance Italy to Enlightenment France, has given pride of place to reason. Once we climb this "high tower of the mind," our view and powers are sweeping. Proud of its autonomy and strength, reason can override our passions and harness our will to achieve rational goals. Reason, in a word, makes us unique and uniquely capable of greatness. Yet reason has never fully recovered its reputation since the publication of Hume's *Treatise of Human Nature*. Hume declared that reason's domain was far more modest than generally held in his time (or, for that matter, in our own age). So modest, in fact, that reason is incapable even of conflicting with passion. Reason alone, he argued, "can never be a motive to any action of the will." True to his naturalist account of human nature, Hume affirms that the "propensities" and "aversions" that lie at the heart of human activity cannot, by their very nature, be the products of reason. As he concludes, "'Tis evident that the impulse arises not from reason, but is only directed by it."[55] This critique applies, as well, to reason's role in desire: what at first seems incredible is, after a moment's reflection, incontrovertible. Reason, in Hume's phrase, does not have "original influence"—like a eunuch in charge of a harem, it can only oversee, but never incite, desire.

Hume was in love and there was little to be done about it. For a month upon Hume's return to Paris, he and Boufflers indeed seemed to live in greater intimacy than they had known before. While their correspondence provides few clues to the character or details of this new relationship—unfortunately, no letters between the two of them survive from this period—Hume's happiness seems manifest. A week after he received Elliot's letter, Hume replied that he had just gone "very contentedly for four days to L'Île Adam," where the comtesse had a chateau.[56] Indeed, as he had earlier confessed, the comtesse had become "the person for whose welfare I would sacrifice my existence."[57]

Little did Hume suspect that within less than two months he would be asked to act on this very vow. In late October the comtesse's husband died. In a terse note to Boufflers, Hume did not bother to offer his condolences, instead underscoring his intimate friend's worldly ambitions. "This late incident, which commonly is of such moment with your sex, seems so little to affect your situation either as to happiness or misery, that I might have spared you the trouble of receiving my compliments upon it."[58] As Hume immediately grasped, the Comte de Boufflers's death had freed his friend to wed the Prince de Conti. Or, at least, "this late incident" freed her imagination to contemplate marriage, since the prince remained scrupulously noncommittal.

Boufflers immediately turned all of her energy and attention to the prince in hopes that he would propose, thus making her the fifth lady of the realm. Learning of the comtesse's sudden embrace of Realpolitik while he was at Fontainebleau, Hume was distressed. A barely suppressed anger courses through his short note to her: "Receive, then, with your usual, I cannot say, with your constant goodness, the prayers of one of your most devoted friends and servants. I hope that every change of situation is to your advantage. In vain would I assume somewhat of the dignity of anger, when you neglect me: I find that this wish still returns upon me with equal ardor."[59]

As the comtesse's matrimonial prospects dimmed, it becoming quickly clear that Conti had every intention of remaining a bachelor, Hume found himself, painfully, transformed into her adviser and confidant. Yet he acquitted himself in this role with great dignity and intelligence. When it became clear that Conti would not marry a woman of inferior rank, Hume urged Boufflers to be reasonable. In effect, Hume was reminding Boufflers that reason, though a slave to the passions, nevertheless served an invaluable function. In this particular case, reason revealed that Boufflers was the victim of a false assumption: that the Prince de Conti, one of the great men of the realm, was free to marry her. Clearly, the prince could no more resist the pressures of his peers and tradition than Boufflers could forget the years she had devoted to his well-being.

Equally consistent with both his feelings and his philosophy, Hume also reflected that the "loss of a friend, of a dignity, of fortune, admits of consolation, if not from reason, at least from oblivion; and these sorrows are not eternal." After trying to reconcile Boufflers to a life of tranquility over grandeur—slim consolation, perhaps, for those incapable of an Epicurean perspective—Hume then urged on her the restorative powers of travel, suggesting a journey to Italy. In a coda of sharp pathos, he noted that "nothing could be so much my choice as to live where I might cultivate your friendship." Should Boufflers wish it, he could "with some probability have the felicity of attending" her to the south.[60]

Boufflers's reply laid to rest Hume's hopes, as well as any illusions he might still have harbored that aristocrats were like the rest of humankind. She curtly dismissed his fears for her health, then continued: "I will not speak to you of my friendship for you, for though it is very sincere, I can discuss it only coldly given my present situation that absorbs all of my being."[61] Hume never again expressed his deepest feelings to Boufflers. Or, more accurately, his deepest feelings soon changed, for, as he had told Boufflers, "these sorrows are not eternal." As an earlier French aristocrat, La Rochefoucauld, had observed, the span of our passions no more depends upon us than does the span of our lives.

CHAPTER SIX

A Stone's Throw from Paris

*Rousseau, Sir, is a very bad man. I think him one of the worst of men: a
rascal who ought to be hunted out of society, as he has been.*
— *Samuel Johnson to James Boswell*

It was midnight when the first salvo of stones struck the cottage. Rattling like
hail against the front door and window, it jolted Sultan from his sleep. Awakened by the dog's howls, Rousseau was groping for his bedroom door when
a large stone sailed through the window, crashed against the door, and rolled to
the foot of his bed. Had he gone to the door a moment earlier, he realized, the
stone would have struck him. Springing through the doorway into the kitchen,
he was met by a terrified Thérèse. They threw themselves against the kitchen
wall, neither knowing what to do or what was happening, while Sultan clawed
madly at the floorboards.

While they huddled together, Rousseau's neighbor had run to warn the local
police official, Jacques-Frédéric Martinet, about the siege. Throwing on his dressing gown, Martinet hailed an armed escort and rushed to the cottage. Yet by the

time they arrived, the mob had already dispersed, returning to the houses where they had lived as Rousseau's neighbors for nearly three years. Upon entering the cottage, Martinet turned pale upon seeing the piles of rocks. "My God. It's a quarry!" he exclaimed.

Though Martinet assigned an armed guard to the house the following day, a delegation of local officials told Rousseau that they could no longer guarantee his safety in Môtiers. In fact, the individual most immediately responsible for Rousseau's well-being, Martinet, seemed "filled with terror at the spectacle of the people's frenzied rage and afraid lest it be turned against him." Rousseau knew that his days as a wanderer were not over.[1]

The events of the night of September 6, 1765, marked the climax of Rousseau's growing difficulties in Môtiers, which had begun just after James Boswell left the philosopher the previous winter. The seismic tremors unleashed by the *Letters Written from the Mountain* at the end of 1764 had upended Geneva, reached Ferney, and surged across the Republic of Letters. Rousseau's enemies took advantage of the controversy; Friedrich Melchior Grimm, Rousseau's former friend and publisher of the *Correspondance littéraire,* a kind of subscription-only gazette covering the events in the Republic of Letters for crowned monarchs and others able to pay the price, dismissed Rousseau's work as a "masterpiece of bitterness, madness, and atrocity."[2] Voltaire went to the astonishing extreme of ending his scurrilous attack on Rousseau, the *Sentiment of the Citizens,* with a call to execute him as a "base revolutionary."

But many of Rousseau's allies also were dismayed by the book. Prince Louis Eugène de Würtemberg, who took his devotion to a peak reached by few others, raising his children in accordance with the education system outlined in *Emile,* begged the philosopher to deny his authorship of the *Letters Written from the Mountain.* The book, he exclaimed, "undermines the foundations of religion, tears apart social bonds, and tends to upset the form of government in Geneva."[3] In Paris, Hume was also uneasy over the apparent incitement to revolution, telling the Comtesse de Boufflers that the "seditious [book] will not do credit to M. Rousseau."[4] The comtesse had the good sense not to relay Hume's strictures to Rousseau, thus saving the Scot from the blistering response Rousseau sent to Würtemberg announcing the termination of their friendship.

Rousseau had called Môtiers home for a little more than three years. Yet despite his sincere if eccentric efforts to win the hearts and minds of the locals, he remained a resident alien in every sense of the word. "I ought, I dare say, to have been loved by the people of this region, as I have been by all those where I have lived," Rousseau claimed in the *Confessions,* "for my open-handed distribution of alms, for being on familiar, perhaps too familiar, terms with everyone, and for divesting myself as far as I could of every mark of distinction that could excite jealousy."[5] Rousseau's unassuming familiarity, however, took unexpected forms. He took to sitting outside the house, wrapped in his caftan while weaving lace ribbons, a skill he had learned from the local women. Handiwork in hand, he would race down the main streets, offering the ribbons (which served as something like primitive brassieres) to young women who promised to breast-feed their own children. Though hardly in need of advice better suited for Rous-seau's aristocratic or bourgeois readers, who farmed out their infants to wet nurses, these perplexed women nonetheless accepted the curious gifts offered by the resident philosopher.

While attempting in his way to meet the locals where they lived, faithful to the idealized portrayal of country life he had provided in *Julie*, Rousseau also sought the company of more cultivated folk. For the first year, he often made his way to nearby Neuchâtel and his protector as governor of the region, Lord Marischal Keith. The elderly Scot, just past seventy years of age, shared Rous-seau's fate as an exile. Having been banished a half-century earlier owing to his association with the Stuart dynasty, the last hereditary Earl Marischal of Scotland and his younger brother found themselves the trusted confidants and employees of Frederick the Great, with the younger Keith becoming Frederick's most val-ued general and the elder serving as ambassador to the Spanish and French courts before being stationed at Neuchâtel in semiretirement.* Rousseau was only one among the many exotic animals that made up Keith's menagerie. A bachelor, Keith had nonetheless collected a remarkable array of "children": Ibrahim the Tartar, said to be related to the Great Lama; Stéphan the Kalmouk; Motcho the Negro; and Emetulla, a Moslem from Armenia captured in a siege by Keith's brother as a girl thirty years earlier, whom Rousseau himself helped to tutor for her conversion to Christianity.[6] After Keith departed for Berlin, Rous-seau befriended the cultivated and wealthy Pierre Alexandre Du Peyrou, a loyal friend who would eventually see an edition of the author's collected writings through the press.

Rousseau's most constant companion, however, was Sultan. The canine, whose virtues were invisible to all other eyes, was the successor of Turc, origi-nally named Duc until Rousseau befriended the Duc de Luxembourg and re-named his dog out of consideration for the nobleman's feelings. The first dog's death in 1761 left the philosopher inconsolable and he refused Luxembourg's offer of a replacement: "It is not another dog I must have, but another Turc, and

---

*The second author of this book was surprised to discover that James Francis Edward Keith is his ancestor, Keith's great-great grandson Alexander Keith Scott being the author's great-great-great grandfather.

my Turc is unique. Losses of that kind are not replaceable. I have sworn that my present attachments of every kind shall henceforth be my last."[7] Yet two years later Rousseau's stoic resolve crumbled in the presence of a puppy, and Sultan thus came to replace the irreplaceable hound.

Rousseau's relations with his neighbors in Môtiers proved more tumultuous than those with his noble and wealthy friends in Neuchâtel or his canine companion. A barometer of the feelings of the townsfolk was the local pastor, Frédéric-Guillaume de Montmollin. Montmollin initially welcomed the famous author. When Rousseau first arrived in the village, he asked Montmollin permission to attend services and take the sacrament, moreover requesting to do so while wearing his unusual costume. Touched by Rousseau's humility and spurred by his own intellectual pretensions, Montmollin agreed. Rousseau quickly became a regular attendee at church. He declared: "I found an extraordinary sweetness in being able to say to myself, here at least I am among my brethren."[8]

Inevitably, though, Montmollin was soon caught up in the literary storm spawned by the *Letters from the Mountain.* All but the most liberal Protestants would have had difficulty accepting the book's rejection of miracles as a basis of faith, and even the most honest minister could not swallow its harsh attack on his fellow clergymen in Geneva. Montmollin was disturbed by the *Letters,* telling a fellow pastor that while his "heart had been sickened" by the book, he felt obliged to allow Rousseau to continue attending services in his church.[9] But he was pushed beyond the limits of Christian charity upon reading Voltaire's portrayal of Rousseau in the *Sentiment of Citizens.* Once he read the libelous pamphlet, Montmollin concluded that his celebrated parishioner had not only misled him but was also fatally misled about his own beliefs.

Determined to rid Môtiers of the heretic in their midst, Montmollin sought the aid of village and regional elders. Yet his task was not easy. Montmollin's most sovereign lord, Frederick the Great of Prussia, denied the pastor's request for Rousseau's expulsion. Yet even Frederick's imperious writ extended only so far. By the middle of May 1765, Montmollin had taken to the pulpit in order to denounce Rousseau as the Antichrist. Although ordered to desist by the king's local representatives, the minister's fiery sermons had already set a spark to the tinder of rural justice. As Rousseau subsequently recalled, the first flames of hatred were already flickering by early summer, when he was "pursued across the countryside, like some sort of werewolf." His refusal to abandon his Armenian dress naturally made him even more conspicuous, eliciting catcalls, jeers, occasional volleys of stones, and, most ominous, men shouting for their guns.[10] These early encounters were so many dress rehearsals for the stoning of the cottage on September 6.

"Although J.-J. Rousseau is not a philosopher, the priests have accorded him that honor despite him, and as a consequence they have treated him as such," Grimm shortly reported after the lapidation in the October 1, 1765, issue of the *Correspondance littéraire*. He then wrote a mock retraction in the next issue of his gazette, taking a hint from a letter sent by his favorite source, Voltaire:

> It seems that the first reports regarding the insults made to M. Rousseau in the village of Môtiers-Travers were extremely exaggerated, and that the similarity of his fate to that of St. Stephen, the first martyr, is not very well attested. If the inquiries ordered by the local justice can be believed, the whole thing comes down to a few pebbles thrown against M. Rousseau's windows by a few drunks who had by chance gathered by his door, without any bad intentions. With a lively imagination it is easy to transform some small pebbles into a hail of rocks and two or three drunks into a group of assassins.[11]

Far from a harmless broadside of pebbles, the stoning may well have represented the defensive reflex of a small community whose social and moral economies had been disturbed by an outsider. Whether rough justice or mere rural intolerance, it was now clear that all the ribbons in the world would not make Rousseau any more acceptable in the Jura than his writings had now made him in Paris or Geneva.

As he stood outside of his cottage the day after the stoning, Rousseau knew he now had to act immediately on his long-planned departure. Fortunately, he had already taken steps to secure a new asylum.

In the summer of 1765 Rousseau had discovered the Île St. Pierre during a botanizing trip with his friend François-Henri d'Ivernois, a well-off merchant residing in Neuchâtel. On this verdant crescent of land lying in Lake Bienne stood a single house, occupied by the local tax collector, stationed there with his wife and a couple of servants to oversee the harvest of wine grapes and wheat grown on the island. Nearby was a smaller and deserted island, covered with willow trees. Rousseau was seduced by the Île St. Pierre's isolation and beauty, and upon his return from the excursion to an increasingly hostile Môtiers he wrote to ask Lord Keith whether he could move to the island. Keith duly saw to the bureaucratic necessities, and the city of Berne, which owned the island, gave Rousseau permission to move there. The timing was fortunate: forty-eight hours after the siege of his cottage, Rousseau was already en route to the insular retreat. He left behind Thérèse, assigned to the packing of their belongings, as well as a straw effigy of himself that his neighbors had erected in the public square.

Some of Rousseau's most lyrical prose recollects his brief asylum on the island, especially in the work he left unfinished at his death, the *Reveries of the*

Nicolas Andre Monsiau (1754–1837), photograph after Louis Michel Halbou (b. 1730), *Jean-Jacques Rousseau Gathering Herbs at Ermenonville, June 1778*, engraving. © Bibliothèque Nationale, Paris / Archives Charmet / The Bridgeman Art Library

Solitary Walker. "They let me spend scarcely two months on this island, but I would have spent two years there, two centuries, and the whole of eternity without being bored for a moment," he reminisced a decade later: "I consider these two months the happiest time of my life, so happy that it would have contented me for my whole existence without the desire for another state arising for a single instant in my soul."[12] He had finally found the solitude he had long sought. "It seemed to me that on this island I would be more isolated from other men than before, more shielded from their insults, more forgotten, more abandoned, in a word, to the joys of idleness and the contemplative life: I should have liked to have been so confined on my island that I need have no further commerce with mortals."[13]

Even after the arrival of Thérèse and Sultan, Rousseau lived a Robinson Crusoe – like existence during those idyllic days. After grudgingly borrowing the tax collector's writing table to attend to the importunate letters that still managed to reach him and impatiently dining with Thérèse and the other residents, he would steal off alone with a copy of Linnaeus under his arm. The amateur botanist would retreat to some new part of the island every few days to survey the world of flora he found there. "Plants seem to have been sown profusely on the earth, like the stars in the sky, to invite man to the study of nature by the attraction of pleasure and curiosity." After hours spent wandering from one flower to the next, he would return, "laden with an ample harvest" to occupy him on rainy days and to decorate his room: "Instead of depressing papers and heaps of old books, I filled my room with flowers and dried plants."[14]

Accompanied by Sultan, Rousseau also rowed along the lake, exploring its "romantic" shores, or drifting aimlessly and falling into daydreams in which he forgot his fellowmen and himself. "At times, filled with emotion, I would cry out loud: 'O nature! O my mother! Here at least I am under your guardianship alone; no cunning or treacherous man can come between us here.'" Whether on water or land, his reveries were akin to raptures. Nature, he claimed, was his temple: below the roof of the sky, surrounded by the walls of woods and carpets of the fields, Rousseau was constantly moved to prayer. As far back as his days at Les Charmettes, his prayers were in fact cascades of praise he was moved to utter outdoors. In the *Confessions,* he observed that while he easily understood the faithlessness of city dwellers, "who see only walls and streets and crimes," he simply could not comprehend how the same might also hold for peasants. "How can their souls not leap in ecstasy, a hundred times a day, to greet the author of those wonders which everywhere strike the eye?"[15]

Of course, such ecstatic leaps do not come easily when one is plowing fields or harvesting grapes. Rousseau unwittingly acknowledged the fact that romanticism is a leisure-time activity when he described his activities on the island: he would "visit their workers and their crops, quite often joining my hand with theirs in work. . . . My morning exercise and the good temper which is inseparable from it made the pause for lunch very enjoyable. But when it took too long and good weather beckoned, I could not wait so long. While they were still at the table, I would slip away."[16] In short, Rousseau's exclamations about the country life, though sincere, are also naïvely ironic. Despite his best efforts, he remained a part-time peasant and nature's tourist, a city dweller unfamiliar with the deadening, backbreaking, and unending labor of those who had no choice but to live off of the land.

This experiential dissonance becomes clearest in Rousseau's attitude toward Lake Bienne. While it was little more than a material resource for the local residents, for Rousseau it was an existential source of the self. In the lake's clear water he recalled the transparency of the childhood world of Bossey, where he felt at one with nature and with himself, a crystalline world he tried to reconstruct through his prose. The worship of nature, with which Rousseau felt an immediate and unmediated relationship, was also the restitution of unmediated access to the true self, or the very absence of self, that he found in solitude.

As he stretched along the bottom of the boat and gazed at the blue sky, the soot and mud, the hypocrisy and lies that civilization had deposited on Rousseau's soul slowly dissolved, leaving behind what was most deeply and purely himself. The slow and constant rocking of the boat, the lapping of water against its hull brought its passenger to a state where his thoughts and self-awareness, those great barriers to pure transparency, would evaporate like the morning mist on the lake. "What do we enjoy in such a situation? Nothing external to ourselves, nothing if not ourselves and our own existence. As long as this state lasts, we are sufficient unto ourselves, like God. The sentiment of existence, stripped of any other emotion, is in itself a precious sentiment of contentment and of peace which alone would suffice to make this existence dear and sweet to anyone able to spurn all the sensual and earthly impressions which incessantly come to distract us from it and to trouble its sweetness here-below."[17]

Ultimately, the boating excursions on Lake Bienne carried Rousseau far beyond the Enlightenment's banks of reason and logic. Yet not far enough. Try as he might to forget the world, the world refused to forget Rousseau. Reveries are frail and short-lived. As Rousseau noted, the "ardent desire to finish my days on the island was inseparable from the fear of being forced to leave."[18] Rousseau was so fearful of having to quit the island that he fantasized a life sentence as a prisoner there, a fate he claimed he would gladly welcome.

A different and more predictable sentence soon arrived, however. On October 16, a month after his arrival, Rousseau received a letter from the local bailiff: the Bernese government was ordering him to vacate the island. Even the cordon sanitaire of Lake Bienne was not sufficient, in the eyes of the authorities, to keep their world safe from Rousseau. Asking for a few more weeks to prepare for his departure, he again was forced to contemplate where he would next haul his weary body.

While Rousseau contemplated his uncertain future, his friends began to act. The celebrated exile received offers of refuge from his correspondents, and even from total strangers who had heard of his plight. A friend from days with "Maman" at Les Charmettes, François-Joseph de Conzié, who had once been one of Rousseau's most enthusiastic and least talented music students, invited his old teacher back to Arenthon, in the neighborhood of the place where he had enjoyed such happiness. There was, however, one condition upon which Conzié insisted. He would be delighted to welcome him, he explained, "provided that you abandon your favorite costume, for you would be immediately recognized. . . . Come straightaway to Arenthon accompanied by your gouvernante, but with the precaution, I repeat, to get rid of your singular costume." Having been informed of Conzié's offer and its condition, the Prince of Würtemberg wrote the philosopher with an inspired suggestion. If Conzié "does not want you to be an Armenian, I am quite happy with that, because I know a costume that is even more commodious than the one you wear, and much warmer. It is the Polish berka."[19]

The man who first sanctioned Rousseau's eccentric sartorial choice, Lord Keith, meanwhile scoured Venice and Berlin, considered Corsica, and wrote to the rulers of Savoy and Silesia to seek asylum for "his" philosopher. Rousseau had told Keith even before the stoning, in January 1765 in the midst of the tumult over the *Letters Written from the Mountain*, that he was considering other refuges: "I see only two countries to choose from, England or Italy."[20] Rousseau was familiar with Italy, yet England had a certain allure for the author of *Julie:* in the novel Rousseau has the English friend of the separated lovers, Lord Bomstom, offer them the refuge of his estate in the Duchy of York and part of his fortune, an offer Julie refuses out of filial piety.[21] Rousseau's concerns in contemplating actual offers of such a refuge were, however, more mundane. "England would be much more to my liking," he told Keith, "but it is less suitable to my health, and I do not know the language: a great inconvenience when one is transplanted there alone."[22] The Marquise de Verdelin was also concerned that Rousseau's linguistic isolation would make England an unhappy retreat. She located a cottage near the estate of Horace Walpole, which Boufflers had visited during her visit to England a few years before. The marquise assured Rousseau that Walpole spoke very good French and was "one of the most virtuous men of his nation." The marquise was right on at least one count: Walpole spoke excellent French.[23]

As Keith pondered Rousseau's options, an old friend entered his thoughts:

David Hume. This was not the first time Hume's services had been sought by Rousseau's friends or his name mentioned to the fugitive philosopher. Just days after Rousseau's arrival in Môtiers, Keith had already broached the subject of the persecuted philosopher to Hume. With great prescience, the old Scot wrote to his fellow countryman that the Jura was "not a country for Jean-Jacques." He then told Hume that "the liberty of England and the character of my good and honored friend D. Hume" were irresistible attractions; should Rousseau go to Great Britain, "he will be a treasure to you, and you to him, and perhaps both to me."[24] Likewise, the Comtesse de Boufflers reached out to Hume at this earlier crisis. Within days of Rousseau's hurried departure from Paris in 1762, Boufflers, who had just launched her correspondence with Hume, sent her "celestial being" a long letter describing the Genevan's travails and character. His dread of dependence upon others, she explained, "may seem excessive but not at all criminal; indeed, it betrays noble sentiments. He flees the world and loves solitude. . . . His desire for retirement has made him enemies. . . . Yet, despite his apparent misanthropy, I do not believe that the man exists who is more gentle, more humane, more feeling for the pain of others and more patient with his own." She then informed the undoubtedly nonplussed Scot that she implored Rousseau to seek asylum in England, promising to ask none other than David Hume for his help: "I am thus carrying out my promise in the confidence that I could not have chosen in all of Europe a man more respected by enlightened opinion or more noted for his humanity."[25]

Boufflers's tactic succeeded brilliantly. Hume immediately lurched into action. "I assure your Ladyship there is no man in Europe of whom I have entertained a higher idea, and whom I would be prouder to serve," he announced: "I revere his greatness of mind, which makes him fly obligations and dependence; and I have the vanity to think, that through the course of my life I have endeavored to resemble him in those maxims."[26] Upon sealing the letter to Boufflers, the exhilarated Scot then fired off a letter to Rousseau himself. In unusually exalted terms, Hume told Rousseau: "Of all the men of letters in Europe . . . you are the person whom I most revere, both for the force of your genius and the greatness of your mind." Developing the personal parallels he had already mentioned to Boufflers, he reassured Rousseau that "my conduct and character entitle me to a sympathy with yours; at least, in my love of philosophical retreat, in my neglect of vulgar prejudices, and in my disdain of all dependence." Inviting Rousseau to settle in Great Britain, which would warmly welcome him despite its "disadvantages of climate," Hume ended with an apology for having written in English: "It is the only language in which I can express myself with tolerable propriety, though I am uncertain whether you will be able to understand my letter without an interpreter."[27]

Delivery of Hume's letter was delayed by the vagaries of Rousseau's movements and the sluggishness of the continental post. More than seven months passed before Hume's offer finally found its recipient, who was by then braiding ribbons in Môtiers under the benevolent gaze of Lord Keith. Replying on February 19, 1763, Rousseau thanked Hume for his offer, but he deflected the invitation to join him in Scotland. Such a voyage would be redundant, Rousseau replied, since the presence of Lord Keith in nearby Neuchâtel allowed Rousseau to "find Scotland in the midst of Switzerland."[28] Rousseau's reply—limited to general, nearly formulaic effusions over the Scot's genius—suggest that he was unfamiliar with the writings of his would-be savior. In fact, the only work by Hume he appears to have read was Prévost's translation of the *History of the Stuarts*, the first published volume of the *History of England*.

Equally intriguing is Hume's attitude toward Rousseau. Despite his protestations of respect and admiration for Rousseau, Hume does not discuss his work at any length. Only when Boufflers asks his opinion of *Emile*, the work that had led to its author's suite of sorrows, does Hume offer a critique. With diplomatic tact, he allows: "All the writings of that author appear to me admirable, particularly on the head of eloquence." Yet for Hume, this quality is as problematic as it is praiseworthy. He recognized the undeniable power of Rousseau's prose: the exiled thinker has given the French language "an energy which it scarce seems to have reached in any other hands." But he was concerned for that very reason. In Rousseau's prose there is "always intermingled some degree of extravagance," a kind of rhetorical high-wire act. In fact, Hume refers to Rousseau's writings as "performances." The author of *Emile*, Hume states, "chooses his topics less from persuasion than from the pleasure of showing his invention and surprising the reader with his paradoxes."[29] Just as Rousseau believed he knew his Scot, then, so did Hume clearly believe he had the number of his Genevan. And just like Rousseau, Hume missed the mark. Rousseau's embrace of paradoxes were not mere extravagances; they were critical to his philosophical enterprise.

Two and a half years after their initial exchanges of goodwill, when Rousseau realized after the flurry of stones that Switzerland was not Scotland, he was ready to listen to his friends. Great Britain and Hume alone could guarantee Rousseau's well-being, Keith wrote Hume in March 1765.[30] Momentarily swayed by the growing chorus in praise of Hume, Rousseau made his choice. "I have decided to go to England, the sole country where some liberty remains to men," he wrote Verdelin in mid-October from his island, asking her to arrange a passport so that he could pass through France, where the order for his arrest still remained in force.[31]

But freedom was just another word for equivocation for the anxious and ill philosopher. Rousseau quickly backtracked, telling another friend a couple of

days later: "I have consulted my situation, my age, my humor, my powers: nothing in all this allows me to undertake at this moment and without any preparations a long and difficult voyage, to go wandering through those cold lands and
to wear myself out in looking for refuge in far off places in a season during which
my infirmities do not even allow me to leave my room."[32] There were also religious doubts. Still upset over the hostility of the Protestant authorities of Geneva,
Rousseau declared with dramatic flair, "I would rather die in a Catholic country
than a Protestant one; the Catholic clergy preach intolerance, but the Protestants
practice it."[33] Then, in a variation of his earlier dream of being imprisoned on
St. Pierre, he announced that he would ask Frederick to lock him up as a prisoner
in a castle, where he would give up writing in exchange for the liberty of reading a few books and walking in the gardens.[34]

After two weeks of making, then unmaking, plans, one more fantastic than
the next, he finally chose not to choose and made his way to Strasbourg to contemplate his decision. As he had done in his earlier departures from Paris and
Môtiers, Rousseau had once again left behind Thérèse to pack their bags. "I have
brought along Sultan, and he is now sleeping on my coat under the table at which
I am writing," he wrote her en route to his way station. "He ran in front of the carriage like a hunting dog, but one that doesn't stop running for ten leagues at a gal-
lop. He is a unique dog, yet he does not allow me to embrace him very often."[35]

Strasbourg's position on the Rhine and at the crossroads of several trade
routes made it an appropriate way station for an indecisive exile. Arriving there
on November 4, Rousseau initially intended to recuperate for a week or so before making his way to Berlin to join Keith in retirement at his new palace, built
by a grateful Frederick on the grounds of his much greater palace Sans Souci.
With Sultan as his sole companion, he took a room at an inn without revealing
his arrival to anyone. "I eat entirely alone in my room with Sultan, who keeps me
faithful company, above all at table, eating just like he runs; that's all there is
to say."[36]

Perhaps too distracted by anxiety and pain to realize that his Armenian dress
hardly helped him remain anonymous, Rousseau was quickly discovered. The
usual parade of well-wishers and celebrity seekers began to appear at his door,
and the philosopher fell into his custom of responding to letters and turning
down invitations. Yet the townspeople seemed to evince genuine warmth for
their guest, and the local opera company hurriedly prepared *Le Devin du village*
to perform in the composer's presence. Rousseau attended the rehearsal of his
opera on November 8, and he told the director how pleased he was with the production and made a few suggestions. His report in a letter to a friend was less
complimentary: "I went this afternoon to see the first rehearsal, and I expected
that it would all be detestable. . . . Behold me, passed from the hands of the the-

ologians into those of the actors; it is just about the same with both, except that
the latter, as bad as they may be, still play their roles better than the former, and
do not massacre people."[37] Instead, they massacred silence, clearly a far less
onerous fate than the one Rousseau faced elsewhere.

While enjoying Strasbourg's hospitality, Rousseau knew that he could not
remain there for long. With the arrival of winter, he had at least to choose a
refuge until the end of spring, when he could travel, yet remaining in French territory was dangerous. Still torn between Frederick's Berlin and Hume's England, Rousseau feared that ill health would make it impossible to reach either
destination. The Comtesse de Boufflers recommended England. So did Lord
Keith, despite his own hope that the philosopher would share his retirement.
"You do not flee men, you only avoid Yahoos, and with good reason," Keith
wrote, reassuring Rousseau about Hume: "David is not one of those, he is a
man. When you find one of them, you must recognize him, and distinguish him
from the Yahoos, and treat him well. . . . He is a public minister; you will be safe
with him, as he is the Houyhnhnm who will protect you from the Yahoos."[38] The
Marquise de Verdelin, who was visiting Rousseau at the time of the stoning and
witnessed at first hand the hostility of Rousseau's neighbors, added her formidable voice to this growing chorus: *le bon David vous attend,* she wrote.

At the urging of the marquise, on October 22 Hume renewed the offer he
had first made more than three years before. Writing in French this time rather
than in English, Hume reassured Rousseau of his sympathy: "Your unrelenting
and singular misfortunes, independent of your own virtue and genius, compel
the interest of anyone devoted to the cause of humanity." This unhappy predicament, however, could be resolved by accepting Hume's invitation to go to England: "I can assure you that in England you will find complete security against
persecution, because of the spirit of toleration that informs our laws, as well as
the respect that everyone has for your character." Briefly discussing the favor-
able treatment Rousseau would receive from London booksellers—as a fellow
author, Hume was acutely aware of Rousseau's dependence upon book sales for
his livelihood—the Scot concluded the letter with a moving declaration: "The
small role you will allow me to play [in your move to England] would make me
extremely happy, and I would count this event as one of the most fortunate in
my life."[39]

Upon reading Hume's letter, Rousseau finally chose England. He was perhaps less drawn by the country's reputation for liberty than repelled by the recollection of Voltaire's virtual imprisonment in Prussia. Fortune also seemed to
have a role: while looking through the books, papers, and other belongings
Rousseau had left to his care, Du Peyrou found a portrait of Hume buried in a
pile of engravings, and sent it along to Rousseau at the end of November.[40]

"I have received M. Hume's letter and I cannot tell you how much I was touched and consoled to see this illustrious man taking such a strong interest in my fate," Rousseau wrote with evident relief to the Marquise de Verdelin on November 14. "Nothing is more capable of increasing my desire to go to England than the honor of going there under his auspices."[41] Then, writing to his benefactor, he announced his acceptance:

> Your acts of goodness, Monsieur, penetrate my heart as much as they honor me. The most worthy response I could make to your offers is to accept them, and I do accept them. I will leave in five or six days to go throw myself into your arms. It is the counsel of Milord Marischal, my protector, my friend, my father; it is that of Madame de Verdelin, whose enlightened beneficence guides me as much as it consoles me; finally, I dare say that it is that of my own heart, which is pleased to owe so much to the most illustrious of my contemporaries, whose goodness surpasses his glory.[42]

On the morning of December 9, 1765, accompanied by Sultan, Rousseau took a coach from Strasbourg to meet Hume in Paris.

CHAPTER SEVEN

First Impressions

I think Rousseau in many things very much resembles Socrates. . . . Both
of them were of very amorous complexions: but a comparison in this
particular turns out much to the advantage of my friend.
——Hume to Hugh Blair

He has not loved truth more than I have . . . but I sometimes put passion
into my researches, and he has put only his wisdom and genius into his.
——Rousseau to Boufflers

Rousseau left Strasbourg as he had arrived: a celebrity despite himself. Ever jealous of his independence, he spurned several offers of private carriages despite his worries about the effects the long trip might have on his fragile health. Instead, in the company of fellow travelers gaping at his costume, the fugitive philosopher headed for the capital by post chaise. One week after having quit Strasbourg, and one year after Boswell had first knocked on his door at Môtiers, Rousseau reached Paris on the evening of Monday, December

16, 1765. By then, though, word had spread that the philosopher was returning to the city from which he had fled nearly four years before: his ostensible desire to steal into Paris thus became an impromptu spectacle.

Rousseau immediately made for the home of Madame Duchesne, the widow of the publisher of *Julie* and *Emile*, Nicolas-Bonaventure Duchesne, who had died earlier that year. He had arranged to stay at her home and place of business on the Rue St. Jacques, the ancient, sclerotic artery cutting Paris into eastern and western halves. Before leaving Strasbourg, he had written to Pierre Guy, his publisher's associate (and newly married husband of the widow), asking him not to tell anyone of his whereabouts.[1]

Rousseau's plan was to recuperate from his journey, as well as to work on the page proofs of his *Dictionary of Music*, which he had been revising for several years. The first comprehensive musical lexicon to be published in any language, the *Dictionary* had its genesis in the articles on music that Rousseau had written a decade and a half earlier for the *Encyclopédie*, the last text volume of which an exhausted Diderot had seen through the press earlier in the year. Given the expenses of a life in which he had to abandon one household only to refurnish the next, Rousseau told one correspondent, Alexis-Claude Clairaut, that he had but one reason for writing the book: "to have bread."[2] Clairaut took the liberty of showing the letter to Hume. The Scot was upset by the news, undoubtedly in part because he increasingly identified with Rousseau's plight. The account, he wrote to Clairaut, "has raised in my heart a movement of pity, mixed with indignation, in imagining that a man of letters of such eminence would be reduced, despite the simplicity of his manner of living, to the last extremities of poverty, and that this unhappy condition was still aggravated by sickness, by the approach of old age, and by the implacable rage of his devout persecutors."[3]

To the litany of woes that afflicted Rousseau, Hume might have added self-inflicted willfulness. Upon arriving in the capital, the Genevan had sworn that he would make every effort to preserve his anonymity: he would not "parade my cap in the streets of Paris."[4] The same day, he wrote to Verdelin, insisting that the only person who could tempt him from his seclusion was the marquise herself.[5] In his peculiar fashion, Rousseau was true to his word: the very next day, he duly avoided the Parisian streets but "paraded his cap" instead in the Luxembourg gardens. And he did so not for a person, but for a dog. After all, Sultan had to be walked. Thus advertising his presence, Rousseau quickly dashed his plans for a secret sojourn in Paris. "J.-J. Rousseau made his entry in Paris on December 17," Grimm reported in the *Correspondance littéraire:* "In the morning, he walked at the Luxembourg in his Armenian dress. . . . This affectation of showing himself in public without any need to do so, in spite of the arrest order, has shocked the government, which has given in to the requests of his protectors by allowing him to travel through the kingdom to make his way to England."[6]

The widow Duchesne's quiet interlude quickly ended: she was now host to Europe's most celebrated recluse. Hurt friends wrote Rousseau to complain that he had not trusted them with the secret of his arrival, and he answered their complaints with complaints of his own. "Madame, always reproaches!" he wrote to Marianne de la Tour, an importunate correspondent who protested that he had done her an unforgettable injustice by not coming immediately to her: "I have not seen you because I am not planning on seeing anyone and because it would not be possible for me to do so even if I enjoyed better health and more leisure."[7] Also disappointed, but for better reason, was Denis Diderot. Writing to Sophie Volland on December 20, he referred wistfully to Rousseau's arrival: "I do not expect a visit from him, but I will not conceal from you that it would give me great pleasure, and that I would be happy to see how he would justify his conduct with regard to me. I do well not to grant access to my open heart, since once someone has entered it he cannot leave without tearing it apart, leaving a wound that never quite heals."[8] Although the philosophical and temperamental differences between Diderot and Rousseau had grown too great to bridge, Diderot's generosity toward his erstwhile friend had not faded: Rousseau, he concluded, was to be pitied, not persecuted.

Rousseau nonetheless soon received an invitation he could not refuse. At the urging of the Comtesse de Boufflers, the Prince de Conti had sent word to the widow Duchesne's, insisting that her guest stay with him for the remainder of his Paris sojourn.

Rousseau had first met the prince in 1760, when he was living as a guest of the Duc de Luxembourg on his estate of Montmorency. Perhaps because he ranked just below the sovereign himself, Conti paradoxically had an egalitarian temper: as an acquaintance explained, he observed "no distinction of rank in society."[9] Impressed by the philosopher, the prince took the unusual step of visiting him twice in his retreat. During the second visit, the two men sat across from one another at a chessboard. Oblivious to the members of the prince's retinue who, by frantic gestures and expressions, tried to warn Rousseau against humiliating his opponent, the philosopher twice trounced one of the most powerful men in France. "My Lord," Rousseau proclaimed: "I honor His Most Serene Highness too much not to beat him at chess every time." Rousseau narrowly avoided a more serious faux pas during these visits: unaware that the Comtesse de Boufflers was the prince's mistress, the philosopher flirted with her until someone took him aside to apprise him of her relationship to Conti.[10] Aware of the philosopher's straitened financial situation, the prince also commissioned

Rousseau to copy the score of his opera *Les Muses galantes* and some other compositions. When Rousseau delivered the bill to Conti for the modest sum of 196 livres and 44 sols, Conti scrupulously paid the exact amount, thus avoiding the fate of the Duc de Richelieu, whose charitable intentions in overpaying the penurious Rousseau 2,400 livres for some music notebooks resulted in the return of precisely 99 livres—along with a testy note asking Richelieu to avoid such mistakes in the future.[11]

Alongside Rousseau's desire to be left alone was the bitter awareness that he could not realize this aspiration without powerful friends. Returned to France, the author of *Emile* and *The Social Contract* remained a fugitive from its law; although wary authorities were for the moment turning a blind eye to his presence, their attitude could change at any moment. Could Rousseau afford to reject Conti's offer? The answer was provided on December 20, when he crossed the Seine, abandoning Mme Duchesne's modest lodgings for the opulence of the Temple.

The Temple was the imposing medieval fortress of the Knights of Malta, located on the eastern edge of the Marais, just north of the Place des Vosges. Alongside the turreted tower of the fortress was the elegant Hôtel St. Simon, which the Prince de Conti occupied in his role as Grand Prior of the Templars. After the Knights were crushed by Philippe IV in the early fourteenth century, the Temple came to serve as a home for the illegitimate offspring of kings and others who simultaneously enjoyed the privilege of birth and the disfavor of sovereigns.* The Prince de Conti carried on this tradition once he lost the favor of Louis XV, who referred dismissively to his rebellious relative as "my cousin, the lawyer."[12] On Mondays he and the comtesse served dinner for up to a hundred guests, while Fridays were reserved for her salon.[13] On other days the couple hosted poetry readings and musical entertainments in the centerpiece of the prince's mansion, the dazzling Hall of Four Mirrors. One such entertainment took place a couple of weeks after Rousseau left the Temple for England, when the ten-year-old Mozart, on his second visit to Paris, astonished guests with his virtuosity on the harpsichord in a scene captured by the celebrated painting by Ollivier. (This was the second time Rousseau had missed the prodigy, who was on the road into

---

*Roles were reversed, however, on the evening of August 13, 1792, when the revolutionaries invited Louis XVI and his family to dine at the Hôtel St. Simon. Fueled by wine and the rhetoric of *The Social Contract*, they called their monarch "Monsieur" with mocking politeness, and then, after the plates were cleared, arrested the king and led away his children and sister to the Tower of the Temple. The Tower became a shrine to monarchists and was duly toppled by Napoleon, leaving only the palace, to which the Princess Royal returned after the Restoration to weep, pray, and plant a willow tree. In a final and ultimately ill-fated attempt to put the Revolution to rest, in 1853 Napoleon III in his turn had the Hôtel St. Simon torn down.

Paris the day in 1763 that the philosopher was on the road out of the city after the order was issued for his arrest.)[14]

Inevitably, Rousseau was swept up in the whirl of social activities at the Temple, including a performance of the philosopher's *Les Muses galantes,* the opera that had had a disastrous premiere thirty-three years earlier. Eager to show off their philosopher, the prince and his hostess paraded an endless stream of visitors through the palace. For six hours a day—three in the morning, three in the evening—Rousseau sat like a potentate from a distant land, receiving one person after another. "I am here in the Hôtel St. Simon like Sancho on his Isla Barataria, receiving petitions the whole day," he wrote to Du Peyrou. "I have the whole world surrounding me from the instant I arise until I go to bed and I am forced to dress in public. I have never suffered so much."[15] A sign of the times: Rousseau had hijacked the royal levee, at which guests would attend the Bourbon kings as they rose from bed.

On December 20, the same day Rousseau arrived at the Temple, he was finally introduced to Hume. Since it was a Friday, the comtesse escorted the two philosophers to her weekly salon, placing them next to each other at the lavishly appointed table. Even the ancient walls of the Temple had rarely welcomed so marvelous a sight: the huge Scot dwarfing the slight Genevan, the two men exchanging pleasantries while the rest of the room hummed with excitement.

No stranger to celebrity himself, Hume nevertheless marveled at the public's fascination with Rousseau. "It is impossible to express or imagine the enthusiasm of this nation in his favor," Hume declared in an excited letter to Blair. "Even his maid, La Vasseur [*sic*], who is very homely and very awkward, is more talked of than the Princess of Monaco or the Countess of Egmont, on account of her fidelity and attachment towards him. His very dog, who is no better than a coly [collie], has a name and reputation in the world." The usually modest Hume could not resist bragging to his friend that he was to leave for Paris soon in order to "settle the celebrated Rousseau, who has rejected invitations from half the kings and princes of Europe, in order to place himself under my protection."[16]

Hume also discovered, he related to Blair, that his new friend's fame was contagious: "As I am supposed to have him in my custody, all the world, especially the great ladies tease me to be introduced to him: I have had *rouleaus* thrust into my hand, with earnest applications, that I would prevail on him to accept of them." Were he to advertise Rousseau's daily walks in the Luxembourg Gardens, Hume half-joked, he could draw an audience of thousands, flocking there just to get a glimpse of the philosopher. "I am persuaded, that were I to open here a subscription with his consent, I should receive 50,000 pounds in a fortnight." Indeed, in a nation that worships genius more than ancient Greece, the Scot exclaimed, "no person ever so much engaged their attention as Rousseau. Voltaire and everybody else are quite eclipsed by him."[17]

Rousseau left no detailed record of his reaction to Hume, but Hume was eager to share his own first impressions of Rousseau. In a long letter to Hugh Blair, written a week after the previous one marveling at Rousseau's contagious celebrity, Hume shared an enthusiastic description of Rousseau, the wide-eyed wonder of which is unparalleled for the skeptical Scot. "As to my intercourse with him," he began, "I find him mild, and gentle and modest and good humored; and he has more of the behavior of a man of the world than any of the learned here." Taking up the issue of Rousseau's unusual dress, he declared that it was not at all an affectation, explaining that he "had an infirmity from his infancy, which makes breeches inconvenient for him." And despite the sneers of disbelief from his foes, who claimed "his solitary humor is all affectation, in order to be more sought after," Hume assured Blair that Rousseau's desire for solitude was no less sincere: this "solitary humor is natural and insurmountable." As evidence for his conclusion, Hume related how Rousseau was surprised by "two very agreeable ladies" and was so flustered "that he was not able to eat his dinner afterward." He further remarked on other occasions when, in the midst of lively conversation with the skittish philosopher, the sudden opening of a door would throw him into a spasm of anxiety and the "distress would not leave him unless the person was a particular friend."[18]

As with many other observers, however, what most drew Hume's attention was what he described as Rousseau's "most expressive countenance." His observation led him to make a revealing comparison between his guest and history's most celebrated philosopher: Socrates.

Parallels between Rousseau and Socrates had long been drawn; the Genevan's persecution at the hands of his fellow citizens recalled for many Socrates' trial in Athens two thousand years before. As early as 1762 d'Alembert lamented Rousseau's putatively Socratic fate, while the Abbé Morellet hailed him upon his return to Paris as the "persecuted Socrates."[19] Not surprisingly, among those attracted to this comparison was Rousseau himself. In his unpublished "Allegorical Fragment" (Le Morceau allégorique), Rousseau presents a philosopher who, having fallen asleep, dreams of a city whose citizens worship a statue hidden behind a veil. Returning to the theme of transparency and obscurity, Rousseau's allegory reveals the reality behind the shroud: the statue's face streaked in violent colors while its feet crushed worshipers below. In the dream, three liberators then appear, each of whom sacrifices his life to free his fellow men from this idol of fanaticism: Socrates, Christ, and a man "dressed exactly like the dreaming philosopher"—which brings us, by the slightest stretch of the imagination, to Rousseau himself.[20]

While Hume would have found such a stretch extravagant, his own experiences, and his sympathy with a fellow sufferer at the hands of the dogmatists and zealots, led him to discover important similarities between Socrates and Rousseau. Like Socrates, Hume explained to Blair, Rousseau was of "small stature" and "would be rather ugly had he not the finest physiognomy in the world." He glimpsed the flashes of brilliance that came from this otherwise unprepossessing man. "His modesty seems not to be good manners; but ignorance of his own excellence. As he writes and speaks and acts from the impulse of genius, more than from the use of his ordinary faculties, it is very likely that he forgets its force, whenever it is laid asleep." Again like Socrates, who claimed to be directed by his *daimonon*, a kind of divine voice, Rousseau's actions seemed inspired. "I am well assured, that at times he believes he has inspirations from an immediate communication with the divinity," relates Hume, who curiously does not add a note of his usual skepticism.[21]

Having, he thought, unraveled the riddle of Rousseau, Hume uses the answer to address the riddle of Socrates himself. Continuing his description of the divinely inspired philosopher, Hume tells Blair: "He falls sometimes into ecstasies which retain him in the same posture for hours together." Hume consciously here recalls the accounts of Socratic contemplation, those moments where his self-absorption appeared queer rather than quaint, and especially the famous description of Socrates in Plato's *Symposium*, where the philosopher misses the first half of the dinner to which he has been invited because he stands lost in thought outside the house. "Does not this example solve the difficulty of Socrates' genius and of his ecstasies?" Whether Hume succeeds in explaining Socrates by way of Rousseau or vice versa, the link he draws does underscore a trait shared by both thinkers: their intense inwardness. Hume thus makes explicit the comparison toward which he has, perhaps only half-consciously, been building. "I think Rousseau in many things very much resembles Socrates," he declares, even turning the comparison to Rousseau's credit: "The philosopher of Geneva seems only to have more genius than he of Athens, who never wrote any thing; and less sociableness and temper. Both of them were of very amorous complexions: but a comparison in this particular turns out much to the advantage of my friend."[22]*

Friend: for the first time Hume dares use the word: "I call him such; for I

---

*In his essay "The Sceptic," Hume concludes his observations on the attractions of virtue and vice by remarking upon those with "amorous complexions" that he would have been well to recall: "I shall add, as an observation to the same purpose, that, if a man be liable to a vice or imperfection, it may often happen, that a good quality, which he possesses along with it, will render him more miserable, than if he were completely vicious. . . . A very amorous complexion, with a heart incapable of friendship, is happier than the same excess in love, with a generosity of temper, which transports a man beyond himself, and renders him a total slave to the object of his passion."

hear from all hands that his judgment and affections are as strongly biased in my favor as mine are in his."[23] Just as Socrates' squat and aging body harbored a soul that seduced Athenian youths such as Alcibiades, so too had Rousseau's "very amorous complexion" begun to seduce the Scot.

Hume's rapid bonding with Rousseau must have surprised his contemporaries. Even more puzzling was that Hume had become attached to someone who was so different philosophically as well as temperamentally. The Scot himself recognized the apparent mystery in a letter he wrote to Blair barely more than a month after meeting Rousseau. "The philosophers of Paris foretold to me that I could not conduct him to Calais without a quarrel; but I think I could live with him all my life in mutual friendship and esteem." The cause for this pessimistic forecast, Hume believed, was Rousseau's religion: the philosophes are displeased with Rousseau "because they think he overbounds in religion; and it is indeed remarkable that the philosopher of this age, who has been the most persecuted, is by far the most devout."[24] The common experience of persecution certainly influenced Hume's feelings. He had more than one occasion to brood on the compassionate welcome given by Dido to Aeneas's shipwrecked crew in one of his most beloved works, Virgil's *Aeneid:* "I, too, have known suffering." This alone, however, could not explain Hume's attachment. During his life he had run to the defense of friends besieged by religious and political extremists, but had done so without the same emotional commitment—or, indeed, exhilaration—he now showed toward Rousseau. And while religious faith was rarely an obstacle for Hume's friendships, it was even more rarely a prod. Hume loved Blair, Robertson, and Home in spite of, not because of, their faith.

A deeper cause must have been at work. Hume hinted at the source in his letter to Blair, when he alluded to the character of Socrates in the *Symposium.* In the Platonic dialogue, Socrates is a man fully, even ludicrously, apart, committed to the pursuit of truth regardless of the cost. Among the consequences of Socrates' *philosophia*, his love of wisdom, was his fundamental indifference to the world and the men and women who inhabit it. Yet many of these same men, most powerfully Alcibiades, loved Socrates—a love, ironically, spurred by the old man's otherworldly character and concerns. The tragic implication of the *Symposium*, embodied by a desperately drunk Alcibiades, is that his particular love for Socrates cannot, by its very nature, be requited. Hume hardly fit the bill of the beautiful and young Athenian, but as he told Boufflers, "I love him much, and hope that I have some share in his affections."[25] Like Alcibiades, Hume was to discover that his love could not be returned.

During his wintry final weeks in Paris, Hume was not only preoccupied with completing his own official duties as chargé d'affaires in anticipation of the new ambassador's arrival but was also busy serving as intermediary between Rousseau and the world. As Morellet observed during his visit to the Temple, Hume showered "constant concern and kindness on the sorrowful philosopher."[26]

Quite suddenly, and with little deliberation, Hume had become not just Rousseau's secretary but also an advance man for the continuing public spectacle. The account of the young Scottish traveler and future diplomat Robert Liston is instructive. Having proclaimed that "no man has a more irresistible curiosity to see great men than I" (he was apparently unacquainted with James Boswell), Liston stationed himself across from the Temple "in order to stare at [Rousseau] as he and David were going into their poste-chaise." Seeing Hume about to enter the carriage, Liston seized the moment: "Now, thought I, now is the time. I run out and got as near as possible. But behold! No Rousseau appeared." Undaunted, he collared Hume, with whom he was acquainted. "I am just come to have a peep at Jean-Jacques, says I; I beg you'll not take notice of me, but let me stare in full liberty." Though weary of such requests, Hume nevertheless invited the young man to meet the object of his adulation. Hume led Liston inside the Temple and introduced him to the Comtesse de Boufflers, who in turn took him to meet the philosopher. Liston spent an hour in Rousseau's company, watching him dine and then helping him into his carriage. "His person is very thin and delicate looking," he reported; "his face, and especially his sharp black eyes promise every thing he has shown himself possessed of."[27]

By early January those eyes were beginning to glaze under the surfeit of attention. As Hume confided to Blair, Rousseau was fraying under the great press of human traffic at the Temple. So much so that Rousseau and Hume questioned their original intention to remain in Paris until the second week of January: "The concourse about him gives him so much uneasiness that he expresses the utmost impatience to be gone."[28] Rousseau urged Hume to hasten their departure, saying that he could not "endure for much longer this public theater."[29] While less eager than Rousseau to leave the city where he had known such affection and respect, Hume recognized the need to move up the date of departure. Moreover, given the turmoil that the exile's stay in Paris had generated, he thought it best for them to leave the city as inconspicuously as possible. Writing to Du Peyrou, Rousseau reported that although the news had been spread that he and Hume would leave on New Year's Day, they would actually depart on January 4.[30]

Once having initiated this diversionary tactic, Hume quietly joined Rousseau at the Temple the day before their actual departure, spending two hours making plans for their voyage. Afterward, Hume visited several friends to bid them farewell. After *le bon David* left her, the Marquise de Verdelin herself wrote Rousseau to bid adieu: "I have just seen Mr. Hume. I commended your welfare to him. He is worthy of the trust; the more I listen to him the more I admire his candor. His soul is made for yours."[31] But another of Hume's friends, Baron d'Holbach, had a very different message. Full of enthusiasm about his budding friendship with his "pupil," as he had begun to call Rousseau, Hume had stopped to see the patron of the "synagogue" where Hume had been a regular guest. Holbach warned him: "Though I am sorry to dispel your pleasant hopes and illusions, you will see before long that you were deceived." With a dramatic flourish, he told Hume: "You do not know your man. I tell you plainly that you are nursing a viper in your bosom."[32]

Confident that he knew his man, Hume proved impervious to such warnings, and he finished plans to escort him to Great Britain. The two philosophers slipped unnoticed out of the Temple on the morning of January 4. Joining them was Rousseau's friend Jean-Jacques de Luze, a relative of "Papa" Roguin who had become part of the protective circle that surrounded Rousseau during his exile in the Swiss Jura. De Luze had business interests in England and had agreed to accompany Rousseau to London in his comfortable carriage before Hume joined the party. The three men and Sultan traveled in two post chaises, swapping places to vary the company as they made for the Channel.

Their route to the coast took them through a number of towns, and they stopped for the first night in Senlis, where they shared a room at a crowded inn—a seemingly uneventful night that would prove decisive in the ending of their friendship. They traveled onward through Roye, Arras, and St-Omer, reaching Calais on January 8. Stopped by the storm-tossed waters of the Channel, the travelers were forced to wait two days before a packet could safely leave the port.

Apart from his boating on Lake Bienne, Rousseau had spent little time on water; in fact, he had never seen the ocean. Nevertheless, he spent most of the twelve-hour crossing, nearly triple the time of a normal transit, on the ship's chilled and lurching deck, with Sultan standing beside him, his eyes battened on the rain-shrouded cliffs of Dover. Hume was struck by Rousseau's unsuspected reserves of strength, reporting to Boufflers that their mutual friend "passed ten hours in the nighttime above deck during the most severe weather, when all the seamen were almost frozen to death, and he caught no harm."[33] Hume, however, spent the voyage below, retching up his guts.

As with any port town, Dover saw its share of odd voyagers. Yet the ship from Calais that docked on the gray, rain-swept morning of January 11, 1766, offered a rare sight. Having hardly set foot onto the slippery dock, a small man swathed in a rain-glistening caftan, pale and weak-kneed, threw himself at a large Scotsman, embracing him and covering his face with wet kisses. For both Rousseau and Hume, Dover seemed to promise the end of a frantic and exhausting experience in Paris, as well as the start of a new and happier life in England.

CHAPTER EIGHT

A Public Spectacle

*I have been an avanturie all over the varld, and am à present en
Angleterre, vere I am more honoré and caress den ever I was
in my own contrie, or inteed any vere else.*
— *French barber in Garrick's* Lethe

The public avidly followed the stages of Rousseau's journey to London.
William Rouet, a retired Scottish professor of Oriental languages and
Hume's fellow lodger at Lisle Street, for one, excitedly reported to his
cousin on January 10, 1766, that the Genevan philosopher was expected in London any day.[1] Several London newspapers reported his arrival on the thirteenth,
with the *Public Advertiser* crowing: "'Tis with pleasure we find he has chosen an
asylum amongst a people who know how to respect one of his distinguished talents."[2] His movements were reported as far away as Holland, where the *Gazette
d'Utrecht* announced: "His enemies reproach him particularly for the singularity
of the *Armenian* dress he has adopted. Rousseau, in turn, justifies himself by
claiming that he needed it first in order to hide himself, and will always retain it

because he finds it quite comfortable."[3] From Ferney, Voltaire fumed over "that monster of vanity and of contradictions, of pride and baseness." His anger undoubtedly sharpened by the fact that his beloved England had welcomed Rousseau, he declared: "I do not know whether he was chased from Paris, as the rumor has it here, or whether he left on all fours or dressed in his Armenian robe."[4]

Hume again marveled at the commotion caused by his new friend and at the public's "great interest in M. Rousseau; and though we are now in the hottest time of our hottest factions, he is not forgot."[5] Rousseau's activities quickly rivaled the daily spectacle of parliamentary politics. That winter, politicians were noisily jostling with one another, making and unmaking alliances. The six-month-old Rockingham ministry was coming undone, in part because of the brewing trouble with America, where colonists were rioting over the Stamp Act passed the previous summer to help pay for the costs of the successfully concluded Seven Years' War.[6] As the returning chargé d'affaires to the French court, Hume reported to the new secretary of state, General Henry Seymour Conway, the brother of Lord Hertford. It was to Conway that Hume also appealed for a royal pension for Rousseau, a subject the Scot had first broached while he and Rousseau waited in Calais.

Hume settled Rousseau in lodgings on Buckingham Street near Charing Cross. Concerned by the turmoil, he decided to stay with Rousseau rather than return to his rooms at Miss Elliot's on Lisle Street. He had made a wise decision: Rousseau's admirers soon stormed Buckingham Street. The hereditary prince, the Duke of Brunswick, came to visit incognito, while Conway and his wife visited Rousseau at Hume's urging. A legion of nobles, members of Parliament, and titled and untitled individuals came either announced or unannounced. Rousseau particularly welcomed the director of the reading room at the British Museum, Richard Penneck, whom Lord Keith had recommended in the highest terms, and he also saw his cousin Jean Rousseau, one of the many Genevans drawn abroad by London's commercial vitality.[7] Others wrote to say that they could not pay their respects in person. Among them was one of Rousseau's most singular fans, the Chevalier d'Eon, the former soldier, spy, and representative of the French court in England, who had fallen out with his superiors across the Channel and was now living in exile in London. As a refugee and renegade, d'Eon believed that he and Rousseau had much in common, embracing the philosopher as his "colleague in politics, master in literature, and companion in misery."[8] As it happened, they were also sartorial soulmates of sorts: while living in England, d'Eon began what became the lifelong habit of wearing women's clothing in public, which led to speculation about his sexual identity that was resolved only by his autopsy.[9]

Rousseau was no less determined to wear his own unique dress. As he had breezily told a Parisian correspondent: "I've thought as a man, I've written as a man and I have been called bad. Well, now I shall be called a woman."[10] In London as everywhere else, his costume drew curious onlookers, and crowds followed him on his daily walks with Sultan along the wide and paved streets of the capital he came to admire. Yet Rousseau preferred to admire the city from afar.

In London for scarcely a week, Rousseau already yearned to leave for the country. But he could not move without the aid of Hume, whom Rousseau characterized — with a hint of alarm — as "so zealous" for him.[11] Hume also noticed Rousseau's desire for solitude. A few weeks after their arrival in London, Hume observed that while few men seemed "better calculated for good company" than Rousseau, he was nevertheless "absolutely determined to retire and board himself . . . among the mountains of Wales for solitude."[12] It seems that Rousseau had been told of a "substantial farmer who inhabits a lonely house amid forests and rivulets, and rocks and mountains," Hume reported back to the Marquise de Barbentane, adding: "I have endeavored to throw a hundred obstacles in the way, but nothing can divert him."[13]*

Yet the Welsh mountains, or any kind of rural retreat, would have to wait. Given his client's peculiar requirements and his "variable and fanciful" temper, Hume's effort to find suitable accommodations was Herculean. Among the friends he recruited in his effort to find suitable lodging for Rousseau was John Stewart, a friend in the wine business. Trawling the English countryside, Stewart reported that some farmers did not have room; others had room, but not for foreigners; and yet others had room for foreigners, but neither the means nor the manners for such an unusual guest. Stewart had located one farmer who had been born in France and raised in England, but unhappily "his house is as dirty as a Frenchman's in France."[14] Then there was the Townsend country estate, the possibility of which fell through when the owners learned that Rousseau insisted that his "maid," Thérèse, must sit at the same table. As an exasperated Hume confided to Boufflers, "this woman forms the chief encumbrance to his settlement." He was baffled by the hold she had over Rousseau, especially as Rousseau himself admitted, Hume wrote, that she was so "dull that she never knows in

---

*Hume's attitude toward Rousseau's desire for isolation eerily mirrors the relationship, more than 150 years later, of another British philosopher and his continental protégé: Bertrand Russell and Ludwig Wittgenstein. The eccentric young Austrian philosopher insisted on leaving his adopted Great Britain for an isolated village in Norway, despite Russell's battery of arguments: "I said it would be dark, & he said he hated daylight. I said it would be lonely, and he said he prostituted his mind talking to intelligent people. I said he was mad & he said God preserve him from sanity. (God certainly will.)" See Ray Monk, *Ludwig Wittgenstein: The Duty of Genius* (New York; Penguin, 1990), 91.

what year of the Lord she is . . . and that she can never learn the different value of the pieces of money in any country. Yet she governs him as absolutely as a nurse does a child. In her absence his dog has acquired the ascendant. His affection for that creature is beyond all expression or conception."[15]

Part of the problem was language: the host had to know French. Rousseau was aware of the difficulties of learning English. "In order to know English it must be learned two times," he explained in his *Essay on the Origin of Languages,* which he had reworked into its final form a few years before, "once to read it and another to speak it. If an Englishman reads out loud and a foreigner glances at the book, the foreigner will not perceive any relationship between what he sees and what he hears."[16]

It quickly became obvious that Rousseau's efforts at acquiring English were as futile as they were idiosyncratic. He had asked Hume to purchase two English translations of *Emile,* which, he explained, would "save him some pains in consulting the dictionary; and as he improved, it would amuse him to compare the translations and judge which was the best." Yet after just a few days with the books, Rousseau handed them back: he simply could not endure reading his own work in any language. "My writings," he exclaimed to Hume, "are good for nothing at the bottom, and all my theories are full of extravagance."[17]

Among the many visitors to an increasingly agitated Rousseau was David Garrick, the most celebrated actor in Georgian England, manager of the Drury Lane Theatre and a friend of Hume's. Rousseau's arrival in London, in fact, coincided with Garrick's own return. The self-styled heir of Shakespeare had taken a leave of absence after a twenty-year run of performing, directing, and writing and had undertaken a triumphal two-year tour of the Continent. Mesmerizing audiences with his mimetic talents, Garrick broadcast far and wide the good news of Shakespearean tragedy and comedy. Undeterred by Rousseau's well-known ambivalence concerning the theater, Garrick paid a visit to Buckingham Road in order to invite Hume and his guest to a command performance scheduled for January 23 at Drury Lane. Their Royal Majesties King George and Queen Charlotte would be in attendance.

The inscription above the Drury Lane stage summed up the nature of Garrick's fiefdom in the oldest theater in London: *Totus mundus agit histrionem* — "All the world plays the role of the actor." A microcosm of English society, the raucous and unruly audience was part of the spectacle. Indeed, until 1762 the very best seats were on the stage itself, where privileged spectators joined in the drama, occasionally chatting with the actors during the play or walking about and generally getting in the way of the action.[18] As for the wealthy spectators in the upper galleries, they were often more preoccupied with the roaming prostitutes than with the declaiming actors. The great majority, though, milled about in the lower galleries, where admission was made even more affordable when the entrance fee, generally one shilling (a third of a worker's daily wages), was halved at intermission. Spectators in the galleries ate, drank, and conversed while the actors, competing for their attention, gestured under the dim lighting of lamps whose smoke gradually filled the room during the performance.

Not surprisingly, foreign visitors to Drury Lane, a bit like the Persian visitors to the Paris theater in Montesquieu's *Persian Letters*, were uncertain whether the audience or the actors provided the evening's spectacle: "The uproar before the play begins is indescribable," one tourist exclaimed. "Not only orange peels but sometimes even glasses of water or other liquids are thrown from the gallery into pit and boxes, so that frequently spectators are wounded and their clothing is soiled. . . . At Drury Lane I wished to look around at the gallery in order to examine its structure, but a heap of orange peels, striking me with considerable force in the face, robbed me of all curiosity. The best plan is to keep your face turned towards the stage and thus quietly submit to the hail of oranges on your back."[19]

The dim line at the Drury Lane between staged and spontaneous spectacle was obliterated on the evening of January 23, 1765, when Rousseau himself became the spectacle. No doubt with Garrick's approval, if not active complicity, news of his invitation to Rousseau spread rapidly. When the theater doors opened three hours before curtain time, a great press of men and women was already outside. With a muffled roar of relief, the well-dressed mob surged into the theater, elbowing and jostling one another to get the best possible seats. According to one newspaper, "The crowd was so great at getting into the theatre on Thursday, that a great number of gentlemen lost their hats and wigs, and ladies their cloaks, bonnets, &c."[20]

A short ride away on Buckingham Street, Hume and Rousseau had little inkling of the furious expectations simmering at the theater. This was for the best, as Hume already had his hands full with a different sort of drama. As the two men prepared to leave their apartments for a waiting coach, Rousseau suddenly declared that he would stay behind. When a stunned Hume asked why, Rousseau replied: "What shall I do with Sultan?" Hume, who knew the emotional hold the dog had over Rousseau, replied that Sultan must be left behind. This would hardly do for Rousseau, who worried that his dog would run after him and get lost in the dark streets of a strange city. Clearly, Rousseau had not recovered from an earlier incident, reported in all the papers, in which Sultan had run away and been found by Hume, who was treated as a kind of hero for rescuing the dog.

Eager to leave for the theater and dreading the prospect of searching the city for the dog yet again, Hume reassured Rousseau that they would lock the dog inside and take the key. With great reluctance, Rousseau obeyed. But as they left their lodgings Sultan began to wail, and the faithful philosopher started to turn back. Though Hume reminded him that king, queen, and, indeed, country waited for him at Drury Lane, Rousseau remained firm. Hume had good reason to worry: was this not, after all, the same man who had already snubbed pensions from two kings? As Rousseau moved to climb back to his lodgings, Hume caught him up in his arms, telling him that they could not disappoint Mrs. Garrick, much less the royal couple "without a better reason than Sultan's impatience." Shepherding Rousseau toward the carriage as one would a recalcitrant child, Hume thus "partly by these reasons and partly by force . . . engaged him to proceed."[21]

True to their habits, Their Majesties King George III and Queen Charlotte had arrived punctually that evening, settling down in the royal box situated directly across from Garrick's own box. The royals were hardly strangers to Drury Lane, where their prudish tastes favored the tame comedies popular at the time, many of which, moreover, had the advantage of being broad and antic enough that the former princess from Mecklenburg-Strelitz could follow the action, if not the dialogue.[22]

As was customary, there were two plays on the evening's bill: one was Garrick's adaptation of the popular tragedy *Zara*, the other was his own farce *Lethe*. For reasons that had as much to do with Great Britain's recent victory over France in the Seven Years' War as with Rousseau's presence—he was, after all, a victim of French injustice—the audience cried for Garrick's anti-French prologue to the tragedy. With a great flourish, Garrick stepped forward before their royal highnesses and honored guests and declaimed:

> The French, howe'er mercurial they may seem
> Extinguish half of their fire by critic phlegm
> While English writers Nature's freedom claim
> And warm their scenes with an ungoverned flame
> 'Tis strange that Nature should never inspire
> A Racine's judgment with a Shakespeare's fire![23]

No sooner had Garrick begun to speak, however, than "a general clap and a loud huzza" billowed from the audience. There was "such a noise, from the house being so crowded, very few heard anything of the prologue." Even after Garrick bowed and left the stage, the bedlam continued: "There was a great disturbance in the gallery, and some called out, Guards, Guards! [so] that they could not go on." James Lacy, Garrick's business partner, mounted the stage and

Sir Joshua Reynolds (1723–92), *David Garrick Between the Muses of Tragedy and Comedy*, oil
on canvas, 1760–61. © Somerset Maugham Theatre Collection, London / The Bridgeman
Art Library

glared at the galleries until the disturbance died down. He then marched off without saying a word, and the play was resumed.[24]

Garrick's choice to stage *Zara* was not surprising; it was, with *Hamlet*, the
most popular work staged at the Drury Lane, performed for twenty-two con-
secutive seasons. But the choice of the play was ironic for this particular evening:
adapted by Garrick from Aaron Hill's earlier version of the drama, *Zara* was a
loose translation of the paragon of eighteenth-century French tragedy: Voltaire's *Zaïre*. Chased across the Channel, in part, by Voltaire's machinations,
Rousseau was now guest of honor at an English production of his archenemy's
play.

Voltaire had first presented *Zaïre* in 1732. He rode the age's wave of Ori-
entalism—a fascination associated, for example, with Montesquieu's *Persian
Letters*—and the work quickly became his most acclaimed and frequently performed drama. This "Christian tragedy" tells the tale of Zaïre, captured as a
young girl by the Turks and raised a Muslim in the harem of the Sultan Orosmane, to whom she is betrothed. A French nobleman, Lusignan, who had been

the Christian king of Jerusalem before being captured and then liberated by Orosmane, discovers that Zaïre is in fact his daughter. To complicate matters, her enslaved companion Nerestan is actually her brother. Lusignan persuades Zaïre, who sincerely loves Orosmane, to return to her Christian faith. In the meanwhile, however, Orosmane, as ignorant of this conversion as he is of the family ties between Zaïre and Nerestan, suspects them of being lovers. In a fit of wild jealousy, he murders Zaïre. When Nerestan reveals the truth of his relationship with Zaire, the sultan kills himself.

The irony of Garrick's choice of *Zara* was even greater than first appears. Nearly a decade earlier, in his *Letter to d'Alembert*, Rousseau had cited Voltaire's play as the most damning piece of evidence for the pernicious impact of the theater on morality. For Rousseau, the theater, rather than being a model of virtue or occasion for emotional catharsis, was a spur to our vices and passions. "Do you wish to know if it is certain that tragedy, in showing the fatal consequences of immoderate passions, teaches us to protect ourselves against them?" Rousseau asks his reader to consult his experience and gives an example: "These fatal consequences are very strongly represented in *Zaïre*. . . . I should be interested to find someone, man or woman, who would dare to boast of having left a performance of *Zaïre* well armed against love." Indeed, "of all the tragedies of the theater, no other shows with more charm the power of love and the empire of beauty."[25] A truly moral society would never stage tragedies, Rousseau concludes—especially one as brilliant as *Zaïre*.

Voltaire was not mollified by the backhanded compliment and dismissed the *Letter to d'Alembert* as the "lunatic's latest vomiting."[26] Yet the apoplectic dramatist failed to address the "lunatic's" central claim: theatrical representation not only encourages and justifies unhealthy emotions but amounts to a kidnapping of our souls. Rather than cultivate the spectator's feelings, the tragedian instead projects and imposes his own emotions: "When we do not live in ourselves but in others, it is their judgments which guide everything."[27] The problem with theater, Rousseau declared, is that it gets in the way of life, coming between man and his world, between man and his own self. Theater is thus little more than modern life writ small. Instead of cultivating the virtues of citizenship and family, tragedians *stage* these virtues, replacing reality with appearance and lived experience with vicarious experience. At the end of a theatrical evening, all we are left with are ticket stubs and stunted lives.

Uncannily, Rousseau's concerns are echoed in Garrick's revision. Fluent in French, the Englishman's great concern was to adjust Hill's translation in order to make Voltaire's own version more natural. It was as though Voltaire's art was too artful, his representation of tragedy too consciously tragic. As if to underscore his point, Garrick has Osman, shaken in his confidence, challenge Zara:

Speak!—Is it artifice?
Oh! Spare the needless pains. Art was not made
For Zara. Art, however innocent
Looks like deceiving—I abhorred it ever.[28]

Rousseau could not have agreed more—or would have, had he English enough
to understand Garrick's claim. While Garrick and his fellow players postured in
outlandish reproductions of Oriental robes and spoke lines originally written in
French, Rousseau sat in Garrick's box, dressed just as exotically, watching a play
he had denounced when performed in his native language, now utterly incapable
of understanding its English version.

Stranger still was Garrick's choice of the comic afterpiece: *Lethe*.* The tale
of "Aesop in the Shades," as the subtitle of the farce announced, is simplicity itself: a series of characters are ferried across the Styx by Charon. Once across,
they tell their stories to Aesop, who decides whether they will be allowed to drink
from the river Lethe in order to forget their woes. The characters range from Mrs.
Riot, a woman given to malapropisms who fancies herself a lady of fashion and
complains of her husband's niggardliness, to Lord Chalkstone, a gouty peer who
comes to Hades not to drink from the Lethe but to survey the Elysian Fields like
some English country garden, complaining to Aesop that they are in very poor
taste indeed and that the famous river of Hades is no better than the Fleet ditch.

Yet the most curious character, at least from the perspective of this evening's
performance, is a fake French marquis, who speaks in a comic mix of English and
French that permits a series of unintended puns and sly misunderstandings.

FRENCHMAN: Monsieur, votre serviteur. Pourquoi ne repondez vous
pas? Je dis que je suis votre serviteur.

AESOP: I don't understand you, Sir.

FRENCHMAN: Ah, le barbare! Il ne parle pas Français. Vat, Sir, you no
speak da French tongue?

The phony nobleman confides to Aesop that he is in reality a Provençal hair-
dresser planning to make his fortune by scamming the gullible English nobility.
"I have been an avanturie all over the varld, and am à present en Angleterre, vere
I am more honoré and caress den ever I was in my own contrie, or inteed any

---

*Rousseau himself wrote a poem about Lethe when he returned to Chambéry after a year in
Lyon as a failed tutor, addressing his poem "To Fanie"—his nickname for Maman, from her given
name of Françoise. In the poem, Rousseau imagines Charon trying to make him drink from the
Styx, but he protests that he will never be able to forget the "divine Fanie." See Leo Damrosch,
Jean-Jacques Rousseau: Restless Genius (New York: Houghton Mifflin, 2005), 156.

vere else," he boasts.[29] As with *Zara*, stage and box bizarrely mirrored each other in *Lethe*, with a bogus aristocrat newly arrived from France speaking the only lines in the plays that Rousseau, himself recently arrived and swathed in an Armenian costume, could have understood—lines that, moreover, were intended precisely to be misunderstood.

The multiplying questions of authenticity and illusion reached a climax not on stage but in Garrick's box. During the performances, Rousseau, and not the actors, or even the king and queen, was the center of everyone's attention. As Hume later wrote to his brother, "I observed their Majesties to look at Rousseau, more than at the players."[30] While curtains afforded inhabitants of the box some privacy, Rousseau had parted them and moved forward, the better to watch—or be watched. As he edged closer and closer to the edge, Mrs. Garrick grew more and more concerned. She had never spent a more uncomfortable evening in her life, she later told her husband's friend Joseph Cradock. According to Cradock, Mrs. Garrick found that "the recluse philosopher was so very anxious to display himself, and hung so forward over the front of the box, that she was obliged to hold him by the skirt of his coat, he might not fall into the pit."[31]

Once returned safely to the ground floor at the end of the evening's performances, Rousseau left with Hume to attend a party at Garrick's home in the Adelphi. Several members of the Literary Club, to which Garrick belonged, were present, including Oliver Goldsmith, whose *Vicar of Wakefield* would bring him fame later that year. (The club's most celebrated member, Samuel Johnson, ostentatiously did not appear that evening.) Upon entering the house, where the beaming actor welcomed his guests, Rousseau displayed not only the warmth and urbanity that had captivated Hume but the spirit of paradox that made his host so uneasy. Bowing to Garrick, Rousseau announced: "Sir, you have made me shed tears at your tragedy, and smile at your comedy, though I scarce understand a word of your language."[32]

How to make sense of Rousseau's behavior that evening?

In his *Paradox of Acting*, written around the same time as these events, Rousseau's estranged friend Denis Diderot outlined two methods of acting. The first method, favored by French actors of the time and resembling modern Method acting, was to inhabit a character so thoroughly that the actor would lose his original self. The alternative favored by Diderot, however, was not to become someone else but to remain oneself, all the while acting like someone else. In a word, actors were meant to act. The paradox of acting, then, is that an actor is the more effective insofar as he distances himself from the role and consciously mimics his character's passions.

Diderot's model was none other than Garrick, whose demonstrations of his art while in Paris and, more important, his discussions of the method he had himself developed, partially inspired the philosophe's essay. Diderot related his astonishment at the actor's skill: "Garrick will put his head between two folding-doors, and in the course of five or six seconds his expression will change successively from wild delight to temperate pleasure, from this to tranquility, from tranquility to surprise, from surprise to blank astonishment, from that to sorrow, from sorrow to the air of one overwhelmed, from that to fright, from fright to horror, from horror to despair, and thence he will go up again to the point from which he started." Inspired by Garrick, Diderot argued that mimesis or mimicry made for a more convincing reality. This paradox was no mere literary conceit. Fully conscious of what he is doing, an actor can be a spectator to his own acting, free to alter the performance so as to have the desired effect on the other spectators.[33] The whole art lies in the illusion.

Wittingly or not, the spectators at Drury Lane that night joined in Diderot's musings. It was not Garrick's performance, however, but Rousseau's that fired the debate. Was the odd little man, in his fur cap and alchemist's robe, acting? If he was acting, which method had he embraced? And if he was *not* acting, well, just what in heaven's name *was* he doing?

Mrs. Garrick harbored little doubt. She declared that Rousseau had simply wished to "display himself."[34] Another spectator that evening reached a similar conclusion. This was Mrs. Bunbury, the former Sarah Lennox, daughter of the Duke of Richmond, whose beauty had once infatuated the newly crowned George III. "His dressing is particularly silly, and, as the papers say, he told Garrick that he made him laugh and cry without understanding a word, in my humble opinion that was very silly too."[35]

With much keener insight, one of Rousseau's former patronesses, the memoirist Stéphanie-Félicité de Genlis, has left us a strikingly similar account of another evening at the theater. Several years after his stay in England, Rousseau told M. and Mme de Genlis one day in Paris that he "never went to the theater and tried to avoid showing himself in public." His friends nonetheless prevailed upon him to join them that evening at the Comédie française with the promise that they would sit in a curtained box. Stepping into their box, Mme de Genlis reached out to close the raised curtain. Yet Rousseau stopped her, insisting that the curtain be kept up for *her* sake; he would simply sit inconspicuously behind his hosts. Puzzled by Rousseau's intervention, Mme de Genlis again tried to close the curtain; again, Rousseau objected. As they argued over the curtain's disposition, Mme de Genlis realized that they were attracting the very attention Rousseau declared himself so keen to avoid. She thus gave in to Rousseau's wish and promptly sat down with her husband. But then their celebrated guest began to wedge his face between and above the shoulders of the perplexed couple. Warned by Mme de Genlis, Rousseau retreated behind her—but scarcely a minute passed before his head again rose above her shoulder. Suddenly, murmurs began to ripple through the audience: "C'est Rousseau! C'est Rousseau!" But as Mme de Genlis noted with satisfaction, Rousseau's antics were then upstaged by the *other* spectacle that evening: "With the first notes of the orchestra, everyone's attention returned to the stage and Rousseau was forgotten." In the end, Genlis concurred with Mrs. Garrick: "He wished to show himself."[36] Predictably, enemies and critics such as Voltaire and Grimm, who had already mocked Rousseau for his ostentatious Armenian costume, echoed the conviction of Mrs. Garrick and Mme de Genlis: the mountebank had changed venues, but not character. Replying to Garrick's description of the evening, Holbach replied caustically that Rousseau was "a philosophical quack, full of affectation, of pride, of oddities, and even villainies."[37]

Hume, in turn, never sought to answer the question Rousseau's behavior posed that evening, at least directly. He knew, of course, that Rousseau understood scarcely a word of English. As Rousseau told the Marquise de Ars the day before his visit to Drury Lane, "I am consumed by useless efforts to learn it . . . but it is no longer possible for me to learn anything."[38] Yet the strange evening at the theater was one among many experiences that made Hume increasingly aware that Rousseau's personality was more complex than first suspected. He agreed that his "pupil" displayed certain affectations that were as extravagant as his language. Returning to the matter of the Armenian costume he had so confidently explained less than a month earlier to Blair, Hume now confided to Boufflers a few days before the performance that the caftan was not dictated by need but was the product of "pure whim."[39] Hume nonetheless did not conclude that Rousseau was always and only whimsical—on the contrary. As he observed in a letter to the Marquise de Barbentane, there were "opposite opinions with regard to the personal character of M. Rousseau: his enemies have sometimes made you doubt of his sincerity; and you have been pleased to ask my opinion on this head." Having had two months to observe his guest, Hume was in a good position to judge: "I declare to you, that I have never known a man more amiable and more virtuous than he appears to me; he is mild, gentle, modest, affectionate, disinterested; and, above all, endowed with a sensibility of heart in a supreme degree."[40]

For Hume, this extreme sensibility was the clue to Rousseau's seemingly contradictory behavior. He elaborated on this trait several weeks later to Blair. Rousseau, he announced, "has reflected, properly speaking, and studied very little; and has not indeed much knowledge. He has only felt during the whole course of his life; and in this respect, his sensibility rises to a pitch beyond what

I have seen any example of. But it still gives him a more acute feeling of pain than pleasure. He is like a man who [was] stripped not only of his clothes but of his skin."[41] In Hume's eyes, Rousseau was a man flayed alive, thrown into the roiling confusion and beauty of our world, deprived of the protective layers of education and etiquette, objectivity and distance, that society wrapped around the rest of us.

Hume was almost certainly unaware of Rousseau's *Essay on the Origin of Languages,* which was published posthumously. But the Scot nevertheless anticipated what might have been Rousseau's own explanation of his behavior that evening. In the *Essay,* Rousseau claimed that man's earliest language was inseparable from music: the two were one when we first stepped into the world. Melody was the Ur-language of our passions, carrying the "complaints, cries of sadness or of joy, threats or moans. All the vocal signs of the passions are within its scope. It imitates the accents of languages, and the turns of phrase appropriate in each idiom to certain movements of the soul; it not only imitates, it speaks, and its language, inarticulate but lively, ardent, passionate, has a hundred times more energy than speech itself."[42] Only when man became a social being—in other words, fully human—did he require a more complex language, for it was only by this means that he could persuade or manipulate his fellow men. In fact, as language evolves, when it becomes, ironically, the vehicle by which Rousseau could convey such insights, it grows ever more distant from the music with which it first entered the world.

The *Essay* thus laments what man lost when he gained language. We might ask, as a result, what a man might gain upon *losing* language—the situation in which Rousseau found himself in England. Do we regain our original selves? When Mrs. Garrick grabbed Rousseau's caftan to prevent him from tumbling into the orchestra pit, she perhaps did not rescue a man who was "lost in translation." This, instead, would have been Rousseau's lot had he been able to follow *Zara* in English. Rousseau instead *found* himself through the *lack* of translation. Put differently, he achieved a different form of translation, in the archaic sense of transport or rapture, precisely because he did not understand the words spoken on stage.

For Rousseau, meaning at its most elemental and authentic—the expression of pure emotion—could be reached only when semantic meaning gives way to melodic meaning. At Drury Lane the obstacle of words dissolved into the transparency of music and melody. The sonority of Garrick's voice, the inflections of his words, the tragic cadence of his speech, combined with his broad, powerful gestures—gesture, for Rousseau, is a form of expression as ancient and natural as music, but also easier to understand and less dependent upon conventions—

was all the meaning he required that night.* Perched on the box's ledge, gloriously unaware of the world above and below, Hume's linguistic innocent abroad was thus moved to tears and laughter. The irony of Rousseau's quip, a few years earlier, when he renounced his native Geneva and dreamed of settling in Scotland, becomes all the more dazzling. There, Rousseau claimed, "I shall have the happiness of living with men whose language I shall not understand."[43]

*Diderot remarks in his *Letter on the Deaf and the Dumb* upon an experiment he himself undertook at the theater that echoes Rousseau's situation: "Formerly I used to visit the theater very often, and I knew most of our good plays by heart. On the days when I proposed to study movements and gestures, I went to the third-class boxes. . . . As soon as the curtain went up . . . I would put my fingers into my ears, not without some astonishment on the part of those round about me . . . and stubbornly kept my ears stopped up as long as the action of the actor appeared to me to be in harmony with the lines I was remembering." Diderot recalled with amusement the surprise of the people round him "when they saw me shed tears in the pathetic parts, and that with my ears continuously stopped." See Arthur M. Wilson, *Diderot* (New York: Oxford University Press, 1972), 31.

CHAPTER NINE

Poses and Impostures

*This is the only portrait of a man, painted exactly according to nature
and in all its truth, which exists and will probably ever exist.*
—*Rousseau,* Confessions

*I believe he intends seriously to draw his own picture in true colors:
but I believe at the same time that nobody knows himself less.*
—*Hume to Boufflers*

From late February to early March 1766, a carriage daily clattered to a halt in front of a house at 10 Soho Square in the fashionable Westminster district of London. Muffled by his caftan and fur hat against the gusts of the winter air that had frozen the Thames solid, Rousseau stepped out. The portraitist Allan Ramsay met him at the door, and the two men entered the house and chatted as they walked to the studio. There, amid dozens of portraits of George III in various stages of composition, Rousseau exchanged his caftan for an even darker robe. Assuming his place in a corner of the studio, he braced his

left arm against a small table and turned to Ramsay, who had taken his place behind an easel. With his lips carefully pursed to cover "the most horrible teeth any
human creature ever had," Rousseau then stooped over a stool and fixed his eyes
on the artist.[1] And stooped he remained for hours — or so he later recalled. Yet
as Ramsay explained, all of this was necessary so that he could portray Rousseau
seated at his ease! During those long sessions, Rousseau must have reflected on
this paradox and the vexed relationship between nature and artifice.

The portrait was Hume's idea.[2] Flush with the excitement of his friendship
with Rousseau, he proposed that they sit for parallel portraits that would commem-
orate their relationship. Soon after their arrival in London, Hume commissioned the
work from Ramsay, his old friend and fellow founding member of the Select Society. Ramsay had done a portrait of his fellow Scot in 1754, soon after Hume had
launched his *History of England*. There, a dapper and (relatively) lean Hume, in
semiprofile, wears a white waistband and brilliant red scholar's cap: he is clearly a
man who knows his intellectual powers yet also wishes to cut a smart figure.

Beyond the complicity of friendship — Ramsay proudly recalled that it was
"by much drinking with David Hume and his associates that I have learned to be
very historical" — Hume had other reasons to enlist Ramsay.[3] By 1766 Ramsay
was recognized as one of the age's great portraitists; his purchase of the Soho
Square residence had been eased by his appointment as Principal Painter to His
Majesty, George III. Ramsay's dislike of pomp and extravagance dovetailed
with the king's own tastes. This extended to gastronomy: George would often
eat his favorite dish of boiled mutton and turnips while Ramsay worked at his
easel, moved for this reason into the royal dining room. The two men chatted
about European affairs until the king, his meal dispatched, rose from the table
and said, "Now, Ramsay, sit down in my place and take your dinner."[4] "Sitting
down in another's place," re-creating the inner life of his sitter without appealing
to heroic themes, was the essence of Ramsay's genius. Whereas his rival Joshua
Reynolds sought to improve on nature by elevating his subjects, the Scot instead
worked with nature, yoking his strokes to her simple demands. If a painting were
to "touch the feelings," it had to go beyond traditional rules of composition.[5] Yet
this arousal of the sentiments must be contained within the limits of common
life. Like Hume, Ramsay espoused simplicity and moderation in art as the surest
path to nature, considering metaphysical posturing and aesthetic acrobatics as
pointless as they were artificial. As Ramsay's many portraits of George reveal,
art was the means not for making the sitter heroic but instead fully human.

Hume, then, knew precisely what he bargained for with Ramsay. In his portrait of Rousseau, the artist captured the peculiar quality that mesmerized so
many contemporaries: an inner intensity so great that even when sitting still,
Rousseau seems on the move. The amber light the subject casts, emphasized by

Allan Ramsay (1713–84), portrait of Jean-Jacques Rousseau, oil on canvas, 1766. © National Gallery of Scotland,
Edinburgh / The Bridgeman Art Library

the somber robe and dark bonnet, not only dissolves the encircling shadows but
threatens to do the same to Rousseau's facial features, which are slightly blurred.
This inner light, neither metaphorical nor mythological, instead reflects the unprecedented enthusiasm his writings had generated.[6] It is, in a sense, the blaze of
celebrity. Rousseau's right hand emerges from the tenebrous background, where
confusion and mystery reign, and points toward his heart.

    In the pendant portrait of Hume, the Scot appears in the diplomatic uniform
he wore in Paris. The red and gold laced uniform contrasts brilliantly with the
man barely wrapped inside. Hume's massive left arm rests on a pedestal of
books, one apparently written by Tacitus, the other unidentified, perhaps suggesting an implicit comparison between the two historians.[7] But the eye then
gravitates to Hume's face, a great orb of flesh that appears half in light, half in
shadow. While Rousseau's expression blazes with white intensity, Hume's is
sensual, peaceful, nearly indolent, bordering on the vacant stare that so many
friends, not to mention strangers, found discomforting. Hume gazes directly at
the viewer, without seeming to register him.

Allan Ramsay (1713–84), portrait of David Hume, oil on canvas, 1766. © Scottish National Portrait Gallery, Edinburgh / The Bridgeman Art Library

Although Rousseau at first declared that he liked his portrait, he later claimed that the awkward stooping pose Ramsay had insisted upon was designed to distort his face and make him look like a "Cyclops," and the portrait would become one charge among many in his case against Hume as their friendship fractured.[8] Hume, in turn, thought that Ramsay had "succeeded to admiration, and has made me a most valuable portrait." This likeness, he suggested to his brother, captured the nature of his friend: "He is surely a very fine genius. And of all the writers that are or ever were in Europe, he is the man who has acquired the most enthusiastic and most passionate admirers."[9] Chief among them himself: while Rousseau grew to hate his own portrait and discarded his engraving of the earlier portrait of the Scot, Hume hung Ramsay's pair of portraits in his townhouse in Edinburgh.

Rousseau commuted to Ramsay's studio from Chiswick, a village about six miles west of London. Depressed by the gray and teeming city, he had retreated to the suburban village after two weeks in his Buckingham Street lodgings. Hume had found the new quarters for Rousseau: an apartment above the local grocer's. Once there, Rousseau reprised his role as rural magus, sitting in his landlord's shop in his Armenian dress and receiving visitors.

There Rousseau impatiently awaited the arrival of Thérèse. He had marooned his gouvernante more than two months ago on the Île St. Pierre to pack up what remained of their household. Once safely arrived in Great Britain, he asked Du Peyrou, to whom he had entrusted Thérèse, to make arrangements for her to join him. Relieved to be rid of the woman and her incessant gossiping, Du Peyrou gladly complied. He packed up Thérèse and bundled her off along with some letters and papers Rousseau needed to write his *Confessions*.[10] Transported to her native Paris, Thérèse must have nonetheless felt quite out of place staying in the imposing palace of the Duchesse de Luxembourg, who, alone among Rousseau's aristocratic friends, was fond of the former laundress.

How to get Thérèse to England, though? The answer was about to present itself.

Reaching the end of his European tour, James Boswell had arrived in Paris near the end of January 1766. Not only did he miss Rousseau and Hume, who had left a few weeks earlier, but he also failed to be at his mother's bedside during her last moments. It was only upon reading an English newspaper that Boswell learned of Lady Auchinleck's death two weeks earlier. Grief-stricken, the young man wandered from one British acquaintance to the next over the next couple of days, alternately weeping, praying, and singing Italian songs softly to himself for consolation.[11]

Burdened with this "melancholy affliction," Boswell learned about Thérèse's arrival in Paris. Grasping at the memories of their flirtation in Môtiers, Boswell immediately called upon her at the Hôtel de Luxembourg. After they exchanged accounts of their distressing experiences, Thérèse confided to him her anxiety about continuing alone to Great Britain to join Rousseau. At one point, she blurted out: "Mon Dieu, Monsieur, if we could go together!" Roused by the call of chivalry, Boswell gallantly replied that he had come to make that very offer.

When Hume learned that the amorous Scot would escort Thérèse across the Channel, he predicted the result. "A letter has also come to me open from Guy the bookseller, by which I learn that Mademoiselle sets out post, in company with a friend of mine," he told Boufflers: "a young gentleman, very good-humored, very agreeable, and very mad." His younger compatriot was always "in search of adventures," Hume added, noting that Boswell "has such a rage for literature, that I dread some event fatal to our friend's honor." Hume reminded Boufflers of the example of Terentia, a Roman woman who was first married to Cicero, then to Sallust, and then, in her old age, to a young aristocrat "who imagined that she must possess some secret, which would convey to him eloquence and genius."[12]

Hume proved prescient. The couple had scarcely left Paris in a post chaise before they fell together in bed at an inn. The results, though, were disappointing: Boswell was unable to perform. He burst into tears, and a tender Thérèse calmed him. Whether she was comforting him for the loss of his mother or his failed attempt is not clear. In any case, though, her solicitude proved a peculiar kind of catharsis: Boswell found "his powers were excited and he felt himself vigorous."[13]

The next day Boswell reported his feats to his journal, feeling "very proud of himself." Congratulating Thérèse on her good fortune in having a "Scotch lover," poor Boswell was mortified by her reply: "'I allow,' she said, 'that you are a hardy and vigorous lover, but you have no art.' Seeing him cast down, she went on, 'I did not mean to hurt you. You are young, you can learn. I myself will give you your first lesson in the art of love.'"[14] The approaching lessons filled Boswell with terror. When the dreaded moment arrived the next evening, Thérèse beckoned but Boswell dallied. He called for a servant to bring a bottle of wine and, rapidly downing a few glasses, he clutched the bottle and advanced toward the bed. Instead of joining Thérèse, however, he paced the floor, asking her questions about Rousseau with the mixed motives of temporizing and curiosity. Finally, as Thérèse grew irritated at his stalling tactics, he drained the bottle and, perhaps for the first and only time in his life, slipped reluctantly into bed with a woman.

"I felt like a child in her hands, not a lover," Boswell later admitted. Instructed by Thérèse, Boswell later reported to his journal that he "made good technical progress." Yet he soon began to wonder whether Thérèse had the necessary credentials as a professor of love, noting that she rode him "agitated, like a bad rider galloping downhill." His curiosity about the amorous arts soon sated, Boswell tried in vain to learn more about Rousseau. When Thérèse resisted the change of subject matter, Boswell concluded that, as a general rule, it was a mistake to seduce an old man's mistress. Perhaps Thérèse also had second thoughts, primly informing Boswell: "Don't imagine that you are a better lover than Rousseau."[15]

It was with great relief that Boswell, after vowing that he would "not mention the affair till after her death or that of the philosopher," delivered Thérèse to Rousseau on February 13. Touched by Rousseau's flurry of kisses, Boswell had nonetheless already begun to lose his earlier enthusiasm for the man he had earlier hailed as "the great chemist of humanity." Rousseau now "seemed oldish and weak," he thought.[16]

While Rousseau and Thérèse shivered for another month in Chiswick, Hume redoubled his efforts to find them a more permanent and secluded refuge. The promise of a retreat in Wales ultimately came to nothing, only whetting Rousseau's appetite for seclusion. Hume observed that despite the "great variety of schemes which I propose to him, the most solitary, the most remote, the most savage place is always that which he prefers. . . . I have endeavored to throw a hundred obstacles in the way, but nothing can divert him."[17]

The choice of asylum was finally decided upon in early March. A friend of Garrick's, Richard Davenport, wrote to offer his services. An enlightened member of England's landed gentry, Davenport applied the lessons he had learned at Cambridge with phlegmatic persistence. Not only had he invented a new kind of plow to work his lands, but he also was raising his orphaned grandson according to the educational precepts of *Emile*. Equally important, Davenport was a man of considerable means. Having recently retired to an estate in the north of England, he owned several other properties in the area, including a recently acquired and rarely visited one in Wootton, a village tucked into the folds of the wild and mountainous northern districts at the border between Derbyshire and Staffordshire.[18]

As usual, Rousseau hesitated over the choice. Finally his acceptance of Davenport's invitation was the result of the intervention of another of his ardent admirers, Daniel Malthus. Malthus wrote Rousseau immediately after the philosopher's arrival in London, reminding him that they had met two years earlier, when the wealthy botanical enthusiast had made the pilgrimage to Môtiers. He now invited Rousseau to come stay with him while he decided where to settle permanently.[19] Rousseau politely refused this offer but accepted an invitation to visit Malthus at his estate, the Rookery, south of London. Accompanied by Hume and Thérèse, Rousseau set out on March 8 to visit his acolyte, who had, two weeks earlier, added to the world population with the birth of his son Thomas, the future economist. Determined to play the role of Rousseau's savior, Malthus had been working tirelessly on the philosopher's behalf to locate a suitable refuge; his praise of the rugged beauty of his native north finally convinced Rousseau to move there.[20]

"Situated amidst mountains and rocks and streams and forests," Hume explained to Hugh Blair, Wootton "pleases the wild imagination and solitary humor of Rousseau."[21] There were nonetheless a few conditions that Hume, with some embarrassment, was obliged to mention to Davenport. "Cannot Mr. Rousseau, if he should afterward think proper, find a means to boil a pot, and roast a piece of meat . . . in order to be perfectly at home?" Along with this odd request, for Davenport had already offered the services of his domestic staff, was one even stranger: would Davenport accept payment of thirty pounds for the annual room and board? This, and not a penny *less,* Hume awkwardly hinted, was their final offer.[22] When made aware of Rousseau's intense dislike of patronage, Davenport, who had initially made it clear that he sought no reimbursement and whose fortune included annual income of more than five thousand pounds, gracefully conceded to the terms insisted upon by his new tenant.

Fatefully, it was also Davenport's goodwill that led to the overwrought final meeting between Rousseau and Hume at the Scot's lodgings on March 18, the eve of Rousseau's departure for his new home. Knowing Rousseau's straitened circumstances, Davenport had arranged for a coach to take Rousseau and Thérèse north to Wootton. Sensitive to Rousseau's fetish of independence, Davenport had told Rousseau that the coach, having unloaded its passengers in London, was returning north empty and could be had "for a trifle."[23] (Davenport may even have mentioned this manufactured stroke of good luck during a visit to Ramsay's studio earlier that month to meet Rousseau while he was standing for his portrait.)[24] He had Hume, participating in this conspiracy of goodwill, inform Rousseau that the squire "has made a bargain for you and Mlle Le Vasseur."[25]

These well-meaning liberties were too much for Rousseau, who soon detected the imposture. As he and Thérèse rode to town from Chiswick in Davenport's coach on March 18, every jolt against the frozen road must have reinforced in Rousseau's mind his humiliation over his treatment. Having devoted his life to truth and independence, regardless of the cost to himself (not to mention others), he was now captive in a coach rented by another without his accord or knowledge. By the time the carriage turned onto Lisle Street, the philosopher was beside himself with shame and rage.

Yet Hume had no inkling of Rousseau's poisoned mood. Ironically, he may have been dwelling on a letter he had just received from Baron d'Holbach. The baron wrote that while Hume may not have had reason, just yet, "to repent of the kindness" shown to Rousseau, he wished the same could be said for their mutual friends, who had good reason to complain of his "unfair proceedings, printed imputations, ungratefulness, etc."[26] Certainly, Holbach's letter must have come to Hume's mind during the fierce interview into which Rousseau launched as he soon as he stepped inside the Scot's lodgings.

The account of the evening that began with Rousseau's fierce philippic against Hume for treating him like a child—and that ended with his suddenly hopping on the Scot's knee, throwing his arms around his neck, and bathing him in tears, oddly enough, like a child—we have from Hume himself. Indeed, Hume was eager to share the story, including his own part in the drama, which he related with a mixture of embarrassment and pride. Re-creating the scene in a lengthy letter to Boufflers, he invited her to share it with their female acquaintances in Paris. The choice of audience was important, for Hume added, "I scarce know a male who would not think it childish."[27] In a similar letter to Hugh Blair, Hume concluded the account of the evening, "I think no scene of my life was ever more affecting," without the coda about its "childish" character. "This man, the most singular of all human beings, has at last left me," he wrote, "and I have very little hopes of ever being able for the future to enjoy much of his company, though he says, that, if I settle either in London or Edinburgh, he will take a journey on foot every year to visit me."[28]

Apart from describing what would turn out to be his last meeting with his friend, Hume took the opportunity in these letters to summarize his attitude toward Rousseau after two months of friendship. While he believed, as he told Boufflers, "that nobody knows himself less" than Rousseau, he was also certain that he, at least, understood this "most singular" of men.[29] "He has read very little during the course of his life, and has now totally renounced reading," Hume informed Blair. "He has seen very little, and has no manner of curiosity to see or remark. He has reflected, properly speaking, and studied very little; and has not indeed much knowledge." Rather than reflection, what Rousseau possessed, according to Hume's analysis, was an extreme sensibility. "He has only felt, during the whole course of his life and in this respect, his sensibility rises to a pitch beyond what I have seen any example of." Struggling to find an analogy, he compared his friend to a man "stripped not only of his clothes but of his skin, and turned out in that situation to combat with the rude and boisterous elements, such as perpetually disturb this lower world."[30]

Hume's description of what is lacking in his friend reveals much of what he himself believed was true philosophy. It was the act of reflection "properly speaking": reflection upon experience, whether the experience was gleaned from books, such as the histories he himself wrote, or from personal observation. Such reflection produces self-understanding, as well as understanding of our fellow human beings and of our world. To embrace "false philosophies" that deny the hold of common life, Hume cautioned, has catastrophic consequences for oneself and others. Before he had met Rousseau, Hume warned in his *Treatise of Human Nature* that such rebellious thinking leads to a "forlorn solitude," a state in which the subject fancies "himself some uncouth monster, who not being able to mingle and unite in society, has been expelled from all human commerce, and left utterly abandoned and disconsolate."[31] Despite his own glimpse into what his heart alone knew in their shared scene of emotional upheaval, Hume was incapable of seeing that Rousseau represented an alternative way of knowing that went, in a certain sense, beyond reason to regions reached only through the imagination and the passions. Rousseau's flayed sensibilities made him Marsyas to Hume's Apollo. True philosophers, for Hume, are at ease in their skins. From Rousseau's perspective, Hume was too much the philosopher, and too much the civilized man as well.

The intemperate weather that accompanied Rousseau's departure, along with the traveler's mercurial temperament, weighed on Hume. On March 22, the day Rousseau happened to arrive in Wootton, Hume, unaware of his whereabouts, sent him a short note asking for news. He added that Davenport, who had visited him that same morning, was no less anxious for news. Hume reassured Rousseau that he and Davenport would "never lose sight of you, till [we] see you contented and easy."[32] But they *had* lost sight of their eccentric charge. The intimacy Hume had known with his friend since December was broken. Another five days passed without news, prompting him to write again: "We have had very bad weather for some time past, which has made me uneasy with regard to you. I hope you [were] able to get through the mountains of Derbyshire without any bad accident."[33]

In the meanwhile, Rousseau had arrived without incident, but also without having sent word along the way. The four-day journey taken by philosopher, gouvernante, and dog led north from London and followed more or less what is today the M1, cutting northwest through the English countryside and then through Derby, the heart of the budding Industrial Revolution. Their coach then traced the fringes of the rugged Peak District, passing through the market town of Ashbourne and swinging south along the River Dove, immortalized a century earlier by Izaak Walton in the *Compleat Angler*. Eventually, the travelers entered the park surrounding Wootton Hall and made their way up the drive, lined with oaks, firs, and hickories, until their coach rolled to a stop on the frost-glazed drive that curved along the graceful Italianate façade of the house.[34]

As with Les Charmettes and Montmorency, Wootton Hall was the sort of asylum most prized by Rousseau: a well-appointed home buried in nature. Rousseau scarcely toured his new lodgings before sitting down to send word to London. In a letter to Davenport, Rousseau was debonair: the house's only fault, he declared, was that it was "too beautiful." He then added that the one thing that would make it yet more agreeable was the occasional visit of the owner.[35] Rousseau was no less reassuring in the letter he then wrote to Hume. Though encased in snow, the estate was enchanting. "You cannot see all the charms I find here: it would be necessary to know the place and to read my heart." A curious sentence: of course the empiricist Hume cannot see the charms of a place he does not know. Equally puzzling is how Hume could see these charms by reading them in his friend's heart, a possibility Rousseau even seems to deny by his conditional phrasing. The ability to read the heart indeed turns out to be the heart of the matter for Rousseau. "You should be able to read at least those sentiments that regard you, which you have so well merited. . . . Preserve our friendship forever, my dear mentor; love me for myself, for one who owes you so much; love me for yourself; love me for all the good you have done for me."[36]

Yet Rousseau's letters also carried the seeds of lingering mistrust and diffidence that would blossom with the spring thaw in Staffordshire. Thus, to Davenport, Rousseau could not help but criticize the squire's good-hearted attempt to pay for the coach. Asking Davenport to send him the bill, Rousseau added that while "generosity is most assuredly a very good thing, I believe that honesty is even better."[37] With Hume, Rousseau was no less wounding. Apparently having forgotten his earlier acceptance of Hume's fervent denials concerning the matter of the coach, he concluded his letter with a clear warning: "If you had a role in this, I counsel you to stop playing once and for all these small tricks from which no good can come when they turn into traps against simplicity." His thirst for moralizing temporarily sated, Rousseau concluded: "I embrace you, my dear mentor, with the same heart that I hope and desire to find in you."[38] For Hume, this farewell was a touching pronouncement of friendship, but a second glance reveals language that is oddly ambiguous.

Upon receiving the much awaited letter, Hume was relieved by Rousseau's safe arrival but puzzled by his friend's inability to forget the absurd affair of the coach, and unable to appreciate Rousseau's need, emotional and otherwise, for independence. Nevertheless, in his reply the Scot gallantly apologized for an act whose sole purpose was to aid Rousseau: "I ask you ten thousand pardons, my dear friend, for the cheat attempted to be put on you: I had not, however, any hand in it, except concealing it." Having promised that Davenport would not again attempt such a ruse, Hume then shared his joy that Rousseau found Wootton to his taste: "Nothing can make me happier than to find that your situation is to your mind."[39]

At the same time Hume wrote Rousseau, Rousseau himself wrote what would turn out to be his last letter to Hume for several months. In a light tone, he informed Hume that his inability to communicate with the servants at Wootton was happily remedied by Thérèse, whose "fingers speak better than my tongue." Rousseau reveled in his linguistic isolation: "I have even discovered in my ignorance an advantage that compensates for it, which is to keep idle visitors at a distance by boring them. Yesterday the parish minister visited me, and seeing that I would speak only French with him, and he himself not wishing to speak English to me, it happened that the visit passed with hardly a word spoken. I have taken a liking to this expedient, and will employ it with all my neighbors, if I have any." Rousseau closed his cheerful letter with a weather report. "It has been frozen here ever since I arrived; the wind cuts into my face; yet despite this, I would prefer to lodge in the trunk of an old tree in this region than the most beautiful apartment in London. Good day, my dear patron, I embrace you and love you with all my heart."[40]

By all exterior appearances, Rousseau's first few months at Wootton seemed to be happy, apart from the frigid weather that kept him indoors. Wootton Hall was relatively small for an estate, yet it was far grander than Rousseau's simple cottage in Môtiers, with two floors of living quarters boasting windows overlooking the fields and hills below. Rousseau at first occupied Davenport's bedchamber on the second floor, with a large adjoining parlor, and then moved to another bedroom separated from its own parlor by a vestibule illuminated by a windowed ceiling he referred to as a "lantern." In addition to a bed, table, and some chairs, his chamber included a harpsichord, which he played on the long winter nights.[41] Delighted with the instrument, he asked Du Peyrou to send some of his music, along with certain letters, left in Paris by Thérèse, that he needed for writing the *Confessions,* the great task that occupied him when kept indoors.[42] Thérèse was installed in a smaller bedroom, which had two beds and an armoire that served as the philosopher's library.

In addition to Rousseau, Thérèse, and Sultan, Wootton housed Davenport's domestic staff. There was his estate manager, Benjamin Walton, who fetched sugar, raisins, and wine for Rousseau from Ashbourne, and an elderly couple with ill-defined duties whose marital squabbles taught Thérèse the few words of English she learned. There was also Davenport's half-blind former nurse, a gardener, a maid, and, finally, two male domestics who performed whatever further chores and tasks were demanded. While Thérèse mimed her needs to the servants, Rousseau found their Staffordshire accent utterly incomprehensible. "I learned thirty words in London which I have totally forgotten here," he wrote to Du Peyrou, "since their awful gibberish is indecipherable to my ear."[43] Rousseau soon limited himself to a list of English words for ordinary foodstuffs—sugar, meat, butter, and such—to which he could point or try to pronounce when absolutely necessary.[44]

As winter finally began to yield to spring, the wild beauty of the region entranced Rousseau. In a letter to one of Daniel Roguin's nieces, Marianne-Françoise de Luze, he portrayed the house and environs: "Imagine, Madame, an isolated house, not large, but well-kept, built half-way up the side of a valley . . . replete with rocks and trees which offer delightful nooks, and which at certain places are far enough from the stream to allow one to walk comfortably along its banks, sheltered from the winds and even from the rain, so that even in awful weather I can botanize peacefully beneath the rocks and, in the company of the sheep and the rabbits." Rousseau splashed the peaks of Staffordshire with the same colors as he had those of Switzerland when still a child. His one regret, he added, was that he could not find scordium, an herb thought to cleanse the blood and reestablish the appetite. "The countryside is beautiful but sad; nature is dull and lazy," he wrote, quickly shifting moods: "We've hardly seen violets, the trees are still bare of leaves and we never hear nightingales. All the signs of spring seem to fly from me."[45]

Rousseau spent his days exploring the gorge through which the Dove ran north of Wootton, or the Weaver Hills to the south. What chiefly interested him on his walks was the local flora, for he was still afflicted with the "botanical fever" he had contracted in Môtiers. His rooms at Wootton soon resembled those he festooned with the pressed flowers on Île St. Pierre. Happy to have his other books packed up and sold in England, Rousseau jealously kept his botanical books, which he scoured to identify the specimens he encountered in this new land. At times, others who shared Rousseau's passion accompanied him. Daniel Malthus, who visited that summer as promised, made a number of outings with the philosopher. Rousseau also shared his passion in person and then in a series of letters with the nearby Duchess of Portland, an avid botanist who specialized in seashells, her collection of the mollusks being so vast that it took thirty-eight days to auction off after her death.[46]

While his chief purpose on his promenades was to collect plants, Rousseau could not help but meet his neighbors as well. As his encounters with the servants at Wootton Hall already made painfully clear, communication was well nigh impossible, and strolling by himself across the landscape he was bereft of even the dubious assistance of Thérèse's miming. We can only begin to wonder what the lead miners in nearby Stanton and other local men made of this exotic apparition speaking an incomprehensible tongue. Young girls occasionally scattered at the sight of the strange man bounding through the woods in his "comical cap an' ploddy [plaid] gown, a' gethering his yarbs [herbs]." Among older residents opinion was split: some claimed Rousseau was an exiled king, while others insisted he was a magician dallying with fairies and "lost sperrits." Yet others, however, simply concluded that "Owd Ross Hall" and his companion "Madam Zell" were strange but well-meaning visitors.[47]

Even in the northern reaches of England, however, Rousseau found that his celebrity had preceded him. During one of his botanizing expeditions, he bumped into Erasmus Darwin. Living at nearby Lichfield, Darwin was a well-known biologist and botanist.* The encounter with Rousseau, whose thought anticipated in certain respects the theory of evolution proposed by Darwin's grandson, may well have been planned. Having learned about Rousseau's excursions, Darwin ambushed his prey while he examined some plants near a cave.

---

*Darwin was also a member of the Lunar Society, an eighteenth-century organization devoted to the scientific progress Rousseau had condemned. Among its members were Josiah Wedgwood, the innovative potter and canal builder, Joseph Priestley, the radical cleric and discoverer of oxygen, and Isaac Watt of steam engine fame. Most interesting with regard to Rousseau was Thomas Day. At about the time Rousseau reached northern England, Day was carrying his Rousseauian schemes to their logical limit, and beyond, by adopting two young orphan girls to raise after the fashion of Sophie in Rousseau's *Emile*, with the intention of taking one as his wife and keeping the other as a spare. Unhappily, however, one girl proved unsuitable and the other ran off with his friend.

According to Charles Darwin, who describes the meeting in a biography he wrote of his grandfather, Erasmus, "who was then a stranger to [Rousseau], sauntered by the cave, and minutely examined a plant growing in front of it. This drew forth Rousseau, who was interested in botany, and they conversed together, and afterwards corresponded during several years."[48] We do not know, however, whether they talked of twigs or technology, scorium or science.

Soon Rousseau found sympathetic company in Staffordshire as well. Scarcely two miles from Wootton Hall stood Calwich Abbey, the home of Bernard Granville, a dyspeptic and well-read squire who conversed in French with Rousseau about music. Rousseau met Granville in April and occasionally visited Calwich. There he became acquainted with Granville's sister Mary, who had spent much of her life in Ireland, where she had befriended the Wesley brothers and Jonathan Swift. Upon her return to England, the good woman brought her daughter Mary Dewes, whose youthful beauty captivated Rousseau. She certainly knew the way to his heart, sending Sultan a collar she had embroidered for the dog, which, she explained to Rousseau, "has entertained me so many times with more skill and intelligence than many of a species that prides itself on their reason."[49] Rousseau was thoroughly conquered by her gesture: "My lovely neighbor, you have made me unjust and jealous for the first time in my life; I have not been able to look at the chains with which you honor my Sultan without envy, and I have seized from him the privilege of wearing them first."[50] Still eager to enroll innocent strangers into his dream life, Rousseau assigned the role of shepherdess to the twenty-year-old. In turn, Mary always recalled Rousseau as "the old shepherd."[51]

As spring was ending, Davenport arrived at his northern estate from London and visited with his guest for the first time since he had settled at Wootton. Davenport wrote Hume in London to say how pleased Rousseau seemed to be with his new situation: "I came on Friday and had the satisfaction of finding Mr. Rousseau in perfect health, he seems to like the place, amuses himself with walking, when the weather is fair, if rainy he plays upon the harpsichord, or writes—is very sociable and an excellent companion."[52]

During June, Davenport made his promised three-week visit to Wootton. The widowed squire came with his two orphaned grandchildren, ten-year-old Phoebe and nine-year-old Davies. They were attended by their governess, Madame Lausanne, who came from the other end of Lake Geneva from Rousseau's native city. During their host's stay, Thérèse was honored as official "cook." This was a notable event, as she had been all but banished from the kitchen by the servants, pushed to rebellion by her incessant and incoherent gesturing.[53] Rousseau was heartened by Davenport's arrival: "He is a very gallant man, full of solicitude and attention for me," Rousseau reported to Du Peyrou, and he went so far as to entrust Davenport with receiving his letters.[54] For his part, in a letter of June 23, Davenport related to Hume that the stretch of rainy days kept his guest "busy in writing, and it should be some large affair, by the quantity of paper he bought."[55]

While Rousseau settled at Wootton, Hume was engaged on his "pupil's" behalf. In particular, he busied himself with negotiating a royal pension for his friend that would serve as a symbol of English liberty, as well as supplement the exile's meager income in his final retirement. He had first raised the issue of the pension in Calais, as the two men waited for the frigid seas to calm so that they could make their crossing. He knew that Rousseau had already refused pensions from two monarchs: one from the King of France proposed after the successful performance of the *Devin du village,* and another, more recently offered, from Frederick of Prussia. The latter offer came after Frederick granted the philosopher's request, channeled through Keith, for asylum in the territory of Neuchâtel. The Prussian king offered a miserly sum of one hundred écus to be given to Rousseau in the form of provisions: wood and coal to heat his cottage. Shortly afterward the idea of a small annuity was advanced, and Rousseau's reply was less than solicitous: "You wish to give me bread. Is there no one of your subjects who lacks it? Hide from my eyes that sword which dazzles and wounds me. It has done all too well in your services and the scepter has been abandoned. . . . May I see Frederick the just and the feared fill his states with a happy people of whom he is the father and Jean-Jacques, the enemy of Kings, come to die of joy at the foot of his throne."[56] Keith forwarded the philosopher's reply for Frederick's eyes only. The matter was dropped.

Knowing Rousseau's prickly history in this regard, then, Hume endeavored to persuade him that accepting a pension from the King of England would not in the least endanger his prized independence. A reluctant Rousseau promised that if such an offer were forthcoming, he would consult his "father," meaning Keith.[57] In this regard, Keith was uniquely qualified: he was the sole person who, about six months earlier, had prevailed upon Rousseau to accept a pension. In this case, Rousseau accepted because he considered the Lord Marischal a generous friend whose gift did not include the unspoken clause of dependence that accompanied princely patronage.

Having raised the issue with Rousseau, Hume then approached General Conway, who agreed that the idea was "honorable both to the King and nation." As secretary of state, Conway then brought the matter to George's attention, and the king agreed to pay Rousseau one hundred pounds a year. "You know that our sovereign is extremely prudent and decent, and careful not to give offense,"

Hume explained to Boufflers, "For which reason, he requires that this act of generosity may be an entire secret."[58] All that remained was Keith's blessing. With his recent service to the crown and his connections in the government, Hume was confident that a deal would be struck.[59]

In the beginning of March the matter seemed to be concluded when Lord Keith wrote to advise Rousseau to accept the offer. "There is nothing to hesitate about here," Keith declared, adding for good measure that Rousseau should have accepted the earlier offer from the King of Prussia.[60] General Conway's illness delayed the final resolution for a month, but by the beginning of April, Hume was anticipating the happy result when he wrote a formal letter to Conway to thank him for his assistance, saying of himself in the third person: "He will keep it a secret, though one of the most laudable actions in the world. He has informed Monsieur Rousseau, who, as he has the greatest sensibility imaginable, must feel the proper gratitude for the obliging manner in which he is treated."[61] The only matter to be settled, then, was whether the pension would be paid through the treasury or, more likely since it was to be a secret, through the King's Privy Purse.[62] Hume promptly informed Rousseau of the result, enclosing Conway's formal offer and telling him he must formally accept the pension and thank Conway for his good offices.[63]

The business of the pension took an unexpected turn with what seemed a minor affair just when everything seemed to be proceeding as Hume had hoped: the circulation and then publication of a supposed letter from Frederick the Great to Rousseau. In fact, this affair dated back to the commencement of Hume's friendship with Rousseau, but it came to a head just as the negotiations over the pension seemed happily concluded.

In the mock letter, "Frederick" offers his kingdom to Rousseau as a place of exile. Mixing magnanimity with irreverence, the faux monarch writes: "I admire your talent and enjoy your reveries, on which, by the way, you dwell too much and too long. . . . Show your enemies that, on occasion, you have common sense. That will bother them without harming you. My states offer you a safe refuge." But the conclusion reveals the peculiar nature of royal generosity as well as Rousseau's embattled attitude toward society: "If you persist in racking your brain to find new misfortunes, choose whatever you like: I am a King, and I can procure them according to your wishes; and, as will never happen for you with your enemies, I will stop persecuting you when you stop finding glory in being persecuted."[64]

The author of this bit of pleasantry was not Frederick but Horace Walpole. Already baffled by Hume's improbable success in the salons, Walpole may have felt further upstaged with Rousseau's triumphal return to Paris en route to England. As Rousseau made his way to Paris in mid-December, then, Walpole decided to recapture the limelight with his satiric letter, reading his production to appreciative applause first at Mme Geoffrin's salon and then at Mme du Deffand's. Not everyone was amused. His recital at the Temple, for example, dismayed the Comtesse de Boufflers, who "abused me heartily," related Walpole. "I acted contrition, but had like to have spoiled all, by growing dreadfully tired of a second lecture from the Prince de Conti, who took up the ball, and made himself the hero of a history wherein he had nothing to do. I listened, did not understand half [of what] he said (nor he neither), forgot the rest, said 'Yes' when I should have said 'No,' yawned when I should have smiled, and was very penitent when I should have rejoiced at my pardon."[65] Applauded or chided, Walpole was an instant success. "Yet, do you know," Walpole wrote to General Conway in mid-January 1766, "my present fame is owing to a very trifling composition, but which has made incredible noise. . . . The copies have spread like wildfire; et me voici la mode!"[66]

Hume himself appears to have been witness to what may have been Walpole's inaugural performance of the letter. With clever detective work, David Edmonds and John Eidenow identify the date on which both Hume and Walpole could have been present—December 12, just before Rousseau arrived in Paris. They further suggest that Hume was not merely present at the creation but possibly even responsible for the stinging witticism in the letter's concluding line.[67] Such at least was the rumor that Boufflers heard, since Hume wrote to the Marquise de Barbentane to ask her to assure the comtesse that he had played no role in the letter, insisting that the pleasantries that made their way into the prank letter all came from Walpole's own mouth, "in my company, at Lord Ossory's table, which my Lord remembers very well."[68] If Hume was guilty, however, it is strange that he himself provides the same evidence and witnesses in his defense that were also used to condemn him. In any case, it is unclear whether Hume was more impatient with Walpole for his prank or Rousseau for his extravagant reaction: as he told Boufflers, "It is a strange inclination we have to be wits, preferably to everything else. . . . I am a little angry with [Walpole], and I hear you are a great deal; but the matter ought to be treated only as a piece of levity."[69]

Rousseau had gotten wind of the letter as he was preparing to leave for Wootton, and unbeknownst to Hume, he began to suspect the Scot himself of complicity in this "piece of levity." Writing Du Peyrou as he was packing for his departure, Rousseau had asked him to find some way of getting the papers from Paris that he still needed for writing his *Confessions*. "M. Hume has given me the address . . . for his friend M. Walpole, who leaves Paris a month from now, but for reasons too long to include in a letter, I would prefer not to utilize this means unless there is no other. People have spoken to me about the pretended letter from the King of Prussia, but they did not tell me that it was spread around by M. Walpole, and when I spoke about it to M. Hume he would neither confirm nor deny it."[70] As with the incident of Davenport's coach, it was Hume's very discretion that led to Rousseau's suspicions.

The publication of the letter in the *St. James's Chronicle* at the beginning of April, shortly after Rousseau had arrived at Wootton, further raised his suspicions. Rousseau replied with a letter to the editor that Hume characterized as "full of passion, and indeed of extravagance, complaining in the most tragical terms of the forgery, and lamenting that the imposter should find any abettors and partisans in England."[71] Rousseau wrongly suspected that d'Alembert was the author of the squib, but Hume had no idea that the exiled philosopher counted him among the "abettors" of the scheme to dishonor him in England.[72] Rousseau's letter itself produced a flurry of letters, poems, and bagatelles, some defending him and others ridiculing him for taking such a satire seriously — after all, this was the price of living in a land that enjoyed freedom of the press.[73] Walpole also wrote a response, which he suppressed for humanity's sake, according to Hume.[74] (And it was just as well that he did: the "Letter from Emile to Jean-Jacques Rousseau" begins, "Alas, my dear tutor, I arrive in this country and for the first bit of news I am told that you have lost your mind.")[75] As he continued to negotiate the increasingly difficult matter of the pension, Hume wrote Rousseau to apologize on Walpole's behalf for the offense given by "that idle piece of pleasantry."[76]

As a veteran diplomat, Hume realized that the satisfaction of his request depended on repairing Rousseau's rapidly fraying amour-propre. He assured Rousseau that his suspicions of a slander-slinging conspiracy were groundless. At the same juncture, however, yet another attack on Rousseau had appeared in the press, giving some credence to the exile's fears, Hume had to admit: the biting "Letter from M. de Voltaire to Doctor J.-J. Pansophe." Voltaire was pursuing Rousseau as far as England. In this bit of satire, which he characteristically disavowed even as he gloried in the resulting mischief, Voltaire offers Jean-Jacques a lesson in good faith, common sense, and modesty, and then points out the supposed contradictions in his writings and, worse, the contradictions between what he preached and practiced.[77]* "Dr. Pansophe, I am told that you intend to go to

*"I forgot to tell you that I am quite angry that the *Letter to Doctor Pansophe* is attributed to me," Voltaire wrote d'Alembert on November 29, 1766, adding, "it is quite amusing, in truth," even though it seems to contain "some naïve things taken from Candide." Given Voltaire's denials that *Candide* was aimed at Rousseau, as Rousseau himself thought, it is at least curious that Voltaire draws a parallel between "Doctor J.-J. Pansophe" and his famously ingenuous character.

England. This is the country of pretty women and good philosophers," Voltaire continued.

> These pretty women and good philosophers will perhaps be curious to see you, and you will make them see you. The gazettes will take care to give an exact account of your deeds and gesticulations, and will speak of the great Jean-Jacques like the king's elephant or the queen's zebra: for the English are amused by the rare productions of every kind, although they rarely admire them. You will be pointed out at the theater, if you go there, and they will say: There is that eminent genius who reproaches us for having lost our natural goodness and who says that His Majesty's subjects are not free![78]

Recalling the theme of common life that runs through the *Treatise*, Hume urged Rousseau to forget such imbecilities and hold fast to what is most important: "My dear friend, if you must fly from mankind, do not at once renounce the amusement and consolation of society, and feel all the pain which may result from the idle opinions of men and those misrepresented." Besides, he added, Conway's profuse praise in his letter of Rousseau's "distinguished genius and merit" attested to "what estimation you are held by all men of character in England."[79]

Hume's shock was great, then, when two weeks later he called upon Conway and learned from the perplexed general that Rousseau had rejected the pension. Although "vividly touched by the favors with which it pleases His Majesty to honor me, and by your goodness," Rousseau wrote to Conway on May 12, he had to speak frankly. "After so many misfortunes, I believed myself prepared for all possible events," Rousseau explains. "Nonetheless, something has happened that I could not have foreseen, and which it is not even permissible for an honest man to foresee." What these unforeseen events might be, Rousseau does not say, but their effect is to make him unable to decide any important matter. "Far from refusing the beneficence of the King from the pride that is imputed to me, I glory in acknowledging it, and the only drawback I can see in this is not being able to do honor to it in the eyes of the public, as I am able to do in my own. . . . Deign, therefore, Sir, to preserve [the goodness of His Majesty] for happier times, when you will know that I defer taking advantage of it only to try and render myself more worthy of it."[80]

Was Rousseau declining the pension or delaying his acceptance of it? What were these terrible unforeseen events that led to his decided indecision? Was he hinting at the conditions under which he would make up his mind to accept the pension? Not only was Hume as baffled as Conway, but he also finally allowed himself the anger that was fanned into flames by this latest example of his friend's extravagance.

Hume made use of that very word in a letter he immediately wrote to Boufflers. "I am afraid, my dear Madam, that notwithstanding our friendship, and our enthusiasm for this philosopher, he has been guilty of an extravagance the most unaccountable and most blamable that is possible to be imagined." Forwarding to her a copy of Rousseau's letter to Conway, whom he said was "so good humoured as not to be angry," Hume concluded that Rousseau refused the pension because it would be given in secret. Yet how could that possibly be, Hume demanded? Had not Rousseau already replied that "he liked it the better on that account, as it was a testimony of esteem from his Majesty, without any mixture or suspicion of vanity?" Hume declared that he would tell Rousseau that "the affair is no longer an object of deliberation: he had already taken his resolution, when he allowed me to apply to the minister; and again, when he allowed the minister to apply to the King; and again, when he wrote to Lord Marischal; and again, when he allowed me to notify Lord Marischal's answer to the minister; and again, when he acquiesced two months in this determination; and that the King, General Conway, Lord Marischal, and I, shall all have reason to complain of him." Clearly exasperated, Hume asked whether there was "any thing in the world so unaccountable?" The philosopher of common life answered his own question: "For the purposes of life and conduct, and society, a little good sense is surely better than all this genius, and a little good humor than this extreme sensibility."[81]

True to his word, Hume wrote to Rousseau: "Your letter to General Conway has given me great uneasiness; as it did also to the General." But apparently he had thought better of telling Rousseau that the die had been cast; instead, Hume wrote that General Conway hoped he would change his mind. "But there was another circumstance of your letter, which gave me still greater uneasiness," Hume continued. "You mention some calamity or affliction which you have met with, and which has thrown you into the most profound melancholy." If it was Walpole's jest, Hume was authorized to apologize to Rousseau on his behalf. "I am yours with great sincerity," Hume closes his letter.[82] He could easily have added "with even greater trepidation."

Nearly a month later, with no answer from Rousseau, Hume contacted Davenport. Noting that the good squire's "guest is not a little whimsical," he asked him to press Rousseau on the matter of the pension. In a second letter that followed on the heels of the first, Hume reassured Davenport that were not Rousseau "the most unaccountable man in the world, I should be very much scandalized and very much offended at this long silence."[83]

Yet Davenport was unable to pry a reply from the recluse at Wootton. As a result, Hume was forced to interpret Rousseau's intentions from his silence: "As I have not received any answer from you, I conclude that you persevere in the same resolution of refusing all marks of His Majesty's goodness, as long as they must remain a secret." He had therefore applied to General Conway, he explains, to have that condition removed from the king's offer. But he must first know whether Rousseau intends to accept, so "that His Majesty may not be exposed to a second refusal."[84]

The reservoir of gratitude Hume had collected during his ambassadorial posting was running dry. What is more, General Conway and his brother Lord Hertford were about to be ushered out of power with the imminent fall of the Rockingham ministry.[85] Finally, with his affairs now in order Hume was planning to leave London for his native Edinburgh. Receiving word from Rousseau was therefore imperative, and he accordingly dashed off a short note to his friend telling him that he needed an immediate reply concerning the pension. Once I leave London, he warned Rousseau, "I shall not then have it in [my] power to be any longer of service."[86] Hume's services, it soon became clear, were the last thing Rousseau sought.

CHAPTER TEN

Hume, Judge of le Bon David

Mr. Hume must necessarily have acted in this affair either as one of greatest or the lowest of men. There is no mean position. It remains to be determined which of the two he is.
— Rousseau to Hume

But would you believe it, that in a piece so full of frenzy and malice, impertinence and lies, there are many strokes of genius and eloquence; and the conclusion of it is remarkably sublime.
— Hume to Mme de Meinières

In March 1766 Boswell returned to his ancestral home, Auchinleck. Although his attitude toward Rousseau had begun to change in the wake of his amorous apprenticeship under Thérèse, his need to be remembered and reassured by others had not. With his habitual mix of audacity and gregariousness, Boswell wrote twice to Rousseau in July, gently reprimanding him for neglecting their correspondence.

In his reply, Rousseau revealed that he was not a clueless cuckold. With brittle aplomb, he thanked Boswell for asking after his and Mlle Le Vasseur's health: both of them were as healthy as their age, circumstances, and, well, certain recent activities permitted. He advised Boswell to pay greater heed to his own health and, in particular, "to have yourself bled on occasion; I believe it might do you good." Either Thérèse had confessed her fling to Rousseau, or she had fibbed, regaling Rousseau with tales of her stubborn loyalty in the face of the hot-blooded Scot's repeated assaults. In any event, Rousseau's mind was clearly elsewhere. In a postscript, he excused his tardy reply to Boswell, explaining that his "letters, both of which passed through M. Hume's hands, were seriously delayed. The first letter had been opened, while the battered state of the second one, which arrived a month after being posted, suggests that it too had been opened."[1] Evidently, not all acts of disloyalty were equally unforgivable: Boswell's transgression was small beer when set against the crimes Rousseau was busily attributing to Hume.

For Rousseau the summer of 1766 was a season of account settling. And no one was more taken aback by this turn of events then Hume himself. While Rousseau rightly sensed Boswell's lack of sincerity, he failed to credit Hume's honesty. The problem for Rousseau, however, was that honesty necessarily amounted to little in a world of appearances. What virtue or value could there possibly be in being true to falsehoods? When one was caught in a maze of funhouse mirrors, the single virtue that counted was sincerity, or fidelity to one's self. The motto that Rousseau took as his own from Juvenal, *vitam impendere vero*, was thus given a revolutionary twist. Living one's life in dedication to the truth was, however, no longer directed at the world but toward the self: conformity to the inner life was our sole virtue in the shadow lands of the modern world.

Rousseau's long-awaited reply to Hume was finally sent on June 23, the same day that Davenport had reported back to Hume in London that a rainy day had kept Rousseau indoors, where he was busily writing.

I would have believed, Sir, that my silence would have said enough if it had been interpreted by your conscience, but since it does not seem to occur to you to understand it, I will speak. You have poorly concealed yourself: I recognize you and you are not unaware of this. Without previous connections, without quarrels, without entanglements of any kind, without knowing one another except through literary reputation, you rushed to offer me your friends and your services; touched by your generosity, I threw myself into your arms, you brought me to England, in appearance in order to obtain an asylum for me, and in reality in order to dishonor me.[2]

As he read the several sheets of Rousseau's closely spaced and neatly written letter, Hume realized with growing horror that events had swerved in an unexpected direction. Like a splinter inside a festering wound, the lodging of Walpole's hoax in Rousseau's imagination had had appalling consequences. The Genevan had concluded that Hume, in appearance his friend, was in reality his greatest enemy.

"You have applied yourself to this noble work with a zeal worthy of your heart, and with a success worthy of your talents," Rousseau continued, "so much was not necessary to assure success. You live in the world, and I live in seclusion, the public loves to be deceived, and you are made to deceive it. I nevertheless know a man whom you do not deceive; it is yourself." Rousseau had pierced the veil that concealed Hume's motives and, in a perverse mirror image of friendship, now claimed that they understood one another perfectly. "You know with what horror my heart pushed aside the first suspicion of your plans. I said to you while embracing you with tears in my eyes that if you were not the best of men, you must be the blackest. Thinking about your secret conduct you must sometimes tell yourself that you are not indeed the best of men, and I doubt that with this realization you can ever be the happiest."[3]

In his allusion to the "affecting scene" that had passed between them the last evening they were together, Rousseau added a crucial element missing in Hume's account. Hume had reported that Rousseau suddenly sat on his knee and tearfully exclaimed, "Is it possible you can ever forgive me, my dear friend? After all the testimonies of affection I have received from you, I reward you at last with this folly and ill behavior. But I have notwithstanding a heart worthy of your friendship. I love you, I esteem you; and not an instance of your kindness is thrown away upon me."[4] Rousseau's version, however, adds that he pointedly asked his ostensible protector whether he was the best or the blackest of men. Completing the infernal syllogism, Rousseau then claimed that the answer could lie only in their hearts: Hume must know the horror with which Rousseau's "heart" rejected these suspicions; Rousseau, for his part, now knew that Hume knew, in his heart of hearts, that he was not the best of men and must therefore be the blackest.

"I give free rein to you and your friends to continue your schemes, and abandon my reputation during my lifetime to you with less regret, quite sure than one day justice will be rendered to both of us," Rousseau wrote, anticipating the tone and argument he would use in his later autobiographical writings, *Rousseau Judge of Jean-Jacques* and the *Reveries*. Alluding to his reasons for not accepting the pension that Hume had labored so hard to obtain for him, Rousseau announced, "As for your good offices in matters concerning my interests, which you have masked yourself, I thank you for them and dispense you of any further obligations. I must no longer have any contact with you, and must not accept any affair in which you are a mediator, even if it is to my advantage." Rousseau brutally concluded, "Farewell, Sir. I wish you the truest happiness, but as we ought no longer have anything to say to one another, this is the last letter you will receive from me."[5]

Hume immediately replied, demanding to know what he had done to deserve such accusations. "As I am conscious of having ever acted toward you the most friendly part, of having ever given you the most tender, the most active proofs of sincere affection, you may judge of my extreme surprise on perusing your epistle: such violent accusations, confined altogether to generals, it is as impossible to answer as to comprehend them. But affairs cannot, must not remain on that footing," he continued. "I shall charitably suppose, that some infamous calumniator has belied me to you. But in that case, it is your duty, and I am persuaded it will be your inclination, to give me an opportunity of detecting him, and of justifying myself, which can only be done by your mentioning the particulars, of which I am accused."[6]

When he declared that it "is as impossible to answer as to comprehend" Rousseau's accusations, Hume revealed his philosophical consistency: understanding was possible only by reducing experience to its separate elements. Hume only now began to measure the intellectual divide between himself and his "pupil." For the Scot, Rousseau's testimony of the heart was an assertion, not an explanation. And while Rousseau insisted on reasons the heart alone can know, Hume stubbornly maintained that such reasons must withstand appeal to available facts and public testimony.

> You say, that I myself know that I have been false to you, but I say it loudly, and will say it to the whole world that I know the contrary, that I know my friendship towards you has been unbounded and uninterrupted, and that though the instances of it have been very generally remarked both in France and England, the smallest part of it only has as yet come to the knowledge of the public. I demand that you will produce me the man who will say the contrary; and above all I demand that he will mention any one particular, in which I have been wanting to you.[7]

In short, Hume demanded a public trial. "You owe this to me, you owe it to yourself, you owe it to truth and honor and justice, and to every thing that can be deemed sacred among men. As an innocent man; I will not say, as your friend; I will not say, as your benefactor; but I repeat it, as an innocent man, I claim the privilege of proving my innocence, and of refuting any scandalous lie which may have been invented against me."[8] But what he could not know, much less comprehend, was that there were no such false accusations or incriminating facts that could be brought to court, or witnesses to be called. Rousseau had already condemned him.

Rousseau had, in fact, started to prepare his case against Hume during his first days at snowbound Wootton. At the time he was writing to Hume to thank him for all he had done on his behalf, Rousseau sent a very different account of his life to François-Henri d'Ivernois, a Genevan merchant who led the city's democratic faction and who had praised *Letters Written from the Mountain* as a "firebrand in a powder magazine."[9] Rehearsing the wild claims he would soon fire at Hume, he shared with d'Ivernois the reasons for his winter of growing discontent, grousing that his reputation had suffered ever since he had left London. Letters forwarded to him by Hume, Rousseau confided, often arrived opened, while those he had given Hume to post never reached their destinations. Most insidiously, Rousseau whispered that "several other facts make me suspect him, even the zeal he has shown for me." Though uncertain about Hume's exact intentions, Rousseau concluded, "I cannot help but think they are sinister."[10]

A week later Rousseau related his suspicions regarding Hume to the Marquise de Verdelin. Along with the incidents he shared with d'Ivernois, Rousseau mentioned for the first time Hume's blank and unsettling stare: "It was impossible for me to sustain his horrifying look."[11] In a long letter a month later to Malesherbes, he again dwelled on Hume's gaze, announcing that he had broken off all communication with him — unbeknownst to Hume, who was increasingly worried over his friend's silence and trying to salvage the pension that Rousseau insisted on sabotaging.[12]

Mutual friends were understandably perplexed. The Marquise du Verdelin, Lord Marischal Keith, even the loyal Du Peyrou all assured Rousseau that he was mistaken. "I am greatly astonished with what you say of David," Keith replied. "You say, *that he serves you with the truest zeal,* and I would still like to believe that his intentions are pure, and that the means he takes are not to your liking rather because he has not judged matters correctly than because of any self-interest on his part."[13] Yet Rousseau was unconvinced, for he knew — or, rather, *felt* — the truth behind these false appearances. Indeed, Hume's protestations of innocence reinforced Rousseau's conviction that his former friend was guilty. From the wilds of Staffordshire at the end of May, Rousseau finally announced to Du Peyrou the break with the man who had brought him there: "I have broken off all correspondence with M. Hume and I have decided that whatever may happen I will never write him. I regard the triumvirate of Voltaire, d'Alembert, and him as a certain thing. I cannot penetrate their scheme, but they have one."[14]

Rousseau thus cast Hume in the same role imposed on the young Jean-Jacques at Bossey: he was condemned by appearances, which Rousseau revealingly calls "facts." The more Hume argued for his innocence, the more Rousseau grew convinced of his guilt. Hume could no more reveal the truth to Rousseau than Rousseau himself could with the Lamberciers. In both cases, language deepened the rift between reality and appearance. Adding to the tragic parallels is the absence of malevolent intent in both the Lamberciers and Rousseau: just as the pastor and his wife were sincerely (though wrongly) persuaded of young Jean-Jacques's crime, so too was the much older Jean-Jacques convinced (again wrongly) of Hume's crime. Hence the pathos of Hume's appeal to Davenport, which he made immediately after receiving Rousseau's letter of accusation: "You and you alone can aid me in the most critical affair, which, during the course of my whole life, I have been engaged in."[15]

"I am ill, Sir, and hardly in a position to write; but you desire an explanation, and you must be given one. It is due only to yourself that you have not had one for such a long time; you did not then want it, so I was silent; now you want it, so I am sending it to you. It will be a long one, for which I am sorry, but I have much to say, and do not want to have to say it twice."[16]

Rousseau's climactic letter to Hume *is* very long, running a full thirty-eight manuscript pages in the best script of the former engraver's apprentice. The letter is also extremely well crafted, having gone through several heavily revised drafts in which Rousseau restructures his account to achieve the maximum effect and tweaks his prose with the same care he devoted to his best works.[17] Rousseau expertly mixes doses of sincerity and self-fashioning, portraying himself as an embattled and frail writer who, were it not for his attachment to truth, would rather do anything else than write. The contrast between the care of the composition and presentation of the letter and its seemingly mad contents must have struck Hume.

Having set the stage for his lengthy missive, Rousseau repeats the promise contained in *Julie:* he will depend on the same sincerity in this present account that infused the "letters" of his novel. He will relate only his feelings, which, by definition, must be true: "As I do not live in the world, I am ignorant of what goes on in it, I have no party, no associates, no intrigues; as I am told nothing, I know only what I feel." Yet this private sentiment is couched in the public genre of the *mémoire judiciaire,* or judicial memoir. Written by lawyers, these enormously popular pamphlets exploited the blurring of the line between fact and fiction—encouraged, ironically, by Rousseau's *Julie*—in presenting the client as the actual author. Moreover, though originally meant to sway legal courts, the memoir, because it was not subject to censorship, soon was used to sway the court of public opinion.[18]

Having spent more than two years in the company of French writers and diplomats, and familiar with their literary strategies, Hume concluded that Rousseau meant to publish his letter. What other inference could he draw from Rousseau's next line: "The first concern of those who deal in dark designs is to conceal themselves from any legal proof; it would not be advisable to confront them through legal processes. Interior conviction allows of another kind of proof that regulates the feelings of an honest man: you know the basis of my own"? To Hume's mind, Rousseau seemed to frame his case against Hume before the public bar of sentiment.

Hume's famous calm now met one of its greatest tests. From all appearances, he must have read the letter through quickly and then, after his initial astonishment wore off, taken it up again, reading with greater deliberation. As he reread the letter, he reached for a pen and carefully noted his reactions to the many charges in the letter's margins.

The sketch of his eventual public self-defense, Hume's comments are infused with outrage and incredulity. Alongside the opening claim that he alone was to blame for not having previously received an explanation, Hume retorted that this is the "first lie." As if explaining himself to his peers, Hume declared: "Mr. Rousseau never gave me an opportunity of demanding an explanation. If he ever entertained any of those black and absurd suspicions, of which his letter is full, he always kept them to himself, as long as we lived together."[19] The vast distance separating the two men widens: whereas Rousseau invited Hume to interpret his silence as proof of Hume's guilty conscience, Hume replied that because of Rousseau's silence he was naturally unaware that he was even being accused, much less found guilty.

Unfolding his charges with a logic as subtle and baseless as the metaphysical systems Hume had combated all of his life, Rousseau then identified the chief witness against his former protector: Hume himself. "You ask me with great confidence to name your accuser. That accuser, Sir, is the only man in the world whom I could be made to listen to if he testified against you: it is yourself."

Portraying himself, as he had ever since his *Discourse on the Sciences and Arts,* as the "enemy to all artifice," Rousseau continued: "I will speak to you with the same frankness as though you were another person in whom I had all the confidence that I no longer have in you. I will present the history of the movements of my soul and of what produced them, and, speaking of M. Hume in the third person, I will make you yourself the judge of what I ought to think of him. Despite the length of my letter, I will not follow any other order than that of my ideas, beginning with the premises and concluding with the demonstration."

In his earlier letter to Rousseau, Hume had asserted his rights implicit in the protocol and evidentiary procedures of an English court. Invoking the spirit of habeas corpus, Hume naturally wished to confront his accusers and be given the occasion to prove his innocence beyond a reasonable doubt. Yet Rousseau rebuffed Hume's request and replied with a kind of philosophical lettre de cachet: having plumbed the testimony of his own heart, he declared appeals or dialogues pointless. Since he was hidden from the world, and since the world was hidden from him by the machinations of those who plotted against him, Rousseau appealed to what he knew best, indeed, the source of his very knowledge: his own sentiments.

Rousseau's letter, in fact, eerily anticipates his last completed work, *Rousseau Judge of Jean-Jacques: Dialogues,* written ten years later. Tellingly, it is the one work in which he discusses his relationship with Hume. The book takes the form of a dialogue between "Rousseau" and "The Frenchman" in which they discuss the accusations leveled at a third party, "Jean-Jacques." As Rousseau explains in the work's preface, "In these conversations I took the liberty of resuming his family name, which the public judged it appropriate to take from me, and following its example, I refer to myself as a third party, using my Christian name to which the public chose to reduce me."[20] Victim of his own runaway celebrity, the infamous "Jean-Jacques" now stands accused, with Rousseau himself serving as his judge. In order to reunite reality and appearance, his true self with his reputed self—to make himself whole once again—Jean-Jacques Rousseau must paradoxically dismember himself. And he must do so in public.

Similarly, in his letter to Hume, Rousseau places his former friend in the position of accused and judge. Like "le pauvre Jean-Jacques" in the *Dialogues,* "le bon David" is cast as the accused, the perfidious Mr. Hume. And, like "Rousseau," the bewildered Scot also serves as his own judge. As for himself, Rousseau partially anticipates the role of "The Frenchman." But he does not assume this task in order to accuse Hume himself. On the contrary, Hume will serve as his own accuser. Instead, Rousseau is witness to and victim of the events he will recount. For unlike the *Dialogues,* in which Rousseau ultimately exonerates Jean-Jacques of all charges, here Rousseau is determined to prove Hume's guilt. As a result, Hume found himself caught in a web of nightmarish logic that would be more familiar to the readers of Kafka and Orwell than those of Richardson or even Sterne.

With his customary flair for drama, Rousseau first explains his decision to accept the offer of asylum in Britain. He was duped, in essence, by Hume's reputation for probity as well as genius: "I found a kind of glory in the prospect of setting a good example for men of letters in the sincere union between two men whose principles were so different."[21]

Expecting probity, Rousseau found perfidy, the foul offspring of wounded vanity and inevitable jealousy. Recalling his welcome in Paris, he dwells on the unhappy effect it must have had on his awestruck host: "He saw, and perhaps saw too much, the reception I received from a great Prince," referring to the Prince de Conti, "and I dare say, from the public. . . . Like me, he must have been touched, but I do not know if he was in the same manner as I was." To Hume's excited report to Blair—"Voltaire and everybody else are quite eclipsed by him"—Rousseau now adds Hume's own name. As a result, the "sincere union" Rousseau expected was, from the start, fraudulent.

Rousseau's reinterpretation of the dramatic crossing of the Channel adds an additional layer of suspense. "Disembarking in Dover, transported by having finally set foot in this land of liberty and by having been brought here by this illustrious man, I threw my arms around his neck and embraced him tightly without saying anything, instead covering his face with kisses and bathing him with tears that spoke eloquently enough." Rousseau again expresses his distrust of language: the truest language, he declared in his *Essay on the Origin of Language,* is composed of gestures, not words. They depend "less on conventions [and] are also more expressive and say more in less time."[22]

Tragically, for Rousseau, Hume seemed deaf—or, rather, blind—to this language. "This was not the only time, nor the most remarkable, that he could have seen in me the signs of a heart penetrated with sentiment. I do not know what he does with these recollections, if they ever come to him, but I have a notion that they must sometimes trouble him." From the embrace long ago at Vincennes with Diderot—"See how my friends love me!"—Rousseau had moved to the embrace on the icy dock at Dover with Hume, who was now, Rousseau believed, whispering to himself, "See how others love my friend!"

Rousseau filtered through a dark glass every gesture made, every word said by Hume. He now even wondered whether the portrait by Ramsay was an early sign of Hume's infidelity. Though not having yet denounced his likeness as little more than a "hideous Cyclops," as he would later do in the *Dialogues,* Rousseau scented hypocrisy, or worse, a conspiracy in Hume's commission for the painting. Hume's "whim," Rousseau claims, appeared "too affected, and I found in it a kind of ostentation that did not please me." Hume hardly seemed the sort of man to collect expensive portraits of his friends, Rousseau muses, but he admits that he could be mistaken.

This would be Rousseau's last tick of generosity. Up to this point, he allowed, Hume benefited from appearances. Anyone acquainted with their affair would see only Hume's solicitude for his new friend and would hear Rousseau's grateful praise of his host. And what else could one make of the royal pension Hume had worked so hard and selflessly to obtain for Rousseau? This was why, Rousseau explains, he had spoken of Hume's good offices with "an overflowing heart." But that same heart had been betrayed, the victim once again of appearance: "In estimating his services by the pains and the time they cost him, they were of an inestimable value, still more so taking into account his good will; but by the real good they have brought me, they were more appearance than true weightiness."

In this world turned upside down—where, in Allan Bloom's description, man thinks only of himself when he deals with others, and thinks only of others when he reflects on himself—Hume alone benefited from the royal pension.[23] Thrusting away the outstretched hand, Rousseau raged that he had not come to England to beg for his bread. Besides, all the good Hume had done for him could have been equaled—or exceeded—had it come from others. Hume's patronage was, in fact, poisonous: enemies, not friends, were spawned by such relationships. And these adversaries were no motley lot: on the contrary, they were Hume's friends. "Who could have excited their enmity against me? It was certainly not I, who knew nothing of them, nor ever saw them in my life. I should not have had a single enemy had I come to England alone."

The external world seemed to Rousseau to have turned against him shortly after he came to England. "A very short time after our arrival in London, I observed an absurd change in the minds of the people regarding me, which soon became very apparent." The newspapers, which had sung his praise upon his arrival, were now slinging insults and falsehoods at him. "Everything that had been published concerning my misfortunes was misrepresented, altered, or placed in a wrong light, and always as much as possible to my disadvantage."[24] These critical or, worse yet, comic reports were not the result of the freedom of the British press, a thoroughly alien notion to a thinker persecuted by theocracies and monarchies, but the machinations of his nemesis, Hume. "I thought it something very odd that, immediately after the return of Mr. Hume, who had so much credit in London . . . his presence should produce an effect so contrary to what might have been expected."

For a public thinker often mauled by the press, Hume surely found it odd to be accused of manipulating England's papers against Rousseau. Whether from the baseless nature of the accusation or ignorance of the freedoms of the English press, Hume was nonplussed. "Am I to answer for every article of every magazine and newspaper printed in England?" he wondered in his margins. "I would rather answer," he continued, "for every robbery committed on the highway; and I am entirely as innocent of the one as the other."

Yet according to Rousseau, far more than the press fell under Hume's baleful influence. Everyone in Hume's orbit, from his host, John Stewart, to Stewart's brother, to the other boarders at Hume's lodgings, to the landladies themselves, had either insulted him to his face or had feigned respect. They had all taken their cue from Hume, who outdid them all when he placed a volume of

Julie prominently in his drawing room when Rousseau first visited his lodgings, even though this book "must be the most tiresome to him," Rousseau asserted (with unintentional accuracy).[25]

Rousseau's accusations grew more elusive and maddening. The librarian of the British Museum recommended to him by Keith was offended by a missed appointment because Hume had insisted he go with Mrs. Garrick to the theater. When Rousseau learned of the fictitious letter from the King of Prussia, he asked Hume whether it was true that Walpole had served as the "editor." The Scot replied with a question of his own: how had Rousseau learned of it? "Until this point, Mr. Hume seems to have walked in the shadows. From now on you will see him in the light and walk without disguise."

As Rousseau traced this sinister web of intrigue, Hume's astonishment deepened. Overwhelmed by the sweeping mixture of madness and eloquence, he demanded proof: How does Rousseau know this? Where did Rousseau see or hear such conspiracies? For Hume, asking for proof was perfectly reasonable, but to Rousseau it was perfectly risible: the Genevan had already ruled such questions out of court. Hume protested his innocence, inscribing the word *lie* time and again in the margins alongside these many mad claims. "Second Lie," Hume writes in regard to the alleged incident involving Stewart, adducing an obliging letter Rousseau subsequently wrote to him, and "Third Lie" to the story of Mr. Stewart's brother. As for the "silly story" about the theater, he recalls nothing at all. Was this, Hume demanded, the basis of Rousseau's suspicions: his friendship with Walpole, Dr. Tronchin's son lodging in the same house by accident, and his landladies' inability to understand a word of French? Only a "black mind," he thought, could invent a story so fantastic, based on nothing more than coincidence and happenstance. Could he not easily explain each of these particular circumstances?[26]

Even the matter of Rousseau's "tampered"-with correspondence was easily, if awkwardly, explained. In the longest note of the published version of the correspondence, Hume described how Rousseau continually complained of the cost of the postage he had to pay for the letters he received, especially the many letters that came from unknown correspondents that he had no desire to read. Though Rousseau finally decided to receive no letters at all, they nevertheless continued to arrive at Hume's lodgings in London. Hume dutifully carried them to Chiswick during his visits to Rousseau, but his guest refused to accept them, asking Hume to return them to the post office and recover the costs. Unable to reason with Rousseau, yet unwilling to entrust the letters to the postal service, Hume decided to cull the important ones to forward to his friend. "I am indeed ashamed to find myself obliged to discover such petty circumstances," Hume concludes his note.[27]

Rousseau's longest note to his letter, in turn, also raises the question of Hume's handling of his letters. Having just arrived at Hume's lodgings on his way to Wootton, Rousseau relates, he was writing a letter that Hume seemed eager to read and offered to post. When Lord Newnham came in and Hume went out of the room for a moment, Newnham offered to put the letter into the ambassadorial pouch. When Hume reentered the room, Newnham was about to apply his seal to the letter, but Hume insistently offered his own. Unable to get Newnham alone, Rousseau watched Hume's servant carry off the letter. "Thus, although I have not received a response to my letter, I do not doubt that it arrived; but I do suspect, I admit, that it was read first."

Hume's response to this charge is potentially revealing, and not entirely to his own credit. "These infamous and black suspicions are built on such a silly foundation, that every circumstance of this story may be either true or false without being of any consequence," wrote Hume in the margins.[28] Yet this is the sole instance in which Hume did not reproduce his marginal notes in some form when he went into print. Did he think it beneath his dignity to reply publicly to this charge? Or was there some truth to Rousseau's charge? While the story of Hume's pocketing the letter may have been absurd, there was, after all, some truth to Rousseau's accusations that Hume had been reading his mail. Although Hume may not have wanted to admit to himself or to others, the "petty circumstances" of his management of Rousseau's correspondence gave some credence to Rousseau's suspicions, if not to his conclusions regarding Hume's intentions.

Yet it was Hume's own behavior that, in Rousseau's eyes, ultimately proved his undoing. Rousseau recalled the final evening between the two former friends. "As we were sitting one evening, after supper, silent by the fireside," he wrote,

> I caught his eyes intently fixed on mine, as indeed happened very often; and that in a manner of which it is very difficult to give an idea. At that time he gave me a steadfast, piercing look, mixed with a sneer, which greatly disturbed me. To get rid of the embarrassment I lay under, I endeavored to look full at him in my turn; but, in fixing my eyes against his, I felt the most inexpressible terror, and was obliged soon to turn them away. The speech and physiognomy of the good David is that of an honest man; but where, great God! did this good man borrow those eyes he fixes so sternly and unaccountably on those of his friends?

Just as Rousseau will separate "Jean-Jacques" and "Rousseau" in his *Dialogues* in order to assess the contradiction between reality and appearance, so he distinguishes "le bon David" from "Mr. Hume." Le bon David seems to be a good man, a man renowned for his honor and genius. Yet the real man beneath, Mr. Hume, was betrayed by the unrelenting stare. While in the *Dialogues* reality

and appearance are, in the end, reconciled to prove Jean-Jacques Rousseau's innocence, here the two worlds converge in order to prove David Hume's guilt.

The impression of this look remained with me, and gave me much uneasiness. My trouble increased even to a degree of fainting; and if I had not
been relieved by an effusion of tears, I had been suffocated. Presently after
this I was seized with the most violent remorse; I even despised myself;
until at length, in a transport which I still remember with delight, I sprang
on his neck, embraced him eagerly while almost choked with sobbing, and
bathed in tears, I cried out, in broken accents, No, no, David Hume cannot
be treacherous. If he be not the best of men, he must be the basest of mankind. David Hume politely returned my embraces, and, gently, tapping me
on the back, repeated several times, in a good-natured and easy tone, Why,
my dear Sir! Nay, my dear Sir! Oh, my dear Sir! He said nothing more. I
felt my heart contract. We went to bed; and I set out the next day for the
country.

As this tortured passage reveals, a Rashomon-like moment confronted Hume.
On the one hand, this was the very same scene that, as he already told Hugh
Blair, had moved him so deeply. The Scot had experienced a kind of catharsis,
feeling both embarrassment and great satisfaction for having wept like a child.
Yet Hume now discovered that Rousseau had felt only anguish and dissatisfaction. Hume's effusions were, to Rousseau's whippetlike sensibilities, little more
than polite embraces and comforting platitudes. It was not life—at least as
Rousseau understood life—but mere playacting. Indeed, for Rousseau, the con-
gruence of Hume's words and actions on this occasion was strikingly similar to
his sorry performance in the parlor game as reported by Rousseau's friend
turned enemy, Madame d'Épinay: when asked to emote with the eloquence of a
Garrick, poor Hume could only stammer, "Well, young ladies; well, there you
are, then!"

The difference, of course, was that for Madame d'Épinay, Hume had not
even bothered to act, while, for Rousseau, the Scot had indeed tried, to his ever-
lasting discredit. Hume was upset less by the critique of his poor acting than by
the attack on his integrity. "This is a fourth lie, the most studied and most pre-
meditated of the whole," he jabbed in the margins.[29]

Hume sensed that Rousseau was preparing this particular scene to serve as
the crux of his case against him. "This entire dialogue in this scene is artificially
constructed in order to prepare and serve as the foundation for a portion of the
tissue of fables in this letter," Hume wrote in his margins. Moreover, he also
feared that Rousseau's apology for suspecting him was not an apology at all: instead, it was a challenge, indeed a trap: "*If he is not the best of men, he would have*

to be the blackest." Given the impossibly high bar set by Rousseau, blackness seemed to beckon to Hume.

Rousseau explains that once he arrived at Wootton, his agony deepened over his patron's character. "But what repose can be tasted in life when the heart is agitated? Afflicted with the most cruel uncertainty, and ignorant what to think of a man whom I ought to love and esteem, I endeavored to get rid of that fatal doubt, in placing confidence in my benefactor." Granted, he allowed, none of these minor circumstances was in itself damning, but their accumulation was, to say the least, surprising. And while Hume could have explained these facts, he chose not to do so. Rousseau thus had no choice but to question Hume's true character. "I wrote him a letter, which he ought to have found very natural, if he were guilty; but very extraordinary, if he were innocent. For what could be more extraordinary than a letter full of gratitude for his services and at the same time of distrust of his sentiments; and in which, placing in a manner his actions on one side, and his sentiments on the other, instead of speaking of the proofs of friendship he had given me, I desired him to love me for the good he had done me!" Although he had not kept a copy of this letter, Rousseau dared Hume to produce the original, stating, "and whoever shall read it, and see therein a man laboring under a secret trouble, which he is desirous of expressing, and is afraid to do it." But what was the effect of the letter on Hume? "None, absolutely none at all."

Hume had failed Rousseau's test—that the Scot had taken it unawares hardly mattered. "I was more struck with his silence than I had been with his phlegm during our last conversation," Rousseau explained. "In this I was wrong; this silence [in response to his letter] was very natural after the other, and was no more than I ought to have expected. For when one hath ventured to declare to a man's face, *I am tempted to believe you are a traitor,* and he hath not had the curiosity to ask for what, it may be depended on he will never have any such curiosity as long as he lives, and it is easy to judge of him from these slight indications."

Attempting to make sense of Rousseau's account, Hume went back to the letter of March 22. When Rousseau confided from Wootton that Hume could not "see all the charms I find here: it would be necessary to know the place and to read my heart," had Hume somehow missed a deeper meaning to these seemingly reassuring words? It was as if the passages Rousseau now referred to were written in ink visible only to the pure at heart. Could that, in fact, have been the intent of the otherwise banal remark that Hume "should be able to read at least those sentiments that regard you, which you have so well merited"? True, the letter ends with a reference to the incident of the hired coach, for which Hume had begged Rousseau's forgiveness, but his accuser does not even mention this sad event as either the cause of his strange behavior on their last evening together or of his suspicions against him. Instead, Rousseau's letter glows with "cordiality." Hume again struck at the margin: "A Fifth Lie: See the letter itself." And as for Rousseau's query as to why Hume didn't have the curiosity to ask why Rousseau thought him a traitor, "A repetition of the fourth lie, and consequently equivalent to a sixth."[30]

Rousseau's suspicions had metastasized. The publication of the pretended letter of the King of Prussia, in which Rousseau thought he saw d'Alembert's hand, finally opened his eyes. "In a moment a ray of light discovered to me the secret cause of that touching and sudden change, which I had observed in the public respecting me; and I saw the plot which was put in execution at London, had been laid in Paris." The pieces now began to fall together: not only was the cunning d'Alembert close to Hume, but Rousseau then recalled "four terrifying words Mr. Hume made use of." But do not bother looking for them just yet, Rousseau warns: he would save them for the letter's climax, where he would fully reveal the depths of Hume's treachery.

And why shouldn't Hume be subjected to such suspense? What did he say or do, after all, when the scurrilous letter in Frederick's name was published? Nothing: the man who had promised the persecuted philosopher his friendship and protection said nothing and wrote nothing. As a result, Rousseau had himself been obliged to write to the newspaper's editor. Had he any other choice? Like his father, Isaac, so many years before, Jean-Jacques resorted to the language of the duel: this implicit challenge to Hume's integrity was the "first slap on my patron's cheek." But Hume rebuffed the challenge by refusing to reply. "He feels nothing," Rousseau inferred from the Scot's failure to respond to the slap.

Rousseau nevertheless persisted. He declared that the "impostor had got his accomplices in England; I expressed myself very clearly to their friend," that is, Hume, "who was in London, and was desirous of passing for mine." In a word, he all but accused Hume, who again was silent. "This was the second slap of the face I gave my patron. He did not feel, however, not yet."

Then there quickly followed the libelous pamphlet written against him by Voltaire, which was quickly translated into English—hardly a coincidence, Rousseau notes. "I made not the least doubt that my dear patron was one of the instruments of its publication." True, Hume was not cited in the pamphlet, but the omission is even more damning. "Mr. Hume was not mentioned; but he lives and converses with people that are mentioned. It is well known his friends are all my enemies": Tronchin, d'Alembert, Voltaire, and all those in England whom Hume had managed to turn against him. "Let anyone discover the clue that has been unraveled since my arrival in London, and it will easily be seen whether Mr. Hume does not hold the principal thread."

The long and painful affair of the pension now came to a head as well. The royal offer having arrived, Rousseau declares that he could not accept a gift obtained through the good offices of this traitor. "This, I must confess, was one of the critical moments of my life. How much did it cost me to do my duty!" Despite the awkward position in which he now found himself, returning a pension he had already in principle accepted, Rousseau did not hesitate to act as a man of honor. "I did my duty, though not without reluctance." He wrote to General Conway, explained his moral predicament as well as he could, and turned down the offer. Yet he refused to mention Hume's name in the letter, much less write to him—an omission Rousseau thought Hume should have seen: "This was the third slap of the face I gave my patron, which is his own fault if he does not feel, he can feel nothing."

Along with every other gesture on Hume's part, Rousseau now saw the pension as bait. "What was his design in it? Nothing is clearer. It was to raise my resentment to the highest pitch that he might strike the blow he was preparing to give me with greater effect. He knew he had nothing more to do than put me in a passion, and I should be guilty of a number of absurdities. We are now arrived at the critical moment which is to show whether he reasoned well or poorly." Having put Rousseau in a position where he had to refuse the pension yet not explain why, Hume next prevailed upon Conway to remove the condition of secrecy, knowing full well that the prickly exile would not accept a public offer. "This was the decisive moment, the end and object of all his labors."

Like a detective admiring the crimes he unravels, Rousseau congratulated the perpetrator: "That last stroke was a masterpiece." He invited Hume to observe how well he, Hume, had arranged everything. If Hume were ignorant of his suspicions, which Rousseau thinks impossible, then all these coincidences were only that, coincidences. Moreover, by refusing to acknowledge Rousseau's suspicions, Hume could claim to be unaware of them.

A man of so enlightened an understanding, of so penetrating a genius by nature, and so dull by design, should see nothing, hear nothing, feel nothing, be moved by nothing; but, without one word of complaint, justification, or explanation, continue to give me the most pressing marks of his goodwill to serve me, in spite of myself. He wrote to me affectionately, that he could not stay longer in London to do me service, as if we had agreed that he should stay there for that purpose! This blindness, this insensibility, this perseverance, are not in his nature; they must be accounted for, therefore, from other motives.

Thus it all comes down to what Rousseau said to Hume that last night in order to test him: "Mr. Hume must necessarily have acted in this affair either as one of greatest or the lowest of men. There is no mean position. It remains to be determined which of the two he is."

Even though it twisted everything he knew to be true and real, the sweep of Rousseau's narrative impressed Hume. It carried the reader from curiosity to doubt, wonderment to awe, climaxing in a peculiar sort of sublimity when its author returned to those four terrifying words, the words whose recollection finally illuminated what had hitherto been obscure. "The critical condition to which he had now reduced me recalled strongly to my mind the four words I mentioned above," Rousseau announced, "and which I heard him say and repeat at a time when I did not comprehend their full force." Only now could he decipher the clues that were lying before his eyes the whole time. Just as the unexceptional question posed by the Academy of Dijon had sparked Rousseau's revelation so many years before, now it was the apparently banal utterance made by Hume that, in a white flash of intuition, made manifest what had hitherto been concealed.

This time, however, the great event occurred on the road to London rather than that to Vincennes, more specifically, at the inn at Senlis. "It was the first night after our departure from Paris. We slept in the same bedchamber, and several times during the night I heard him cry out in French with great vehemence: *Je tiens J.J. Rousseau.* 'I have you, Rousseau.' I do not know whether he was awake or asleep." Rousseau could not recall those words without shuddering. Hume may well have shuddered, too, but for very different reasons. As he jotted in the margin, if Rousseau did not know whether he was awake or asleep when he pronounced those terrible words, how could he be certain that he himself was awake or asleep when he had heard them?*

Hume's question neatly captured the Alice in Wonderland quality to Rousseau's interpretation of their friendship. While the letters "edited" by Rousseau in *Julie* convinced his readers that this fictional world and characters truly existed, his letter to Hume tried to persuade the reader that the factual world and its inhabitants did not exist, at least not in the way they were perceived by others. The reality behind our everyday lives, Rousseau claimed, was very different. Hence his shudder in recalling Hume's terrible gaze that mirrored the sinister intent of those four words.

These words, the tone of which dwells on my heart, as if I had but just heard them; those long and fatal looks so frequently cast on me; the patting me on the back, with the repetition of *O, my dear Sir,* in answer to my

---

*If only Hume had known the story of one of Rousseau's botanizing trips a few years earlier. Along with several friends, Rousseau made an excursion to Mont Chasseron and spent the night in a peasant's barn. In the morning, the philosopher was asked whether he had slept well, to which he replied, "As for me, I never sleep," whereupon an exasperated companion blurted out, "Good God, Monsieur Rousseau, you amaze me. I heard you snoring all night—it is I who never slept!" (Maurice Cranston, *The Solitary Self: Jean-Jacques Rousseau in Exile and Adversity* [Chicago: University of Chicago Press, 1997], 89–90).

suspicions of his being a traitor: all this affects me to such a degree after what preceded, that this recollection, had I no other, would be sufficient to prevent any reconciliation or return of confidence between us: not a night indeed passes over my head, but I think I hear, *Rousseau, I have you,* ring in my ears as if he had just pronounced them.

Hume exploded upon reading this passage: "Without scruple, I may set down this as the twelfth lie, and a swinging one it is." He then carefully noted that "this letter was sealed with Mr. Rousseau's usual motto, *Vitam impendere vero*—'Dedicate life to truth.' Did ever anybody yet know a pretender to superior virtue that had common honesty?"[31] The two men had reached an odd impasse: Hume, the skeptic, now insisted upon the commonsensical, the facts of the matter, while Rousseau defended a certain relation of ideas. The rub was that the validity of this particular relation of ideas went no further than Rousseau's mind. He was in the throes not of an epiphany but an apophany: his world was infused with immense but mysterious significance, while the most commonplace of gestures, words, or acts were endowed with tremendous, yet elusive meaning.[32]

"Yes, Mr. Hume, I know you *have me*," Rousseau concludes in exalted defeat, as if he had been kidnapped rather than escorted into glorious exile that night at Senlis. Hume's caper, however, had ensnared the "mere externals" of Rousseau's worldly standing, even his physical self. But the Scot's ability to affect Rousseau's "reputation, and perhaps my security," could never touch his actual innocence. The sensible part of mankind will "perceive that nothing but my invincible aversion to all kinds of falsehood . . . could have prevented my dissimulation at a time when it was on so many accounts my interest."

From the letter's eloquence and careful organization, Hume surmised that Rousseau was preparing his case for public opinion. Indeed, he himself couldn't help admiring the production. "But would you believe it," he wrote to a French correspondent, "that in a piece so full of frenzy, malice, and impertinence and lies, there are many strokes of genius and eloquence; and the conclusion of it is remarkably sublime."[33] How could Rousseau *not* publish, having represented this affair as but one more instance of the world's injustice? How could he not have lamented, with the practiced sigh of someone who, as Walpole's squib claimed, was making a career out of imagined persecution, that "the sensible part of mankind are few nor do they make the greatest noise in the world"?

As it would soon become clear, the *sensible* part of mankind—as opposed to those committed to *sense*—were the many, not the few, and they would rally not to Hume but to the man who served as their intellectual midwife, Rousseau. Rousseau in fact anticipated this turn of events at the end of his letter, where he once again foreshadowed the logic of the *Dialogues*. He presents himself as *le pauvre Jean-Jacques,* the innocent Jean-Jacques, who condemned by appearances, abandons hope for proving his innocence and virtue to his contemporaries and instead dedicates his life to truth in his very solitude. "Every circumstance of the affair is equally incomprehensible," Rousseau despairs. "On each side there is a bottomless abyss! And I am lost on either one side or the other: I am the unhappiest of mankind if you are guilty, I am the most vile if you are innocent."

Jean-Jacques was once again innocent, yet found guilty. In closing, he offers Hume a choice that parallels the one he had presented to Hume on the last evening they spent together. "If you are guilty, do not write me any longer. . . . If you are innocent, dare to justify yourself. . . . Once again, if you are innocent, dare to justify yourself; if you are not, good-bye forever." Yet the court to which the accused had to present his case was Rousseau's heart, which already knew the verdict.

Hume sensed the futility of finding a reply that would satisfy both Rousseau and reality. On July 22, in what would be his last letter to his former "pupil," Hume explained that he would answer only one article of the accusation: his version of their final conversation that fatal evening before his departure.

And so Hume once again retold the story of his guest's reaction to Davenport's "good natured artifice" regarding the chaise. "You entertained, however, suspicions of his design, while we were sitting alone by my fireside; and you reproached me with concurring in it. I endeavored to pacify you and divert the discourse; but to no purpose. You sat sullen and either [were] silent or made me very peevish answers. At last, you rose up, and took a turn or two about the room; when, all of a sudden and to my great surprise, you clapped yourself on my knee, threw your arms about my neck, kissed me with seeming ardor, and bedewed my face with tears."[34]

Their stories coincide up to this point, but then Hume offered his own account of what was said during this contested scene: "You exclaimed, 'My Dear Friend, can you ever pardon this folly? After all the pains you have taken to serve me, after the numberless instances of friendship you have given me, here I reward you with this ill-humor and sullenness. But your forgiveness of me will be a new instance of your friendship and I hope you will find at bottom that my heart is not unworthy of me.'" Hume's account does not repeat Rousseau's cri de coeur: that David Hume is either the best or blackest of men. Instead, Hume simply reminded his accuser how much this moment touched him. "I own, that I was very much affected; and I believe there passed a very tender scene between us."[35]

Having outlined the supposed facts of the case, Hume then took a page from his discussion of the existence of miracles in the *Enquiry,* the quality of testimo-

nial evidence. "This incident, Sir, was somewhat remarkable," Hume lectured
Rousseau, "and it is impossible, that either you or I could so soon have forgot it."
So memorable, in fact, that only one of the versions—"so different or rather so
opposite"—can be true. As a result, one of them had to be a liar. Having challenged Rousseau's honesty, Hume warned him against counting on the fact that
the scene passed privately between them, with no witnesses. Do not go down
that path, Hume threatened, for he had immediately related the story in letters to
Davenport, Boufflers, and others—all of whom, as either friends or admirers of
Rousseau, would never conspire to blacken his name.[36]

Just as in his demolition of miracles, Hume turned to experience as the most
compelling reason to dismiss Rousseau's account. "The story, as I tell it, is consistent and rational. There is not common sense in your account." As for his infamous stare, Hume would have none of it: "What! Because sometimes, when
absent in thought, I have a fixed look or stare, you suspect me to be a traitor, and
you have the assurance to tell me of such black and ridiculous suspicions! Are not
most studious men (and many of them more than I) subject to like reveries of fits
of absence, without being exposed to such suspicions?"[37]

At the end of the letter, Hume wistfully reminded his friend of all he had
done for him: "I had, beyond my most sanguine expectations, provided for your
repose, honor, and fortune." Regretting that Rousseau had nevertheless turned
against him, Hume ended their correspondence and friendship: "Adieu, and
forever."[38]

Between Hume's and Rousseau's accounts lies the same immense distance, as
Gilbert Ryle once observed, as between a blink and wink, an involuntary twitch
and a deliberate sign.[39] While Hume presents his tale on the public stage of history, Rousseau unfolds his story on the private stage of the heart. Rousseau's
rendition of the evening hinged not upon testimony or documents but on the
meaning of a stare. He was able to interpret the tabula rasa of Hume's blank face
because he knew not only his own heart but Hume's as well. Rousseau's intense
sensibility collapsed the bulwarks between his own self and others. By providing the history of his own heart's movements, Rousseau heard the beating of
other hearts as well.

On the other hand, Hume stood firm against this flood of subjectivity. Conscious of the limits of our ability to understand one another and ourselves, to see
beyond what is available to the careful sifting of sensory experience, Hume insisted upon the commonsense explanation of experience. As if anticipating his
encounter with Rousseau, he had declared in his *Enquiry Concerning Human
Understanding* that the human imagination is "naturally sublime, delighted with
whatever is remote and extraordinary." Fortunately, he continued, we are also

endowed with correct judgment, which helps us avoid "all distant and high enquiries [and] confines itself to common life, and to such subjects as fall under daily practice and experience."[40]

Neither man was able, in the end, to credit the other's account of understanding and self-understanding. For Rousseau, the highest good was sincerity: it guaranteed the self's integrity and girded our existence.[41] Ever since his experience on the road to Vincennes, Rousseau had condemned the reign of appearance and hypocrisy over our lives. Given his diagnosis of contemporary society, the cure could not be, as we have seen, the cultivation of reason. Instead, we had to cultivate the sentiment of existence. Not that of others, but of our own selves—sensing one's own existence in one's own self, rather than shifting this sense of being to others. This, and not reason, is the foundation of our natural lives as self-sufficient and independent beings. "To exist," the Savoyard Vicar of Rousseau's *Emile* declares, "is to sense; our sensibility is incontestably anterior to our intelligence, and we had sentiments before ideas."[42]

The consequences of this stance were revolutionary. From the ancient Greeks to Rousseau's fellow philosophes, reason was considered the means to achieve *eudaemonia*—the happy or flourishing life. Just as Hume did, but to very different ends, Rousseau demoted reason and, in its stead, proposed the ideal of honesty or integrity. Rather than adherence to external or objective truth, it instead meant loyalty to one's own self.[43] In contradistinction to the Copernican Revolution, in which we moved from a man-centered to sun-centered conception of the physical universe, Rousseau's revolution turned our moral universe inside out: truth was no longer located outside ourselves, but instead was within our self.

For a thinker who questioned the very existence of the self, Hume could hardly sympathize with, and perhaps not fully appreciate, Rousseau's claim. Yet his stance concerning the self is no less radical than Rousseau's. The Genevan had transformed the self into a celestial tuning fork that vibrates with the sentiment of existence. In the hands of Hume, however, the self becomes a necessary fiction. Just as in his treatment of cause, Hume argued that the notion of the self—the certitude that each of us owns a personal identity—is simply a term of convenience we give to the consistency of dumb experience. Our memories provide the psychological mortar that connects the repetition of perceptions to one another, as well as to the notion of an extended and independent self. Hume asserted, "had we no memory, we never should have any notion of causation, nor consequently of that chain of causes and effects which constitute our self or person."[44] When dealing with so extravagant an individual as Rousseau, Hume might have added, even our memories provide meager material for understanding causes and effects.

An Enlightenment Tragedy

The league that has formed against me is too powerful, too skillful,
too ardent, too well-reputed for me in my present position, without any
other aid than the truth, to show my face to the public.
——Rousseau to Pierre Guy

He is at present composing a book, in which it is very likely he may
fall on me with some atrocious lie. I know that he is writing his memoirs,
in which I am sure to make a fine figure.
——Hume to Boufflers

I n the *Treatise,* Hume compares the emotional impact of his skeptical inves-
tigations to having "struck on many shoals . . . having narrowly escaped
shipwreck."[1] That youthful experience was a ship in a mere squall when set
against the shock of Rousseau's behavior. Rousseau's accusations were like great
waves: the first was the accusatory missive of June 23, 1766, followed by the
broadside of the thirteen lies of July 10. What sort of man is this? Were these the

letters of a fiend or a madman? How, or whether, to respond? While Hume pondered the riddle as the summer wore on, however, he found himself pulled irresistibly by the tide of events.

"You will be surprised, dear Doctor, when I desire you most earnestly never in your life to show to any mortal creature the letters I wrote you with regard to Rousseau," Hume wrote Hugh Blair on July 1 after receiving Rousseau's first accusatory letter: "He is surely the blackest and most atrocious villain, beyond comparison, that now exists in the world; and I am heartily ashamed of any thing I ever wrote in his favor."[2]

Embarrassed that he had thoroughly misunderstood his man, Hume remained confident of his innocence in the affair. "My only comfort is that the matter will be so clear as not to leave to any mortal the smallest possibility of doubt. You know how dangerous any controversy on a disputable point would be with a man of his talents."[3] Since the accusations against him were transparently false, he reasoned, the motives for the accusation must be likewise false. In short, Rousseau was lying. Were not his letters to Rousseau discrete and civil? As he told Davenport two days after writing Blair, "It would be of no consequence for me to have copies of them, were he not the most dangerous man in the world, on account of his malice and his talents. I cannot take too many precautions against him."[4]

Even after being surprised by the first, brief letter of accusation in June, Hume had clearly already begun rehearsing his defense. With a historian's reflex, he began gathering his correspondence with Rousseau as evidence for his case and practicing his argument with his own correspondents. "This letter needs no commentary," Hume declares in a note to Boufflers, nonetheless adding his commentary: "I only desire you to remark with what impudence and malice he has perverted that story which I formerly told you, and which I then thought to his advantage. I mean the disgust about the hiring of the chaise." As for the last evening together, which had become the linchpin in the conflicting accounts, Hume copied out his response to Rousseau for Boufflers. He demanded that Rousseau name his accuser, although Hume confesses to Boufflers, "I have, from decency, supposed in my letters to him, that some calumniator has belied me, I know it could not be so." He could only conclude that his was "a deliberate and cool plan to stab me," citing the letter from Davenport written to him at the very same time, reporting that the philosopher "was very cheerful, and gay, and sociable, and enjoyed himself extremely, and was in no distress at all." No answer from Rousseau had arrived, but Hume did not expect one: "It is impossible that he can make me any apology for so black a proceeding."[5]

Hume nonetheless immediately learned that such an apology was far from what he would receive. No sooner had he posted his explanation to Boufflers on the morning of July 15 than Rousseau's second, lengthy letter reached his lodgings that afternoon. After reading Rousseau's own account of their proceedings, Hume reached for his own correspondence tablet and wrote to Blair, d'Alembert, and Davenport, sharing his reaction with all three. As he exclaimed to Davenport, "I received today a letter from Rousseau, which is as long as a two shillings pamphlet; and I fancy he intends to publish it. It is a perfect frenzy. I am really sorry for him."[6]

"Frenzy." As Hume began to wonder about the true motives of his accuser, for a fleeting moment he believed his poor friend to be perfectly mad, predicting that Rousseau would "be shut up altogether in Bedlam."[7] Bedlam and Hume were not strangers. Along with his youthful collision with the "Disease of the Learned," Hume had the opportunity to study insanity at close quarters during his stint, from February 1745 to April 1746, as tutor and "gentleman companion" to the mad Marquess of Annandale, a remunerative but exasperating year. Then, three years later, Hume himself had a spell of delirium during his service with the British embassy to Turin in 1748. Overcome by an unspecified disease, the feverish Scot ranted, according to a witness, "with much seeming perturbation, of the devil, of hell and of damnation." Teased by his friends once he had recovered, who thought a philosophical skeptic should have mastered himself, Hume reprimanded them: "Why you boobies, what would you have a madman? Do you suppose philosophy to be proof against madness? The organization of my brain was impaired, and I was as mad as any man in Bedlam."[8]

For philosophical no less than for personal reasons, Hume always maintained his interest in the subject. In the *Enquiry Concerning Human Understanding*, he uses madness in an argument to prove that liberty is consistent with necessity. "Were a man, whom I know to be honest and opulent, and with whom I live in intimate friendship, to come into my house, where I am surrounded by my servants, I rest assured that he is not to stab me before he leaves it in order to rob me of my silver Standish; and I no more suspect this event than the falling of the house itself, which is new, and solidly built and founded." In short, we have no less confidence in the regularity of behavior in the human realm than we do of events in the natural realm, and our thoughts and passions progress with the same customary movement from cause to effect as do billiard balls rolling along the felt of a table. But when we meet a madman, what are we to think or do about him? *"But he may have been seized with a sudden and unknown frenzy,"* Hume's imaginary interlocutor objects. "So may a sudden earthquake arise, and shake and tumble my house about my ears." Such exceptions, Hume replies, do not disprove the rule of the natural course of events, natural or human. "A man who at noon leaves his purse full of gold on the pavement at Charing Cross may as well expect that it will fly away like a feather as he will find it untouched an hour after."[9] Experience, in other words, has repeatedly shown that the purse will be quickly taken if dropped on the pavement.

Given Rousseau's extreme sensibility, Hume considered that his ward's occasional delirium should not be altogether unexpected. Yet his rage quickly stifled this sympathetic impulse. As he warned Davenport: "I would not, however, have you imagine that he has such an extreme sensibility as he pretends . . . so that these complaints of his misery and sufferings are a mere artifice. I find in many other respects that he lies like the devil. You cannot imagine what a false and malicious account he has the assurance to give me of the transaction between him and me the last evening he was in town, which I related to you."[10]

The break between Hume and Rousseau floored Hugh Blair: one of Hume's oldest friends, he was also a great admirer of Rousseau. "Your letter astonished me beyond measure," Blair replied. "I have bewildered myself in conjectures." Nevertheless, whatever the reasons for the surprising behavior of this "very sad fellow," Blair insisted that Hume must restrain his desire to publish in self-defense. "For God's sake do not be in a haste in publishing any thing about him. Nothing but necessity should oblige you to this," Blair counseled. "You know the ill natured pleasure the world enjoys in a paper war between two persons of such fame and eminence as you and him. Both parties often suffer in such personal contests; and how clear so ever the right on your side, yet envy to you will raise partisans for him."[11]

Hume's other Scottish friends echoed Blair's call for restraint, if not always his charity. Writing from Paris, Adam Smith declared that he was "thoroughly convinced that Rousseau is as great a rascal as you, and as every man here believes him to be." Yet the rascal should simply be ignored. Reminding Hume that publicity would make laughingstocks of all Scots, he advised Hume to treat the letter with the scorn it so richly merited. "Stand this ridicule, expose his brutal letter, but without giving it out of your own hand so that it may never be printed," he advised. He suggested that there was *less* to all of this than met the public eye and asked Hume to step back a bit. "I shall pawn my life," he reassured Hume, "that before three weeks are at an end, this little affair, which at present gives you so much uneasiness, shall be understood to do you as much honor as any thing that has ever happened to you."[12]

Smith would have lost this wager: the "little affair," far from waning, was rapidly waxing. Even before he had received Rousseau's long letter of July 10, Hume had confided his fears to Baron d'Holbach, the very man who had warned Hume a half-year before that he had taken a viper to his breast. Holbach resisted the temptation to tell his friend that he had told him so, instead urging him to remain equal to his public reputation. "Europe expects David Hume to continue his admirable work," he declared. A "literary war" with Rousseau was a decidedly undesirable scenario. Holbach's reasoning, however, is revealing: he worried less over the bruises the two men would inflict on each other than over the decisive role that the public would assume. The public, Holbach told Hume, "is a poor judge of quarrels it is asked to decide; leave such polemical disputes to those who have nothing better to do with their time." Nevertheless, the philosophe ended his letter on an equivocal note: "If you decide to publish despite our advice, contact Monsieur Suard at the office of the *Gazette de France*."[13]

At the same time he was advising Hume to ignore Rousseau's barrage of insults, the baron was busily sharing them with all of their Parisian acquaintances. Having devoured Hume's letter, which included a copy of Rousseau's accusatory letter of June 23 (Hume also later sent Holbach a copy of Rousseau's second letter), the baron plunged it into his pocket and then made a round of salon visits. One of the first people he seems to have run into was Jean-Baptiste-Antoine Suard, the editor of the *Gazette de France*, whom he had recommended to Hume as translator and editor. In her memoirs of her husband, Amélie Suard recalls that she and her spouse were attending Mme Necker's salon when Holbach burst in and announced that he had just received a letter.[14] "You are quite right, Monsieur le Baron, Rousseau is a monster," Hume's lost letter of June 27 is reported to have begun.* And apparently it proceeded in the same fashion, with the usually placid Hume venting his spleen against "the blackest and most atrocious villain that ever disgraced human nature."[15]

The news quickly reached the salon of Julie de Lespinasse, where the reaction was immediate. She wrote in tandem with d'Alembert—Julie penned the first paragraph, then passed the tablet to d'Alembert. Hume's closest French friends shared their shock and dismay at the turn of events. While Julie lamented the futility of Hume's well-intentioned efforts on Rousseau's behalf, d'Alembert could not help but note that Voltaire had been right all along in thinking that Hume courted disaster by befriending Rousseau. Like Holbach, d'Alembert also asked Hume to think twice before going public: "This sort of quarrel serves only to further provoke stubborn fanatics, while providing onlookers the occasion to badmouth men of letters."[16]

No less violent was the response at the Temple. Having learned from Holbach's report of Hume's quarrel with Rousseau, Boufflers wrote to demand why her friend had not first sought her advice. Equally important, she insisted that Hume not only had injured her but was injuring himself: "Your sweetness, your

---

*According to Holbach's reply of July 7, 1766, Hume had written twice: on June 27 and July 1. Neither letter survives.

natural goodness, the indulgence you naturally possess, lead one to expect and to desire from you efforts of moderation that surpass the power of ordinary men. Why, then, did you hasten to divulge the first movements of a grievously wounded heart which reason cannot yet overcome?" She was especially aggrieved to learn (incorrectly, it happened) that Hume had instructed Holbach not merely to tell everyone in Paris about his quarrel with Rousseau, but Voltaire as well. "After this passionate stroke, after all you have said and written to me, the reflections I might communicate to you, the advice I might be able to offer you, would be use-less. You are too confirmed in your own opinion, too engaged, too steadfast in your anger to listen to me."[17]

"Nothing could more rejoice me than the sight of your handwriting after such long silence," Hume replied to Boufflers with awkward gallantry on August 12, declaring that he would "kiss the rod which beats me." He admitted that he did write Holbach first, "without either recommending or expecting secrecy," but claimed that he was surprised by the extent and speed with which news of the feud had spread. "I little imagined, that a private story, told to a private gentle-man, could ever run over a whole kingdom in a moment: if the King of England had declared war against the King of France, it could not have been more sud-denly the subject of conversation." As for his reaction to Rousseau's accusations, Hume insisted that his hand had been forced. Moreover, events had since justified his decision: he then told Boufflers of the "studied oration, or invective, against me, of eighteen folio pages" he had since received from Rousseau. When you see the letter, a copy of which is now in d'Alembert's hands, Hume added, you will "have reason to suspect him an arrant madman."[18]

By then the affair had spun out of everyone's control. In sending a copy of this second letter to d'Alembert, Hume again depicted for the benefit of his French advisers the events of his final evening with Rousseau. Needless to say, Hume had thought that he parted with his "pupil" on the best of terms, and had been reassured by the seemingly warm letter he received from Rousseau after his arrival at Wootton. Indeed, he admitted to d'Alembert, this letter had particu-larly pleased him for it proved wrong "some of my friends in Paris, who had assured me that I would not get to Calais with this man without quarrelling." Sadly, Hume was now forced to confess that d'Alembert, Holbach, and the oth-ers were right after all.[19]

Rousseau's long letter astonished d'Alembert. "My first reaction in reading it was to have admired its rhetoric," d'Alembert replied to Hume. "The second was to have laughed; and to say, while shrugging my shoulders: 'Behold a man who has used the strength of Hercules to snap a wisp of straw.'" But Hume was not entirely innocent, d'Alembert wrote, offering an odd indictment seemingly designed less to blame Hume than to praise himself. "I recall that one day you were speaking while seeming to stare right through me," he reminded Hume, "and I advised you as a friend to rid yourself as much as possible of such a stare, and that it would play a bad trick on you someday. And now, as I foresaw, it has happened."[20]

Having established his prescience, d'Alembert had won Hume's trust. He now exhorted Hume to publish the correspondence. Matters were already too advanced, he announced, and "the public is too occupied by your quarrel." Of course, d'Alembert himself was partly responsible for having "occupied the public." In fact, a good number of the relevant "public" were literally looking over d'Alembert's shoulder as he wrote. Along with Julie de Lespinasse, a war council had gathered at the salon, one that included the physiocrat Anne-Robert-Jacques Turgot, the historian Charles-Pinot Duclos, the Encyclopedist Jean-François Marmontel, and the Abbé André Morellet, whose savage wit on behalf of the philosophes led Voltaire to admiringly nickname him Mords-les—"Bite-'em." Like d'Alembert, they all recommended publication. Julie de Lespinasse's voice floated above the chorus of men: "She does not think, any more than I do or any of your friends, that it suffices to send five or six copies of this history to various people," reported d'Alembert.[21]

Like Holbach, d'Alembert also could not help but share the contents of the letter with his circle of friends. D'Alembert had even taken the liberty to send all the relevant documents to Voltaire, assuring Hume that "this whole history will surely divert him greatly."[22] A tactless remark: whatever his feelings toward Rousseau, the prospect of Voltaire's enjoyment of this turn of events could hardly comfort Hume. But d'Alembert, like Voltaire, was also prompted to act by weightier concerns. Eager for an opportunity to strike back at the dangerous apostate from the church of the Enlightenment, he now had just the weapon with which to do so. While another vitriolic exchange between Rousseau and Voltaire, or Rousseau and Diderot, or even between Rousseau and himself, would not have been surprising, d'Alembert understood that the quarrel with le bon David introduced something new and helpful for the good cause.

Offering sober counsel in face of the advice to rush into print—oddly enough, given his role, even if inadvertent, in provoking the quarrel—was Horace Walpole. Having been informed about d'Alembert's letter by Hume, Walpole replied by return post on the same day with a warning about the men who themselves had once warned the Scot about Rousseau. "Your set of friends are what a set of literary men are apt to be, exceedingly absurd," opined Walpole. "They hold a consistory to consult how to argue with a madman; and they think it necessary for your character to give them the pleasure of seeing Rousseau exposed, not because he has provoked you, but them."[23] In short, the philosophes were using Hume to settle their own scores with Rousseau.

As Hume hesitated amid this contradictory advice, a fissure formed in the Lespinasse coterie. Turgot, who had no particular quarrel with Rousseau and who admired his work, wrote Hume to inform him that he had second thoughts about the wisdom of publishing the correspondence. He confided that he had spoken with Malesherbes, France's chief censor as well as Rousseau's correspondent and sometime protector. Both men agreed that before Hume acted, he must first determine Rousseau's motivation. If it were a matter of "folly" stemming from his unfortunate susceptibility to suspicion, Hume should remain silent out of humanity. If, on the other hand, Rousseau had indeed consciously lied and betrayed him, Hume might be justified in defending himself. In any event, Turgot reminded Hume that his own reputation was safe and advised against taking his case before the unreliable court of public opinion.[24]

At this critical juncture, then, the usually resolute Hume uncharacteristically adopted an indecisive course more reminiscent of Rousseau. Or, more precisely, Hume decided to let others decide. Replying to Turgot's counsel to assess Rousseau's motivations, a frustrated Hume reported: "My friends to whom I have shown the letters of this . . . (I leave you to fill the blank) are also of different sentiments among themselves. All of them allow that there is a strong mixture of frenzy and of wickedness in them; but some maintain, that the former ingredient prevails and some the latter." The furious Scot made clear, perhaps unwittingly, that his mind was in effect already made up: "But on the whole, what epithet could you give to a man like this, when you must allow, that it is safer to take a basilisk or a rattlesnake into your bosom than to have the least intercourse with him?" Far from clasping the asp to his breast, Hume had tossed it away. The matter was out of his hands, Hume announced to Turgot: he had already sent d'Alembert a packet of his correspondence with Rousseau, including his own commentary, sealed with the request that their mutual friend publish it if he saw fit.[25]

While Hume spent the summer of 1766 sending letters to seek advice in this unexpected affair and reluctantly pondering publication, Rousseau was receiving letters demanding an explanation for his accusations. "Mr. Hume has sent me, Sir, the outrageous letter you wrote him," wrote the Comtesse de Boufflers in late July. "I have never seen one like this. All your friends are in consternation and reduced to silence. Eh, what can be said on your behalf, Sir, after a letter so little worthy of your plume?" Clearly, very little, as she immediately made clear: "You raise yourself up against all reason, you who have rejected the evidence itself, and deny the testimony of your very senses. Mr. Hume a dishonorable man? A traitor? Great God!"[26]

Holding fast to his version of events, Rousseau was in no mood for Bouffluers's scolding. "One thing in the letter you have had the honor to write me, Madame, brings me great pleasure," replied Rousseau mordantly, "which is to learn from your tone that you are in good health." In contrast to the contrite Hume, Rousseau would have none of his patroness's words of chastisement. "You say, Madame, that you have never seen a letter like the one I wrote Mr. Hume: that may be so, for I myself have never seen one like the one that gave rise to it. This letter at least does not resemble the ones Mr. Hume writes, and I hope never to write any that resemble them." Rousseau then turned to the subject that lay at the heart of his dispute with Hume and, more broadly, his age: the status of truth and human understanding. How could Boufflers, he asked, accuse him of reject- ing the evidence and denying the testimony of his senses? This is what she would have him do, for he only knows what he has sensed, what he has experienced, what he has felt. "The decision I have made to moan very softly and to remain silent is the result of the respect I owe to myself."[27]

Predictably, however, Rousseau was all too vocal in his vows of silence. "M. Hume is a man unmasked," he declared at the beginning of August to his Parisian publisher Pierre Guy. While the guilty party has been flushed into plain view, paradoxically it is Rousseau himself who has been trapped. "The league that has formed against me is too powerful, too skillful, too ardent, too well- reputed for me in my present position, without any other aid than the truth, to show my face to the public. To cut off the heads of this hydra would only serve to multiply them, and I would destroy one of their calumnies only to have twenty others still more cruel immediately succeed them," Rousseau wrote, al- luding for perhaps the first time to the "universal plot" against him that would increasingly consume his later writings. "What remains for me to do is to stand firm in my resolution regarding the public's judgments, to keep quiet, and to try at least to live and die in peace." His peroration completed, Rousseau asked Guy to show the letter to his friends in order to reassure them of his stoic resolve in the face of the "league" against him and of his resolve to remain silent, espe- cially in the event of Hume's publication of their correspondence.[28]

Ironically, the tragedy was set into motion by Rousseau's very resolution of silence, for while the philosopher kept his vow, never publishing a word about their quarrel, Hume and everyone else took his pronouncement as a declaration of hostilities.* Hume was particularly apprehensive about Rousseau's work on his memoirs. "He is at present composing a book, in which it is very likely he may fall on me with some atrocious lie," he worried to Boufflers. "I know that he is writing his memoirs, in which I am sure to make a fine figure."[29] As Hume

---

*Rousseau did briefly allude to his quarrel with Hume in his *Dialogues* when discussing Ram- say's portrait of him, but he never published that work.

explained to Davenport, either the *Confessions* would be published after his own death, in which case "there would be no body to tell the story or to vindicate my memory," or they would be published after Rousseau's death, in which case "my apology, being wrote against a dead man, would lose much of its authenticity." After apprising Davenport that he had collected and collated his correspondence with Rousseau, giving one copy to Lord Hertford and putting another "in a sure hand at Paris," Hume closed his letter by regretting the whole affair and lamenting Rousseau's fate: "Unhappy Man!"[30]

The news of Rousseau's letter to his publisher guaranteed the tragedy. Though unread, its mere existence was taken by one and all as a sign that the exiled philosopher himself proposed to go into print. On September 1 Holbach wrote Hume to inform him that he had once again changed his mind about publication. Rousseau's letter to Guy required a public response, he proclaimed, and a justification was even necessary, "given the great number of partisans and even of fanatics that your adversary has throughout Europe and above all here."[31] From across the Channel, Hume agreed with Holbach's assessment and reluctantly allowed the correspondence to be published. "I found myself obliged to make the rupture public, in order to prevent the effects of his malice against me," he wrote to Davenport after finally making his decision, ruefully commenting: "I am sorry, that that affair has made so great a noise all over Europe."[32]

"My friends at Paris have thought it absolutely necessary to publish an account which I sent them of my transactions with Rousseau, together with the original papers."[33] Writing this to his publisher William Strahan, with whom he had begun arranging an English edition of the account, Hume thus shifts the onus of the decision to his Parisian supporters. Hume was following this strategy in all of the letters of this period explaining his conduct. For example, in a letter to Horace Walpole in late November, Hume wrote: "I readily agree with you, my dear Sir, that it is a great misfortune to be reduced to the necessity of consenting to this publication. . . . But I hope it will be considered that the publication is not, properly speaking, my deed, but that of my friends, in consequence of a discretionary power which I gave them."[34] While technically accurate, Hume's account begs the question of his motives and responsibility in the affair. As soon as the angry Scot elected to share Rousseau's letters with his friends in Paris, he found himself caught in the fog of literary war.

Hume's "transactions" with Rousseau were in the form of letters, preserved in the published account, which concludes with a justification for having been obliged "to give it to the public."[35] This collection of letters, conveyed to Holbach and d'Alembert, also contained an accompanying narrative that connects the letters and provides commentary. When Hume decided to share the Rousseau correspondence with others, he engaged in a rapidly evolving epistolary commerce that blurred the line between public and private. It was a form of commerce that Hume himself may not have fully understood.

When Hume guiltily voiced surprise to Boufflers that "a private story, told to a private gentleman" could spread so far so fast, he revealed two critical elements to the nature of the controversy: the rapid pace of publicity in the Republic of Letters and his own unfamiliarity with this very phenomenon. Hume's letters to Holbach and d'Alembert were almost immediately shared with the city's *gens des lettres* and quickly became the stuff of conversation. The end of the affair delighted some observers. Mme du Deffand, who had always scorned Rousseau, finding him to be a fool and a phony, could scarcely muster more respect for the "peasant," her cruel nickname for Hume.[36] In other drawing rooms, it caused consternation. Mme de Meinières, having learned the contents of the letters to Holbach, wrote Hume to condemn Rousseau's capricious and vain behavior. But she also added that the "public" expected that le bon David "would react only to a real crime, and otherwise ignore such flawed, odd, and ridiculous behavior."[37]

To what extent, however, did Hume consider his letters "public"? As Hume told Boufflers, he had written to the baron "without either recommending or expecting secrecy," yet he also characterized their content as "a private story, told to a private gentleman."[38] That he repeated this characterization to Horace Walpole— "a private letter, which I wrote somewhat thoughtlessly to a private gentleman at Paris"—suggests that Hume realized that he had acted with less deliberation than he perhaps should have in the initial heat of passion.[39] We can probably safely assume that his lost letter to Holbach contained a similar statement to the one Hume sent to d'Alembert: "Please consult our common friends" about the possibility of publication, he implores, adding: "Since the detailed account I have just given you is the only one I have sent to Paris, I would not be at all angry if all my friends were acquainted with it."[40]

To our modern sensibilities, Hume's remarks sound like someone speaking out of school, making public what is intended to be private.[41] In the eighteenth-century Republic of Letters, however, correspondence was fundamentally an extension of conversation: letters were seen and shared in salons and were considered public documents unless a correspondent explicitly asked that one not be shown to others. As Dena Goodman notes, the salon "was the distribution point, the nexus of intellectual exchange."[42] Hume may not have fully mastered the modus operandi of the Parisian world he admired but in which he remained a tourist. When he asked d'Alembert to share the correspondence with their "common friends," he may, in fact, have been trying to restrict the circulation of the letters to the intimate circle whose advice he was soliciting.

The repeated use of the term *public* by Hume's friends over the possible dangers of publication reflects the Republic of Letters' preoccupation with marketing. Despite its abstract connotation, public opinion was becoming a social and political reality in France by the 1760s, while it was already well established in Great Britain. It was, in the words of Turgot's nemesis, the Swiss banker Jacques Necker, the "spirit of society, this constant communication among men." The informed opinion of men and women, acting as citizens of the Republic of Letters, challenged and ultimately displaced the royal court as the arbiter of ideas and ethics. Variously called the court, tribunal, or judge of truth by Voltaire and his contemporaries, public opinion was portrayed as a "political force that was peaceful, universal, objective, and rational."[43] Near the end of his life, Rousseau himself noted the emergence of this phenomenon: "Among the features that distinguish the century in which we are living from others is the methodical and serious spirit that has shaped public opinion for the past twenty years."[44] Here, as in so many other respects, Rousseau served as both creator and critic of the future. Thanks to his entwining of reality and literature, especially through the letters that compose his novel *Julie*, Rousseau revolutionized the reader's relationship with books. Just as life and literature were largely inseparable for Rousseau, he made this the case for his readers as well. As Robert Darnton observes, Rousseau "threw himself into his works and expected the reader to do the same." The "new rhetorical situation" introduced by Rousseau had dramatic consequences for the character of his public quarrel with Hume.[45]

Dimly aware of the way in which the "public" was in danger of being hijacked by Rousseau, time and again Hume's French correspondents reminded him of their worries over the largely untested powers of that newfangled thing, public opinion, or what d'Alembert called the "beast." Telling Hume that all of Paris was speaking about nothing else, Meinières shared her concern over "the unrest in the republic of letters." The "most enlightened people in Europe" had stooped to "exchanging blows with fools and tearing themselves apart with scandal."[46] Holbach initially shared this fear, warning Hume that such a confrontation hardly "suits a sage like you who was made to enlighten the world rather than amuse it with pointless quarrels."[47]

In the end, d'Alembert ultimately advised Hume to publish the correspondence because the news was already too widely known. For better or worse—and some correspondents feared the latter—the *querelle* had already become an *affaire*. There was already "so much noise," d'Alembert reported, that Hume had no choice but to respond. Indeed, Hume was urged not to tarry. Given the growing intensity of the public's interest, the best defense was a rapid, clear but moderate offense: present all the relevant facts and documents and assume a calm tone. "This is what we think," declared d'Alembert, "and, it seems to me, all *gens des lettres* and reasonable people think as well."[48]

To Hume, the opinion of this world was not at all a matter of indifference. On the contrary, he dreaded the consequences the affair would have on his reputation, particularly in France. He had spent a lifetime piecing together his philosophic persona, he had been embraced across the Channel as le bon David, and he had striven to remain above the critical ruckus that invariably followed his books. Yet now, nearly overnight, his public personality threatened to collapse in a pile of bitter recriminations and baseless accusations. As he told one of his French translators, Jean-Charles Trudaine de Montigny, it was not a question of defending his writings: he had always let his books speak for themselves. No, this was a different matter altogether: "Imputations are here thrown on my morals and my conduct; and though my case is so clear as not to admit of the least controversy, yet it is only clear to those who know it, and I am uncertain how far the public in Paris are in the case."[49] Hume repeated this concern to Turgot: "I would not have any secret in this whole affair. It concerns too much my character to have it buried in darkness."[50]

Hume's preoccupation with Rousseau's intentions did not simply reflect wounded vanity. It also came from his conception of man as a social being: all that we value in others, and in turn value within each of us, is social. Hume insisted that experience, and thus our values and sense of self, rise from the deep well of common life. To deny this axiom of human nature — to stake out, as did Rousseau, a heroic pose that denied the lifesaving purchase of custom — was foolhardy. And so, if he had to be a fool, "as all those who reason or believe anything certainly are," Hume had once observed, "my follies shall at least be natural and agreeable."[51] To Hume's mind, Rousseau's folly was anything but natural and agreeable. Rather, it seemed to be the result of a perverse desire to stand apart from the world. Hume struggled to plumb the origins of Rousseau's antics. He repeatedly portrayed the Genevan as either malicious or mad, or both. In fact, the two qualities were closely related in his eyes: "It is by means of his madness that his other bad qualities appear in their full light, and perhaps become more dangerous on that account."[52]

Hume's conviction that Rousseau swung between these two unhappy and unhealthy poles rendered nearly inevitable the publication of the correspondence and commentary. Though a careful thinker and a steady diplomat, Hume nevertheless had helped create his own difficult situation. By having amassed so great a force, rallied so emotional a following, warned so often that his nemesis was a lunatic and scoundrel, Hume helped realize the outcome he most feared.

CHAPTER TWELVE

So Great a Noise

Opinion governs the world, but it is the wise
who ultimately govern opinion.
— *Voltaire*

After months of hesitation on Hume's part and the solicitous stewardship
of the friends in Paris who had urged him to publication, the *Exposé suc-*
cinct de la contestation qui s'est élevée entre M. Hume et M. Rousseau avec
les pieces justificatives reached the Paris booksellers on the afternoon of October
21, 1766.[1] The collection of Rousseau's and Hume's correspondence with accompanying commentary was rapidly (and poorly) translated a month later in
England as *A Concise and Genuine Account of the Dispute Between Mr. Hume and*
Mr. Rousseau.

The danger of appealing to an audience fashioned in large part by Rousseau
was acknowledged, if only implicitly, in the affirmation of authenticity in the
English title: not only was the account concise, it was genuine. In a world awash
in epistolary novels masquerading as reality, the English translator emphasized

that this was a collection of letters that was quite real. The editor of the French edition, Jean-Baptiste-Antoine Suard, shared the same fear. Worried that the reader might be unable to tell a book from its cover, he wrote an introduction that appealed directly to common sense and objective truth. By "offering to the public the genuine pieces of his trial," the editor claimed that truth was in his client's corner. For any reader who wished to examine the evidence, he added that the original letters would be deposited with the British Museum.* All Rousseau could ever produce in reply, the editor added, were "suppositions, misconstructions, inferences, and new declamations." What chance did these rhetorical "phantoms" have to be believed, Suard concluded, by men "of sense and probity"?[2] He protested too much: the shifting status of sense and sensibility was beyond his control. As became quickly apparent, while truth may be one, interpretations are many.

Though still in his early thirties, Suard had already made himself indispensable in the Republic of Letters. A translator, essayist, and editor of the official *Gazette de France* and quasi-official *Gazette littéraire de France*, Suard made up for his lack of originality and creativity with ambition, energy, and polished manners. He represented both the bright and dark sides of the High Enlightenment: the broad acceptance of its ideals along with the institutionalization and ossification of its spirit.[3] A cohort of insiders and bureaucrats was replacing Voltaire's generation of free spirits and radical thinkers. Enlightenment Paris was now represented by men like Suard—individuals more adept at playing the game than at reinventing the rules. For better and for worse, he was the right man for the job.

Suard quickly translated and edited the papers and letters sent to him by Hume and effortlessly saw the manuscript through the press. He first wrote Hume two weeks after the *Exposé succinct* appeared, assuring him: "Your cause seemed to me to be that of all honest men and above all that of the friends of philosophy."[4] In his reply, Hume thanked Suard for his editorial skill and tact, particularly in the softening of some of his expressions, and again sought to explain himself: "My paper, indeed, was not wrote for the public eye; and nothing but a train of unforeseen accidents could have engaged me to give it to the press." Having established his innocence, then, Hume resolved to "keep an absolute silence for the rest of my life." He would do so even if, as he fully expected, Rousseau replied. Indeed, he reckoned that the case was closed: "Could I look on Rousseau as one of the classics of your language, I should imagine that this story, silly as it is, might go to posterity, and interest them as much as it has done

---

*As it turned out, the museum refused the letters and they were ultimately placed with the Royal Society in Edinburgh.

our contemporaries. But really his writings are so full of extravagance that I cannot believe their eloquence alone will be able to support them."[5]

By emphasizing in his editorial preface the unassailable quality of the evidence in the eyes of all men "of sense and probity," Suard was appealing to an enlightened audience, a readership that shared the epistemological values of the Republic of Letters. And this particular audience largely reacted as anticipated, hardly surprising since its leading members had already served as Hume's initial audience for gauging the proper response to the drama Rousseau had initiated.

The skeletal genius presiding over this world, Voltaire, closely followed from Ferney the unraveling of the friendship. Just as he promised to the chagrined Hume, d'Alembert had written Voltaire in mid-July to apprise him of the quarrel between the two philosophers. "How many stupid things all the enemies of reason and of letters are going to say about this matter!" d'Alembert predicted.[6] Voltaire let fly a flurry of letters pronouncing sentence on Rousseau as "a vile calumniator." "He is more guilty than anyone toward philosophy; others have persecuted it, but he has profaned it."[7] Not content to take the high road of defending philosophy, Voltaire chose to vilify Rousseau in the pettiest manner, warming up an old rumor he had eagerly spread a year earlier that Rousseau had been employed twenty years earlier not as secretary to the French ambassador to Venice but as a lackey. Voltaire may not have at first known that this was a false charge, but he certainly knew it by the time he served it up again. It hardly mattered that Rousseau had, in the meantime, written the old man to call him a liar.[8] "As for Jean-Jacques," Voltaire wrote, once again to multiple correspondents in the same words, "I have always held that he should be shown at Bartholomew's Fair for a shilling: it would be all too comical."[9]

With the appearance of the *Exposé succinct,* Voltaire himself entered the fray with an open letter to Hume, "Letter from Monsieur de Voltaire to Monsieur Hume," dated October 24, 1766, in which he commiserated with Hume, declaring that Rousseau's charges against his former patron constituted "the proceeding of ingratitude against generosity." After reviewing his own sad history with the ungrateful Genevan (now admitting that he had been misinformed about Rousseau's service as a lackey, but nevertheless managing to turn his actual role as secretary to his disadvantage), Voltaire addressed Hume's situation. "To speak truthfully, Sir, all these little miseries are not worth worrying about for two minutes; all this will soon fade into eternal oblivion. . . . Jean-Jacques's follies and his ridiculous pride will do no harm to true philosophy, and the respectable men who cultivate it in France, in England, and in Germany will not be less esteemed."[10]

Rousseau had not harmed true philosophy in Voltaire's mind in part because his charges had no standing in the court of reason. "I believe that the quarrel be-

tween Mr. Hume and Jean-Jacques has ended with the public disdain that
Rousseau has attracted and by the esteem that Mr. Hume deserves," he explained
to a professor at Cambridge, commenting on the twisted logic of Rousseau's
letter to Hume and mocking the "three arguments that he calls *three slaps on his
patron's cheek*." Voltaire's judgment was unequivocal: "This man appears completely mad to me."[11] Like Hume and his fellow philosophes, then, Voltaire saw
in Rousseau's behavior, as in his prose, only frenzy and extravagance. "I do not
find any genius in him. His detestable novel *Heloise* is absolutely lacking in it,
Emile as well, and all his other works are those of an empty ranter spun out in an
often unintelligible prose. . . . Jean-Jacques is a miserable imposter, who has
stolen a bottle of elixir and mixed it with a barrel of vinegar and distributed it to
the public as a remedy of his own invention."[12]

Another barometer of enlightened opinion is provided by Grimm's *Correspondance littéraire*. With some exaggeration and greater delectation, Grimm
began the October 15, 1766, edition by announcing: "It has been about three
months since the news of J.-J. Rousseau's falling out with M. Hume first reached
Paris. What excellent fodder for the idle! A declaration of war between two of
Europe's great powers could not have made a greater noise than this quarrel. . . .
All other news was struck from the list of conversation topics for more than a
week in Paris, and the celebrity of the two combatants . . . completely absorbed
the public's attention." While Grimm demurred from judging this "strange
trial," he stated that he knew Hume well and knows Rousseau only too well,
adding a lengthy chronicle of the Citizen of Geneva's serial shattering of friendships. His own experience with Rousseau, as a result, put him in the uniquely
competent position to say, with his typical cruelty, what he would have done in
Hume's place:

> Receiving the sweet and honest letter of June 23, which I could have and
> ought to have paid little heed, I, fat David Hume, would have first rubbed
> my eyes; then, remaining somewhat stunned, my countenance [*regard*]
> would have became as fixed and as prolonged as that day, forever terrible
> and memorable, when David looked at Jean-Jacques; but, this gesture of
> surprise having passed, I would have put that letter in my pocket. The next
> day, I would have written to my friend Jean-Jacques to thank him for the
> good opinion with which he honored me and for the fine coloring he was
> able to give to my services and my tender efforts on his behalf, and then I
> would have bid him farewell for the rest of his glorious life.

Grimm was not finished. He primly declared that he would never have aired in
public his business with Rousseau, yet he then deliberately exposed the identities
of the individuals involved in bringing together the two philosophers in the first

place, the Comtesse de Boufflers and the Marquise de Verdelin. By contrast, Hume had decorously suppressed their identities in his own account. Nor does Grimm's professed pity for Rousseau ring true. Comparing him to Don Quixote tilting at windmills, Grimm concluded his account: "Jean-Jacques has come two centuries too late; his true lot was to be a reformer. . . . In the sixteenth century he would have founded the order of the Brothers Rousses or Roussaviens, or Jean-Jacquistes; but, in our own century, one does not make proselytes, and all that burning prose does not lead the idle reader to put aside his book in order to follow the prose writer." In short, for Grimm and his readers, the reasonableness of Hume's account proves his innocence in an age when reasoned arguments, and not passionate appeals, ought to move people.[13]

Yet Voltaire, Grimm, and Suard were whistling in the dark: not only was their audience already deeply steeped in literature that toyed with the distinction between fact and fiction, but it was also deeply influenced by the Rousseauian appeal to sentiment as the final arbiter of truth. Indeed, the literary situation in 1766 is eerily similar to that of our own day, when the line between fact and fable, particularly in autobiography, is so blurred as to be scarcely distinguishable. Rousseau anticipated the reasoning of some twenty-first-century memoirists when, in his lengthy letter to Hume, he wrote: "I am told nothing, and I know only what I feel. . . . The first concern of those who engage in bad designs is to secure themselves from legal proofs of detection: it would not be very advisable to seek a remedy against them at law. The innate conviction of the heart admits of another kind of proof, which influences the sentiments of honest men."

While both writers invoked the claim of honesty, the word meant very different things to the opposing camps. For Suard and, of course, for Hume, honesty entailed scientific and empirical method—above all, a rigorous fidelity to texts and contexts. On the other hand, Rousseau measured honesty by inward feeling and the subjective criterion of sentiment. The distance between the Enlightenment and Counter-Enlightenment can be measured in this confrontation of methods.

Intriguingly, the vehicles in this collision of worldviews were identical: the epistolary genre. The vehicles' drivers, however, steered them in radically different directions. Hume and Suard fastened upon the genre's appeal to veracity, or at least verisimilitude, underscored by the accumulation of documents, their careful annotation and placement in a public institution. The private, in short, was made fully public. Rousseau, however, exploited the intimate nature of letter writing: addressing himself to the private reader, Jean-Jacques spoke simply and sincerely from his heart. The public, in other words, was whittled down to the private.

A surge of letters from readers, appearing as pamphlets or in the pages of such journals as the *Mercure de France,* which had previously sparked Rousseau's illumination on the road to Vincennes, poured through the breaches blown in the wall that had once separated the realms of sense and sensibility. Both the medium, epistolary, and the messages, invitations to the readers to share their responses, created an unprecedented situation. What many readers happened to think about the affair confirmed the worst fears of Holbach and d'Alembert concerning the public. Ironically, their belief in the individual's ability to arrive at the truth through the exercise of reason proved to be their downfall.

Many of the readers did, in fact, hit upon the truth: the problem is that it was not the same truth held by Hume and his defenders. One reader, writing under the pseudonym T. Verax, made a heavy-handed show of using the empirical method: "Detesting equally the bile of satire and the indulgence of partiality, I will try to develop for you between these two snags the different sensations that I experienced in reading all the documents of this important dispute. If my judgment seems erroneous to you, impute it only to my senses, and pity the falsity of my perceptions, because I have neglected nothing to enlighten myself." And yet he reached a startling conclusion: it was Rousseau, not Hume, who was innocent. It was the creator of *Julie,* and not the historian of England, who was "full of candor, integrity, and sensitivity."[14]

While T. Verax was not alone in his judgment, others tended to adopt Turgot's more nuanced interpretation that Rousseau, though mistaken, was not malicious. As one anonymous correspondent concluded, Hume "will have difficulty persuading his readers that the author of the *Heloise* has become an infamous impostor and a monster of ingratitude. Those who have admired M. Rousseau for years know that his heart is too true and his morals are too pure to give way to such actions which always reveal a black character and an evil soul."[15] That the writer should cite, without apparent irony, Rousseau's fictitious collection of letters as proof of his transparency and sincerity reveals just how dramatically the Genevan had redefined the terms of the debate.

The debate raged across the Channel as well. This was a predictable turn of events, given the public notoriety of the two antagonists, the reach of the Republic of Letters, and the sustained attention Rousseau's visit had received from the British press. It also gave the lie to Grimm's catty remark that only in Paris could such an affair rivet the public's attention, whereas in Great Britain the public was "foolish enough to be more interested in the formation of a new government."[16]

One correspondent to the *Saint James Chronicle* who identified himself as an "orthodox, hospitable Old Englishman" tried to find common ground between the two sides. While Hume seemed innocent of Rousseau's accusations, he was guilty of undue severity toward his former friend: "If Mr. Hume's heart had ever been indeed the friend of Rousseau, his philosophy and coolness might have treated Mr. Rousseau as a man under a strong and great mistake; this would have been more for Mr. Hume's glory, and would have given him an entire advantage in the affair." Instead, all Hume had shown is that "a philosopher, when provoked, is not a better man at bottom than the poor mere bigots of every religion."[17]

A second correspondent echoed this disappointment in the treatment of Rousseau: "There is one thing that Mr. Hume appears to have quite forgotten in his behavior to Mr. Rousseau, which is his inferiority, his misfortunes, and his extreme sensibility, naturally great, increased by these." The letter writer then noted that while Hume had written eloquently on the subject of sympathy, "there are very few that are capable of acting up to even justice in this respect."[18] Yet another reader, writing as "A Friend to Rousseau," joined the fray from the shores of Loch Lomond, "a retreat which," he wrote, "would be highly pleasing to that illustrious exile, Rousseau," to scold his fellow Scot. Rather than lambasting Rousseau for his well-known sensitivity, Hume should have made the Genevan "an object of his care and pity."[19]

Rousseau's predicament inspired yet another Briton to rally the Genevan's spirits through verse:

> Rousseau be firm!—tho' malice, like Voltaire,
> And supercilious pride, like d'Alembert,
> Though mad presumption W----le's form assume,
> And baseborn treachery appear like H--e,
> Yet droop not thou - these specters gathering round,
> These night-drawn phantoms want the power to wound,
> Fair truth shall chase the unreal forms away;
> And reason's piercing beam restore the day;
> Britain shall snatch the exile to her breast.
> And conscious virtue soothe his soul to rest.[20]

Needless to say, such defiant doggerel could not go unanswered for long in the burgeoning media circus. A satirist quickly lambasted Rousseau in a parody of the earlier poem:

> R----, be firm . . . though satire, like Voltaire,
> And genius, in the shape of d'Alembert,
> Though Walpole's form sly ridicule assume
> And honest friendship wear the guise of Hume
> Yet *feel* not thou! Nor hear the silver sound
> Of annual pension of one hundred pound
> Rank arrogance shall chase all help away

> And pedant sophistry turn night to day
> From land to land a wretched exile fly
> Then, mad with pride, curse all mankind, and die.[21]

Boswell, not one to be outdone, wrote his own poems, one of which masquer-aded as Hume's reply to Rousseau:

> Ungrateful dog, whose wild caprices
> Have made all Europe grin and sneer
> To see two sages pull to pieces
> Each other whom they held so dear.[22]

The irrepressible Scot also conjured up an idea for a cartoon titled "Savage Man" that was printed in the *London Chronicle*. Perhaps unaware that Boswell was its source, Hume described the cartoon to Boufflers: "M. Rousseau is represented as a Yahoo, newly caught in the woods, I am represented as a farmer, who caresses him and offers him some oats to eat, which he refuses in a rage; Voltaire and d'Alembert are whipping him up behind; and Horace Walpole making him horns of *papier maché*. The idea is not altogether absurd."[23]

Walpole was hardly alone: there was a wave of parodies of royal letters, even a mock court indictment. Among the many charges laid against Hume in one was that "the said David Hume must have published Mr Walpole's letter in the newspapers, because, at that time, there was neither man, woman, nor child, in the island of Great Britain, but the said David Hume, the said J-J Rousseau and the printers of several newspapers."[24]

In general, the wits sided with Hume—humor was one element missing among Rousseau's defenders—as did most journals and newspapers. While the editors gave ample space to both sides, their comments reflect a widespread im-patience with Rousseau and his supporters. Thus the editors of the *Gentleman's Magazine* regretted the social mischief caused by his behavior. Not only could it lead to a chilling effect on the Republic of Letters, but might well discourage "benevolence, and repress liberality; many may be left to struggle with adversity unassisted, in consequence of such a return for assistance as Mr Rousseau has made to Mr Hume."[25]

That Europe's wags and pundits were arrayed against him did not surprise Rousseau. On the contrary: it confirmed the truth of his cause. Wit, as Rousseau had long insisted, was but one of the many rotten fruits of a corrupt and false so-ciety. More than ever he felt Alceste's pain, a pain that was shared by his legion of disciples. Their hero shared the fate of Molière's misanthrope: he was "a good man who detests the morals of his age and the viciousness of his contem-poraries; who, precisely because he loves his fellow creatures, hates in them the

"The Savage Man," anonymous engraving after a suggestion by James Boswell, 1766. © *London Chronicle*

evils they do to one another and the vices of which these evils are the product."[26] The division of public opinion in the journals reflected the tectonic shift taking place in European sensibility. Two cultures were facing off: one devoted to the ideals of the High Enlightenment opposed to a more recent generation of readers inspired by the proto-Romantic teachings of Rousseau.

Whether sardonic or sententious in their criticism of Rousseau, the official press in France no less than in Great Britain was unable to stem the exile's groundswell of popular support. As a result, while the *Courrier d'Avignon* chastised Rousseau's "bitterness," it recognized that Hume nevertheless "did not have the general support of the public."[27] Correspondents from the provinces as well as Paris made clear their sympathies. From Picardy, a writer to the *Journal Encyclopédique* questioned the legitimacy of the charges against Rousseau, then quickly excused himself: "Pardon, Sirs, these questions from a man who is neither author, nor wit, nor eloquent; but who seeks to instruct himself, and who will succeed in doing more surely by the reading of your wise writings than by any other means." As impatient as their British colleagues, the journal's editors snapped that if their provincial subscriber had carefully read all the documents, only one conclusion could be reached: the journal's own, of course. But why bother with such benighted readers: "Eh! Sir, what could we say that would not be used against [Rousseau]. All the facts reported in this pamphlet and proven charge M. Rousseau severely. All the accusations he makes against M. Hume are ridiculous, absurd, and totally devoid of credibility."[28]

Whether the Picard's diffidence was sincere or the product of Rousseauian rhetoric probably meant little to the journal's directors: either way, Rousseau's influence had reached far and deep. If the quarrel were truly a trial of sorts, the jury was stacked against Hume. Within a remarkably short span of time, Rousseau had created through his writings, especially *Julie,* a new audience of readers. Taught by Rousseau to read against the grain of Enlightenment values, this readership was asked to abandon, not exercise, reason; cultivate, not contain, sentiment; trust their hearts, not their minds. Consequently, the more the denizens of Saint Germain and Soho Square ridiculed Rousseau, the more innocent he appeared to his followers. In the end, the levee between authenticity and appearance was breached most by the claims made by its most intrepid defender, Rousseau.

Dena Goodman notes the ironic turn of events that confronted Hume's defenders: "That the public responded to the philosophe's appeal to reason did not mean that they used the reasoning principles to which the philosophes appealed."[29] In short, enlightened thinkers were hoisted largely with their own petard. In the rough and tumble of public opinion, petitions on behalf of objective reason could not compete with the attraction of inner certainty, particularly when it was shared with others. Not only did Rousseau insist that sincerity is the greatest of human virtues, but he acted upon this axiom's corollary: sincerity requires the individual to bare his soul to others. As a result, he enjoyed a peculiarly modern form of immunity, at least in the eyes of his readers, to the charge of wrong-headedness. Rousseau was hailed for his loyalty to his subjective state of mind, and not to any objective standard of truth.

Rousseau learned of the publication of the *Exposé succinct* in early autumn, while still writing and botanizing in Wootton. In rapid succession, one of Rousseau's political allies, Toussaint-Pierre Lenieps, wrote from Geneva to exhort the exiled philosopher to respond to Hume's attack, while at the same time, another, Du Peyrou, asked Rousseau not to respond, at least not immediately. As strong as his case may be, Du Peyrou worried, it was not clear that it would persuade the public.[30] Even Hume, concerned about Rousseau's response, sent a copy of the *Exposé succinct* to his adversary through Davenport, hoping that its receipt would dissuade Rousseau from going to the public with his accusations. Referring to a letter he had forwarded to Rousseau in which the writer exonerated Hume by declaring himself the author of two journalistic pieces Rousseau had attributed to Hume, the Scot concluded, "He will see, from this instance what weapons I have still in my hand to confound him, if he should make such an attempt."[31]

In his reply to Davenport, Rousseau declared that Hume had no reason to tremble. "I will continue whatever may happen to leave it to Mr. Hume to make all the noise he wants all by himself, and to keep, until the very end, the silence that I have imposed on myself in this matter. I infinitely prefer to be the unfortunate Jean-Jacques Rousseau, delivered over to all this public defamation, than the triumphant David Hume in the midst of all his glory."[32] At this point, Rousseau's reaffirmation of his martyrdom is far less surprising than his success at maintaining his silence about the affair.

Rousseau's self-portrayal had much truth to it: he was well on his way to becoming the "unfortunate Jean-Jacques." Increasingly isolated at Wootton, Rousseau was forced indoors by the shortening and colder days with the onset of fall. He was still unable to communicate with anyone there except Thérèse, whose own relations with the servants went from bad to worse. Apart from his visits at Calwich Abbey, which grew less frequent with the first snow, Rousseau's only connection with the outside world was through the post, yet that conduit of communication also grew ever more restricted: the few correspondents he retained in his vaunted isolation became fewer still after his accusations against Hume.

His "father," Lord Keith, had already greeted Rousseau's suspicions against Hume with incredulity, trying to make Rousseau see that their mutual friend had served him with "zeal and friendship." When he learned of the quarrel, he was despondent: "I regret and I will regret all my days that I was not in England to prevent this, as I certainly would have, by showing you everything David wrote me, for you would have seen that his friendship was true."[33] Claiming his old age as an excuse, Keith terminated his correspondence with the philosopher, whereupon Rousseau wrote back to declare his continued affection and complain that the elderly Scot had taken away, in all of his current misfortunes, "a unique and sweet consolation."[34] Keith could not betray Hume, so he would not answer Rousseau's plea. "I do not see any other part to take for myself than to stop a correspondence in which I have sentiments at such variance with those of M. Rousseau," Keith confided to Du Peyrou on Christmas Eve.[35] Rousseau nevertheless persisted without success to hold on to the man who, after "Maman," played so important a role in his world. "It is a done deed, Milord," he wrote the following spring: "I have forever lost your good graces and your friendship without it even being possible for me to know and to imagine from whence comes this loss." What particularly pained him, he added, was to have learned that Keith's excuses of age and illness were just that, excuses, for he continued to write to "everyone else and I alone am excepted."[36]

The Comtesse de Boufflers, torn between her two philosophers, finally also broke off with Rousseau.* A ruptured friendship with Du Peyrou was repaired more quickly. Angered at his faithful follower's muted reaction to his accusations against Hume, Rousseau ended their friendship in late October only to rethink matters and apologize almost immediately for his intemperate action. After a flurry of letters — critical enough for Rousseau to draft and redraft each several times — the philosopher pronounced himself totally reconciled with his friend.[37] Du Peyrou, however, was less convinced of Rousseau's change of heart. He continued to act with caution, later telling Paul Moultou, with whom he was editing the philosopher's collected writings, that he could never credit what Rousseau said about Hume.[38]

Rousseau was clearly bothered by the controversy. In a letter to his fellow botanical enthusiast the Duchess of Portland, he proclaimed his lack of aptitude for botany due to old age and failed memory. Yet he then pronounced himself nevertheless "crazy enough to persist, or rather I am wise enough." As he explained to the Duchess:

> Because for me this taste is an affair of reason. I sometimes have need of art to preserve myself in this invaluable calm in the midst of the agitations which disturb my life, to keep at bay those heinous passions which you do not know, that I have never known except in others, and which I do want to permit to approach me. I do not wish, if it is possible, that any sad recollections trouble the peace of my solitude. I want to forget men and their injustices. I want to be moved every day by the marvels of him who made them to be good, and whose work they have so scandalously degraded.[39]

Man is naturally good and society corrupts him: Rousseau clung to the principle of his philosophical system in the midst of his troubles, plumbing the memories of his youth and surveying the spectacle of nature for both evidence and solace. In his letter to the duchess Rousseau first sketched the themes of solitude and memory amid the plants that he would perfect in his last work, the *Reveries of the Solitary Walker*.

Oddly, the rupture between the two philosophers did not interrupt the negotiation over Rousseau's pension. Writing in January 1767, Davenport asked his guest to clarify his earlier refusal of the pension to General Conway, adding that he was sure that the king would grant it.[40] Rousseau replied that he would not write to Conway, since to do so would effectively be to demand the pension;

---

*Their correspondence was briefly resurrected a year later when Rousseau, then under the Prince de Conti's protection, tried to patch up things with her in his inimitable manner, writing: "Madame, you are not exempt from blame toward me" (Rousseau to Boufflers, February 25, 1768, *CC*, 32: 146–47). Their reconciliation did not last, however, and Rousseau ultimately came to blame her for her role in the "infernal affair" with Hume.

he would accept it if offered, but would not ask.[41] Despite their quarrel, Hume himself finally intervened, giving Conway his "consent and even full approbation" for renewing the offer and even urging him "to do so charitable an action." Hume nonetheless could not help but interpret what he saw as Rousseau's coy interest in the pension as evidence for his own case: "This step of my old friend confirms the suspicion which I always entertained, that he thought he had interest enough to obtain the pension of himself, and that he had only picked a quarrel with me in order to free himself from the humiliating burden of gratitude towards me. His motives, therefore, were much blacker than many seem to apprehend them."[42] Conway duly wrote Davenport on March 18, informing him that the pension would be offered.[43] "And thus the affair is happily finished," Hume told his friend William Robertson, "unless some new extravagance come across the philosopher, and engage him to reject what he has anew applied for. If he knew my situation with General Conway he probably would; for he must conjecture that the affair could not be done without my consent."[44]

Hume was at least half right: Rousseau did finally accept Conway's offer.[45] Yet a "new extravagance" came upon his former friend that rendered moot the entire matter.

Winter lay at the roots of Rousseau's final extravagance. By late December, Rousseau's uncertainty as to whether Davenport wanted him to stay at Wootton was worsened by the granite-gray clouds and snow-swathed hills of Derbyshire.[46] Davenport reassured Rousseau that he would always be welcome there, but events overpowered his kind intentions. By March 2, 1767, Rousseau was complaining to his host of the "terrible winds" that aggravated a stubborn toothache.[47] The same day, he wrote Du Peyrou, declaring that his situation "becomes every day more critical, and approaches the point where it frightens me," alluding to an unspecified episode that had happened two days earlier.[48]

The "critical situation" could only have meant, at this point, the rapid deterioration of Thérèse's poisoned relations with the servants: the imperious woman's efforts to assume control of the household finally led to a declaration of war between her and the staff. Rousseau soon wrote Davenport again, this time to announce that he had decided to go to London for Thérèse's health, adding: "I am moreover convinced that despite my love for the country, given my age and the loss of my memory for learning the language, I should not longer think of remaining in the provinces."[49] Davenport urged the philosopher to stay, and offered him the use of a house he owned in the more friendly climes of Cheshire with the promise to visit after Easter.[50] The encouragement and offers were all in vain: when Davenport finally arrived at his seat near Wootton in late April, Owd Ross Hall and Madame Zell, to the evident relief of his domestics, had already fled.

Not surprisingly, the couple did not leave a forwarding address. Clearly disappointed, Davenport announced the news to Hume: "I have got a most severe fit of the gout and have lost my philosopher."[51] The squire's gout could hardly have been improved upon discovering, several days later, the letter Rousseau had left to explain his sudden decampment. "The master of a house, Sir, is obliged to know what happens in his own, above all with regard to strangers he has received there. If you do not know what happens in your house since Christmas with regard to me, you are to blame; but the least excusable injury is to have forgotten your promise, and to have gone calmly to settle yourself at Davenport without having troubled yourself to find out whether the man who awaited you here in accordance with your wish was at his ease or not. . . . Tomorrow, Sir, I leave your house."[52]

Abandoning all their belongings and money, Rousseau, Thérèse, and Sultan chose the most improbable of escape routes. From Wootton the odd trio made their way east to the trading town of Spalding, perhaps because Rousseau wished to leave his papers with Jean-François-Maximilien Cerjat, a fellow Swiss who lived nearby and had been recommended to him by Du Peyrou.[53] Whether Rousseau contacted Cerjat is unknown, but he did write the lord chancellor, Baron Camden, begging to be put under his protection and asking for safe escort to Dover.[54] The newspapers followed Rousseau's travels, and so did Hume, who wrote Davenport: "You are probably told . . . that your wild philosopher, as you call him, has at last appeared at Spalding in Lincolnshire, whence he has wrote a most extravagant letter to the chancellor, demanding a messenger to conduct him to Dover. . . . In short, he is plainly mad, after having been maddish."[55]

After a few days in Spalding, where he waited for an answer from a nonplussed government, Rousseau suddenly bolted for Dover. Holing up at an inn, he penned a letter to Davenport, saying that as soon as he arrived and saw the sea he believed himself free—so free, in fact, that he almost decided to return to Wootton. At least, that is, until he saw a piece in the paper about his sudden departure from Wootton that renewed his suspicions about his landlord's view of him.[56] Even for Hume, the coda to the affair seemed swinging ever farther from Sophocles to Aristophanes. He could not resist tweaking Davenport: "So you are a traitor, too, it seems; pray, do you speak in your sleep? But you may cry as loud as you please, *je tiens Jean-Jacques*. He has got out of your clutches and is now in the wide world."[57]

Unhappily, reality again outdid satire. While barricaded in Dover, Rousseau wrote to Conway, suggesting that the plot against him was so extensive that the government must be involved. What is curious about this extraordinary letter, as Edmonds and Eidenow note, is that Rousseau adopts the third person in speaking of himself.[58] Acting like an advocate before the bench, Rousseau offers a kind of plea bargain for his client—Jean-Jacques?—that would allow him to leave unmolested. He also provides his client with an alibi in the form of an alternative explanation of his behavior that is surprisingly rational, as though Rousseau could think clearly about himself only at the distance afforded by the third person.

> Behold, Sir, the man you propose to let go in peace, and who engages his faith, his word, all the feelings for honor he has professed, and all the sacred hopes which provide here below for the consolation of the unhappy, that not only does he forever abandon the project of writing his life and his memoirs, but will also never let escape, either from his mouth or from his pen, a single word of complaint against the misfortunes that have happened to him in England, who will never speak of Mr. Hume, or who will speak of him only with honor; and when he is pressed to explain himself concerning the indiscreet accusations which, under the influence of the strongest of his difficulties, sometimes escaped from him, he will reject them without any mystery at all concerning his temper, embittered and carried to the point of mistrust and clouded by his continual misfortunes.[59]

Hume also noted the shift to the third person in this letter, so similar to the long accusatory letter he received in which he found himself demoted from the second to the third person. "Nothing can be more frenzical than this letter," he wrote Turgot. "He adds, as if a ray of reason then broke in upon his soul, speaking of himself in the third person: 'He forever abandons the project of writing his life.'" In the end, Hume concluded, Rousseau was mad and perhaps had always been mad. "I inform you of all these particulars that you may see the poor man is absolutely lunatic and consequently cannot be the object of any laws or civil punishment."[60] Whether he was the proper object of the publication of their correspondence, Hume does not say.

Desperate to leave England, Rousseau was thwarted by winds, kept in Dover as he had been in Calais on his journey to England more than a year before. In a fit of madness that he later recognized to be such, Rousseau rushed from a dinner party and ran aboard a ship where he harangued a bewildered crowd, only to be overtaken by Thérèse, who led her companion back to their dinner host.[61] Finally, philosopher, gouvernante, and canine set sail on May 22. Catching up with the errant thinker shortly after his arrival in France, the Prince de Conti managed to persuade him to accept the hospitality of his chateau at Trye in Normandy, in truth keeping him there as a virtual prisoner for his own protection. He also persuaded Rousseau, who after all still had an arrest warrant hanging over his head in France, to take an assumed name. Jean-Jacques Rousseau, Citizen of Geneva, having shed his caftan in Wootton, shed his name in France and thus became M. Renou.

CHAPTER THIRTEEN

How Philosophers Die

I am dying as fast as my enemies, if I have any, could wish, and as easily and cheerfully as my best friends could desire.
— *Hume to Dr. Dundas*

I consecrate my last days to studying myself and to preparing in advance the account I will give of myself before long.
— *Rousseau,* Reveries of a Solitary Walker

By 1776 little had changed for Boswell: now a husband and father, he still ran as frantically from death and as he did into the arms of women, seeking certitudes in the bedroom missing from the church pew. On Sunday, July 7, doubts about the final disposition of his soul brought him to Hume's door in Edinburgh. Along with the rest of the Republic of Letters, Boswell had learned that his old friend was dying from stomach cancer.

Seven years earlier, shortly after his quarrel with Rousseau finally died down, Hume had finally decided to settle in Edinburgh, disappointing the Comtesse de

Boufflers's hopes of his rejoining her in Paris. Whether satisfied in his literary ambitions or spent by the controversies they sparked, Hume swore off any new works. Instead, he jokingly told friends of his "great talent for cookery, the science to which I intend to addict the remaining years of my life," singling out his recipe for sheep-head broth as particularly delicious.[1] Hume's good humor, however, could not hide his gradual loss of weight and spasmodic waves of abdominal pain. In a February 1776 letter congratulating Adam Smith on the publication of the *Wealth of Nations*, Hume wrote: "I weighed myself the other day, and find I have fallen five complete stones"—seventy pounds. "If you delay much longer, I shall probably disappear altogether."[2] A few months later, he went to Bath for the waters, and a specialist found a tumor in Hume's gut "about the bigness of an egg."[3] Friends and doctors all sought to reassure him, but Hume would have none of it. He appreciated the cascade of optimistic diagnoses and wishes, but he remained realistic, dismissing such chatter as "very silly expectations."[4]

Ushered into the drawing room, Boswell meant to test Hume's lifelong disregard for faith and religion. Yet the genial inquisitor caught his breath: Hume was splayed across the couch, a gray suit loosely wrapped around his deflated frame, his gaunt and pale face topped by a small wig. Putting down a book on rhetoric, Hume smiled and calmly observed that his end was near. Struck by his host's "placid and even cheerful" demeanor, Boswell pulled up a chair and contrived to introduce almost immediately his great obsession, the question of immortality, and asked Hume whether he had changed his ideas about the Christian faith.[5]

The great infidel, Boswell quickly learned, had not changed his ideas at all. Hume remarked that he had lost his religious faith when a university student, and that it was unlikely he would have a change of heart in the time remaining to him. Besides, true morality positively forbade such a change. Enjoying Boswell's mixture of fascination and discomfort, Hume announced that all religions, and not just Christianity, were bad for morality. Echoing Dr. Johnson's famous declaration that patriotism is the last refuge of the scoundrel, Hume laughed: "They all make up new species of crime and bring unhappiness in their train. When I hear a man is religious, I conclude he is a rascal, though I know some instances of very good men being religious."

Hume's remark cut close to Boswell's bone. Earlier that year, the libidinous Scot had contracted his eleventh case of gonorrhea—an impressive feat even in that mercury-doused age. Boswell asked Hume whether he did not believe in the possibility of a future life in which we would have to answer for our sins. Gesturing at the fireplace, Hume smiled: "'Tis possible that a piece of coal, put upon the fire, will not burn, but to suppose so is not at all reasonable." Hume's skepticism hardly satisfied Boswell, who preferred to see the laws of experience violated before his expectations of salvation. He blurted, "Does the thought of annihilation never give you any uneasiness?" Hume shrugged: "Not at all, Mr. Boswell. No more than the thought that I had not been."

Hume's sally made Boswell smile. Of course, bedeviling a dying man with repeated reminders of his imminent demise was bad manners. But Boswell could not accept Hume's calm acceptance. Adopting a different tack, Boswell testified that he believed in the Christian religion with the same certainty he did history. The new tactic, however, did not impress the author of *The History of England* and the *Natural History of Religion*. Hume replied that Boswell was the victim of a category mistake: "You cannot believe [your faith] as you believe the Revolution of 1688." Inevitably, Hume could not satisfy Boswell's desperate search for spiritual solace. In his analyses of the springs of religious belief, Hume had always understood but was unmoved by such motives. But he did not wish to remind his visitor about his writings on religion. Availing himself of Boswell's insistence that, surely, it is more pleasing to anticipate a future state than mere nothingness, Hume simply replied: "I do not wish to be immortal. I am very well in this state of being, and the chances are very much against my being so well in another estate. I would rather not be more than be worse."

As they spoke, Boswell heard another guest being led to the drawing room. From the whispering voices on the other side of the door, he knew that one of Hume's doctors was asking about the state of the patient. The agitated Boswell realized that there were just moments left to prod—provoke if need be—Hume into revealing a hiccup of doubt, a hint of belief. Leaning toward his host, he cried, "If I were you I should regret annihilation. Had I written such an admirable *History* as you have, I should be sorry to leave it." Hume smiled once again: "I shall leave that *History*, of which you are pleased to speak so favorably, as perfect as I can." His grin widened as he added that even Dr. Johnson "should be pleased with it." As he rose from his chair, Boswell laughed: "I fear Dr. Johnson does not allow you much credit. 'Sir,' he says, 'the fellow is a Tory by chance.'"

Unlike Johnson, who could not even credit Hume the right reasons to be a fellow Tory, Boswell struggled to understand the reasons for his friend's calm acceptance of death. He was certainly not soothed by Hume's parting words: "If there were a future state, Mr. Boswell, I think I could give as good an account of my life as most people." As Boswell wrote in his journal later that day, "I was off my guard; for the truth is that Mr. Hume's pleasantry was such that there was no solemnity in the scene; and death for the time did not seem dismal. It surprised me to find him talking of different matters with a tranquility of mind and a clearness of head which few men possess at any time. I left him with impressions which disturbed me for some time."

Boswell was not through with his dying friend, however. Over the next few weeks, he tried twice again to see Hume but failed both times because the philosopher was too ill to receive visitors. His last attempt was on August 21, fortified this time by being "elevated with liquor." He was turned away at the door. Four days later, Hume died.

Knowing the fascination that attended the notorious skeptic's passing, Adam Smith, serving as Hume's literary executor, prepared a careful account of the event for posterity that took the form of a letter to Hume's publisher. "It is with a real, though a very melancholy pleasure, that I sit down to give you some account of the behavior of our late excellent Mr. Hume, during his last illness," Smith begins. After reciting the philosopher's cheerful attitude at the certain prospect of death, Smith recounted his last conversation with his friend. Hume related that he had been reading Lucian's *Dialogues of the Dead*, the second-century satirist's reflections on human vanity, in which he at one point imagines Charon ferrying passengers across the Styx—so similar to Garrick's *Lethe*, which he had watched side by side with Jean-Jacques Rousseau a decade earlier. "'I could not well imagine,' said he, 'what excuse I could make to Charon, in order to obtain a little delay,'" Smith quoted Hume. "'I have done everything of consequence which I ever meant to do.'" Unable to come up with a weighty excuse, Hume amused himself in inventing jocular pretexts. "'Upon further consideration,' said he, 'I thought I might say to him, "Good Charon, I have been correcting my works for a new edition. Allow me the little time that I may see how the public receives the alterations."'" After the surly boatman refuses the request, Hume tries again: "'"Have a little patience, good Charon, I have been endeavoring to open the eyes of the public. If I live a few years longer, I may have the satisfaction of seeing the downfall of some of the prevailing systems of superstition." But Charon would then lose his temper: "You loitering rogue, that will not happen these many hundred years. Do you fancy I will grant you a lease for so long a term? Get into the boat this instant, you lazy loitering rogue."'"[6]

Hume did not loiter long after this final conversation. "Thus died our most excellent, and never-to-be-forgotten friend," Smith concluded his account, playing Phaedo to Hume's Socrates: "Upon the whole, I have always considered him, both in his life time, and since his death, as approaching as nearly to the idea of a perfectly wise and virtuous man, as perhaps the nature of human frailty will admit."[7]

Despite Smith's account of Hume's demise—or perhaps because of it— Boswell was despondent when he learned of the philosopher's death the next day, drinking himself silly and seeking out a "comely, fresh-looking girl" and "madly ventured to lie with her on the north brae of the Castle Hill." The following morning, hung over and depressed, Boswell and a friend walked to the dismal, rain-swept cemetery on Carlton Hill in Edinburgh, where they inspected the "kirk hole" prepared for Hume's coffin. Seeking shelter from the pelting rain behind a nearby stone wall, the two men reemerged to join the procession that carried Hume's body to its final resting place.

Once the coffin was lowered into its grave and covered with muddy earth, Boswell retreated to the shelter of the Advocates Library, the former home of the Select Club. His clothes still soggy, Boswell pulled down a copy of Hume's *Essays* and sat at one of the tables. Among the essays he reread in this pensive frame of mind was "The Sceptic." The piece, perhaps closest to Hume's own beliefs, concludes with the observation that while "we are reasoning concerning life, life is gone; and death, though perhaps they receive him differently, yet treats alike the fool and the philosopher."[8]

Scarcely two months after Hume died, Rousseau nearly followed him.

After returning from England, Rousseau spent nearly three years in the Prince de Conti's chateau in Normandy, protected from the law and from himself, continuing his work on the *Confessions*. Predictably, the author who boldly revealed himself in his autobiography grew weary of living under an assumed identity, or lock and key. He begged to be released, and the prince finally reluctantly agreed. After wandering for a year in and near Lyon, and marrying Thérèse in recognition of her decades of loyalty, Rousseau returned to Paris in 1770 and once again became Jean-Jacques Rousseau.* Although the arrest warrant issued by the Parlement of Paris eight years earlier was still in effect, he was assured that he would not be molested by the authorities as long as he refrained from publishing any more works. "The return of this extraordinary man . . . has for some days provided a subject of conversation in Paris. . . . His presence drew a huge crowd, and the common people flocked to the square to see him pass by." So reported Grimm, who continued to follow Rousseau's movements with morbid fascination, adding maliciously: "He has discarded his misanthropy at the same time as his Armenian garb, and has become polite and simpering."[9]

Stripped of his Armenian garb if not his notoriety, Rousseau spent his mornings copying music and afternoons botanizing in the nearby woods of Vincennes and Boulogne. After lunch on October 24, 1776, he left his apartment on the rue Platrière and walked north toward Ménilmontant, intent on gathering his daily harvest of flowers and plants.[10] Ménilmontant—long since absorbed by Paris, sitting just above Père Lachaise and harboring the Parc des Buttes-Chaumont, a late-nineteenth-century example of Arcadian kitsch partly inspired

---

*Since Rousseau was a Protestant, his marriage was not legally valid in France.

by the Rousseauian cult of nature—was still, in Rousseau's time, a genuine village whose vineyards and fields overlooked the city.

Finding several species of flora, including the rare *cerastium aquaticum* (chickweed), which he carefully preserved between the pages of his notebook, Rousseau was still at home neither with others nor with himself. He imbued the surrounding countryside, as he had done sixty years before at Bossey, with his own inner melancholy. The bare tree branches and stripped grape vines "offered everywhere the image of solitude and approach of winter." Bittersweet thoughts passed through Rousseau's mind as he walked across the fields. He saw himself "at the end of an innocent and unlucky life. . . . Alone and abandoned I felt the cold blast of the first winter winds." As he approached the village, the plant-filled notebook held close to his breast, Rousseau sighed: "What am I doing in this world? Though made to live, I am instead dying without ever having lived."[11]

Rousseau did not know how close he was to the truth. Toward dusk he was walking down the main street that plunged from Ménilmontant into Paris. Deep in thought, he saw too late a huge Great Dane that was galloping alongside a carriage careening down the same street. The dog upended Rousseau, throwing him headfirst to the ground and knocking him unconscious. Ironically, the vehicle for this bizarre event carried the leader of the Paris Parlement, Le Pelletier de Fargeau. Despite his reputation as a dour Jansenist, Le Pelletier had just spent the afternoon outside Paris in a tryst with his mistress and was scrambling to return to the city in time for an official meeting.[12] Foiled in its attempt to arrest Rousseau fifteen years before, the Paris Parlement thus finally appeared to have gotten its revenge. "M. Jean-Jacques Rousseau has died from the after-effects of his fall," reported the *Courrier d'Avignon:* "He lived in poverty; he died in misery; and the strangeness of his fate accompanied him all the way to the tomb. It pains us that we cannot speak about the talents of this eloquent writer; our readers must sense that the abuse he made of those talents imposes the most rigorous silence on us now."[13]

Yet it soon became clear that the obituaries were premature. Bloodied and shaken, Rousseau was still alive, soon regaining consciousness from the collision. In a sense, however, he had died, only to be reborn. Upon awakening from his fall, the very first thing Rousseau noticed was not the knot of curious bystanders staring down at him but the sky and glittering stars above them. In the *Reveries,* he attempts to describe this state of being:

> I was born into life at that instant, and it seemed to me that I filled all the objects I perceived with my frail existence. Entirely absorbed in the present moment, I remembered nothing; I had no distinct notion of my person nor the least idea of what had just happened to me; I knew neither who I

was nor where I was; I felt neither injury, fear, nor worry. I watched my blood flow as I would have watched a brook flow, without even suspecting that this blood belonged to me in any way. I felt a rapturous calm in my whole being.[14]

The moment rivaled the earlier moment on the road to Vincennes, but with this crucial difference: in the first epiphany, Rousseau translated the world, while with the second rapture Rousseau was translated or enraptured *by* the world. The wandering philosopher viewed the accident as a form of deliverance: a providential moment leading from spiritual death to rebirth. The Great Dane hurled Rousseau back to an earlier moment with another dog, Sultan, when the two companions shared the undulations of the water's surface on Lake Bienne. Once again, Rousseau lost all sense of time and shed his state of self-awareness.

Learning how to die had always been one of Rousseau's great concerns. He had long claimed that the discovery of death, and its inevitable train of terrors, was one of the tragic consequences of our climb from savagery to civilization.[15] As one commentator observes, Rousseau's realization that "life can be extinguished turns life, which is the condition of living, into an end in itself."[16] Besieged by our imagination, made captives to our illusions, we forget what our ancestors understood, even if they could not articulate it: death was part of life, and not a rupture with it. "Naturally man knows how to suffer with constancy and dies in peace. It is doctors with their prescriptions, philosophers with their precepts, priests with their exhortations, who debase his heart and make him unlearn how to die."[17]

Two years after his accident, in May 1778, Rousseau moved with Thérèse and his unfinished manuscript of the *Reveries* to Ermenonville, the country estate of the Marquis de Girardin, an admirer who had invited the philosopher to retire among his carefully designed gardens. On the morning of July 2, after he had returned from his daily promenade and as he was finishing a bowl of café au lait, Rousseau felt a tingling sensation in his feet and was stricken by an intense headache, collapsing to the floor unconscious. Carried to bed by Thérèse, he died later that day, the victim of a massive apoplexy. Despite the many variations, all of them sentimental and self-serving, that Thérèse subsequently offered of his last moments, it is most likely that Rousseau died quite unlike how he lived: in silence. Caught unawares by death, Rousseau was deprived of the occasion, granted to Hume, for a final phrase or grand gesture. Having begun his life, as he claimed in his *Confessions*, "nearly dead," Rousseau finally completed his improbable journey. This time, though, he was not there to interpret it.

Socrates famously said on his own deathbed that to philosophize is to learn to die. The central aspect of learning to die is recognizing our finitude, including the limits of our understanding: the greatest lesson of death's inevitability, as a result, is learning to live. In antiquity, philosophy was not a theoretical discipline: it was an art of living.[18] Indifferent to the science of making a living—hardly ignoble in itself—it was about the making of a life. As a result, those who practiced philosophy were held to a different standard from the rest of us. In their pursuit of life's great questions, philosophers taught, in their various ways, how best to live and how best to die. If his fellow Athenians had not sentenced him to death in 399 BCE Socrates would perhaps be a mere footnote in the history of philosophy rather than having become the text for two millennia of philosophical footnotes.

There are, clearly, important parallels between Hume and Rousseau. Both men were equally skeptical about the pretensions of philosophy; they both philosophized about the futility and potential dangers of philosophy; they both argued that reason was not all that it was cracked up to be; and they both claimed that the remedy to the human condition lay not in reason but in nature. Yet much more separated than joined the two thinkers. This becomes clearest in their respective preparations for death and how, at the ends of their lives, they came to understand each other.

"If there is any study still appropriate for an old man, it is solely to learn to die," Rousseau wrote in the *Reveries,* but his own interpretation of the ancient prescription of philosophy is revealing. "I consecrate my last days to studying myself and to preparing in advance the account I will give of myself before long. Let me give myself up entirely to the sweetness of conversing with my soul, since that is the only thing men cannot take away from me. . . . I write my reveries only for myself."[19] If we take Rousseau at his word, we are not meant to hear this sigh of despair. His habit as a child of peopling his world with imaginary beings now gave way to the creation of a world of just one being: Jean-Jacques. The thrust of Rousseau's claim is patent: he approached death in the company of no one other than his own self. Just as with his experience on Lake Bienne, he strove during his final days to be, like God, sufficient onto himself. Until the very end, Rousseau conversed with himself alone.

Hume, in turn, like Socrates, continued to live in the heart of a great city, not in bucolic isolation, and conversed with his friends. There were those who came to his bedside, like Boswell and Adam Smith, and those who could not come to Edinburgh, like the Comtesse de Boufflers, but who still corresponded. Less than a week before his death, Hume wrote to her in Paris, sharing her sorrow upon learning the news that the Prince de Conti had died just a few weeks before, and then briefly described his own condition: "I see death approach gradually, without any anxiety or regret." He concluded his letter, "I salute you, with great affection and regard, for the last time."[20] As his life slowly ebbed, Hume had not turned sentimental. Instead, he reaffirmed the philosophical principles he had taught and practiced his entire life.

The same philosophical difference plays out in their attitudes toward each other. For his part, Rousseau remained as completely uncurious about Hume's life after they parted as he had been about his writings before they met. When he wrote from Dover to promise Conway that his third-person client, that is himself, would never speak ill of David Hume, he kept his word to remain silent. Or nearly so. Hume expected to play the villain in Rousseau's *Confessions*, and he felt impelled to publish their correspondence in large measure because of these memoirs, but he is in fact unnamed in a book that is consumed with naming names. Yet Hume becomes quite present at the book's end thanks to Rousseau's very silence, for he chose to end the chronicle of his life on the eve of his meeting with Hume. In the final pages of the *Confessions*, Rousseau relates that he was fleeing Switzerland and unaccountably headed for England, having put himself in the hands of "the two ladies who wanted to dispose of me" (Boufflers and Verdelin), who handed him over to their unnamed "friend." With this word, Rousseau ends his narrative.[21]*

Hume's faded fingerprint can also be detected in a draft of one of the most critical passages from the *Confessions:* the story of the purloined ribbon, so fraught with the themes of the terrible chasm between reality and appearances, truth and lies, that run throughout Rousseau's works. Recounting the story from his youth, Rousseau still trembles at the recollection of the "diabolical audacity" with which he falsely accused poor Marion of the crime he himself had committed. In particular, he recalled that his dead employer's nephew dismissed him and Marion with the warning that the conscience of the guilty part would revenge the innocent. "His prediction was not empty, there is not a single day in which it fails to come true."[22] In the original draft of this passage Rousseau continues: "But my punishment is not entirely internal, and David Hume is now doing only what I once did to poor Marion."[23] As he recalled his youthful crime in the gloomy north of England, Rousseau found himself once again the victim of appearances, the retribution of the conscience from within being complemented by punishment from without.

---

*But not the book, for a further silence remained. Having ended the chronicle of his life up to this point, Rousseau leaped forward in time to Paris and the last reading he gave of his *Confessions*, in May 1771, before he was ordered to stop by the police. "I completed my reading this way and everyone was silent. Mme d'Egmont was the only one who appeared moved; she visibly trembled; but she very quickly recovered and kept silent as did the whole company. Such was the fruit I drew from this reading and from my declaration." While the author seems to have taken this silence as assent to his declaration that he had revealed his natural disposition, his audience, perplexed and embarrassed by the work's revelations, may have been relieved that they would hear no more.

Rather than putting himself in Hume's shoes, Rousseau thus forces Hume into his own worn shoes, and, characteristic of his life and thought, turns his reflections back on himself. It is ironic, then, that Hume himself tries on his former friend's star-punched shoes—and, remarkably, does so a quarter of a century before they even meet. In the concluding section of Book One of the *Treatise of Human Nature,* where Hume reflects upon the melancholy and even madness brought on by his skepticism, he writes: "I am first affrighted and confounded with that forlorn solitude, in which I am placed in my philosophy, and fancy myself some strange uncouth monster, who not being able to mingle and unite in society, has been expelled all human commerce, and left utterly abandoned and disconsolate."[24] This "strange uncouth monster" begotten by the attempt at human understanding demands our sympathy, and Hume did come to sympathize with Rousseau, whose own endeavor at understanding, so different in many ways from Hume's own, had thrust him into forlorn solitude.

In the same year that Rousseau started the *Reveries,* Hume also wrote an autobiographical account, titled "My Own Life." The essay begins with typical self-deprecation: "It is difficult for a man to speak long of himself without vanity; therefore I shall be short." Hume's account runs scarcely seven pages—stunning brevity for so celebrated a thinker. In his appraisal of his literary and philosophical works—a survey that omits all mention of his friendship with Rousseau—Hume does not turn to the subject of himself until the closing paragraph. There, he proposes an epitaph of sorts: "I was, I say, a man of mild dispositions, of command of temper, of an open, social, and cheerful humor, capable of attachment, but little susceptible of enmity, and of great moderation in all my passions."[25]

In the end, while Rousseau sought the same self-sufficiency as God, Hume knew that most gods—or, at least, Job's God—do not feel the need, as did *le pauvre Jean-Jacques,* to justify his ways to men. As Hume confided to Davenport, Rousseau was "too wise to be confined, too mad to govern himself."[26] Hume's belief in Rousseau's madness sheds crucial light on his philosophy and actions during this period. A critical element of Hume's historical and philosophical method is his claim that human beings are fundamentally alike across time and place. Yet Hume also shows great sensitivity to the varieties of human nature.[27] He argues that while the springs to human behavior are constant, they are expressed in manifold ways: the only things that do not change are the sources of change itself. Rather than a cause for despair, this insistence upon this common ground of humanity is liberating. It lays the foundation for human sympathy, the common ground on which we can join, converse with, and understand one another. In an important sense, we *see* one another thanks to this commonality of character. Every human creature, Hume affirmed, "resembles ourselves and by that means has an advantage above any other object in operating on the imagination." In fact, "the minds of men are mirrors to one another, not only because they reflect each other's emotions, but also because those rays of passions, sentiments, and opinions may be often reverberated and may decay away by insensible degrees."[28]

It is inevitably and perfectly human to mirror the weaknesses no less than the strengths of our fellow beings. As W. V. Quine quipped, the Humean predicament is the human predicament. Even Rousseau's madness was not alien to Hume's understanding: he had known the cost of philosophical melancholy and delirium all too well. In his correspondence, Hume repeatedly revealed this sympathetic understanding. As he told Blair, Rousseau's "sensibility rises to a pitch beyond what I have seen any example of. . . . He is like a man who were stripped not only of his clothes but of his skin."[29]

To be sure, Hume never completely abandoned the idea that malevolence was an ingredient to Rousseau's behavior. Nevertheless, when he wrote Turgot on May 22, 1767, the same day Rousseau sailed from Dover, Hume allowed that his former friend had become "an object of the greatest compassion." He asked Turgot to do what he could to protect Rousseau from the machinations of the philosophes and royal bureaucrats, insisting "that the enemies of this unhappy man may have their vengeance fully satiated by his past misfortunes, and may no longer aggravate afflictions too heavy to be borne."[30] Hume continued to follow Rousseau's peregrinations from afar. "He is surely the most singular and incomprehensible, and at the same time the most unhappy man that ever was born," Hume wrote to Boufflers at the very end of 1768, having learned of Rousseau's "elopement from the Prince of Conti," and concluded his letter with a request that she keep him informed of the exile's wanderings.[31]

But did Hume's compassion for Rousseau ever lead to a fuller appreciation of his former friend's thought? To the end of his days, the Scot remained convinced that Rousseau's writings were outrageous fancies. Hume acknowledged Rousseau's eloquence and invention but insisted that his books were "at the bottom full of extravagance and of sophistry."[32] For social, cultural, and perhaps linguistic reasons, Hume saw mostly smoke and mirrors where others saw the fire of genius. Rousseau's writings were, for Hume, the stuff of fanciful imagination, and they succeeded so well because their readers wished them to be true. This may be one of the reasons Hume reacted so violently to Rousseau's letter of accusations. Rousseau held tremendous moral sway over his legion of readers—as Hume told his brother, Rousseau "of all the writers that are or ever were in Europe is the man who has acquired the most enthusiastic and most passionate admirers."[33] Especially for a man like Hume, who had worked so diligently to build bridges between the "conversible" and intellectual worlds, such preeminence entailed responsibilities. Hence Hume's earlier indignation, expressed to Boufflers, over Rousseau's *Emile:* how unfortunate that in "even in so serious a subject," namely education, their mutual friend "indulges his love of the marvelous."[34]

There are, clearly, limitations to Humean understanding of Rousseau's writings. He seemed indifferent to or unaware of the radical and profound elements in Rousseau's critique of modernity and was perhaps blinded to the Genevan's insights by the criteria he himself proposed in "Of the Standard of Taste" for evaluating texts. So intently focused on the rhetorical styles with which authors appealed to their audiences, Hume inadvertently, perhaps inevitably, paid less attention to the substance of the text.

Yet such limitations can be seen in a different and better light. Hume embodied, to a remarkable degree, what the twentieth-century German sociologist Max Weber called the ethic of responsibility. This ethic recognizes the dignity and particularity of every human being and accepts our inevitably flawed and limited nature. Above all, the ethic of responsibility fully roots us in the world of men and women, not ideals and abstractions: such an ethic leads us not away from, but back to our fellow creatures. In a moving passage in the *Treatise,* Hume declared, "Let all the powers and elements of nature conspire to serve and obey one man: let the sun rise and set at his command: The sea and rivers ever may be useful or agreeable to him: He will still be miserable till you give him some one person at least, with whom he may share his happiness and whose esteem and friendship he may enjoy."[35]

Rousseau, on the other hand, personifies Weber's alternative to the ethic of responsibility, the ethic of conviction: the passionate certainty in the rightness of one's cause, even at the expense of the values encompassed by the ethics of responsibility. In his lifelong pursuit of the "great truths" conveyed by his illumination on the road to Vincennes, Rousseau paid a tremendous personal and social price: a long and tragic cortege of failed relationships and betrayed friends stretched in the wake of his writings. In his *Letter to d'Alembert,* which marked the final rupture with his Parisian friends, Rousseau announced that he would devote his life to truth. Yet this commitment to truth had less to do with outer reality than with inner conviction. In David Gauthier's phrase, truthfulness for Rousseau "has its foundation, neither in moral sentiment nor in the reality of things, but in the demand to reveal his own nature."[36] The intellectual and social consequences of this demand have since been measured in Rousseau's life and the lives of his readers.

As Hume discovered as a young man, we cannot depend on philosophy alone to make sense of our world and lives. We stray at great risk from the springs of life that alone can slake the delirium induced by unbounded confidence in reason. Hence Hume's distaste for the solitary thinker: "After his death," he writes, such a man "may have a place in the calendar; but will scarcely ever be admitted, when alive, into intimacy and society, except by those who are as delirious and as dismal as himself."[37]

Society saves us from ourselves; it necessarily forms our characters; it makes for everything that is worth living and dying for. As Terence Penelhum has written, David Hume's persona no less than his writings was the result of sustained, conscious, and intense effort: his was the "deliberate achievement of a man who knows better, not less well, than his opponents what a hard taskmaster philosophy can be."[38] He died as he lived: as a philosopher, but above all as a man.

Notes

CC   Jean-Jacques Rousseau, *Correspondance complète*, ed. Ralph A. Leigh, 51 vols. (Geneva: Voltaire Foundation, 1965–95).

LDH   David Hume, *Letters of David Hume*, ed. J. Y. T Grieg, 2 vols. (Oxford: Oxford University Press, 1932).

NLDH   David Hume, *New Letters of David Hume*, ed. Raymond Klibansky and Ernest Campbell Mossner (Oxford: Oxford University Press, 1954).

1. AN ENLIGHTENMENT QUARREL

1. The above account is based on Hume's account of the evening as related in two letters: Hume to Hugh Blair, March 25, 1766, *LDH*, 2: 314; Hume to Marie-Charlotte Hippolyte de Campet de Saujon, Comtesse de Boufflers, April 3, 1766, *LDH*, 2: 317.

2. Susan Neiman, *Evil in Modern Thought: An Alternative History of Philosophy* (Princeton: Princeton University Press, 2002), 248.

3. The literature is vast, but an excellent starting point for the lay reader is Roy Porter's brilliant survey *The Enlightenment* (London: Palgrave, 2001). Peter Gay's phrase is from his two-volume work, *The Enlightenment*, vol. 1, *The Rise of Modern Paganism*

(New York: Norton, 1966), and vol. 2, *The Science of Freedom* (New York: Norton, 1969).

4. Robert Darnton, *The Literary Underground of the Old Regime* (Cambridge: Harvard University Press, 1982); Jonathan Israel, *Radical Enlightenment* (Oxford: Oxford University Press, 2001).

5. Francis Bacon, *The New Atlantis,* in *The Great Instauration and New Atlantis,* ed. Jerry Weinberger (Arlington Heights, Ill.: Harlan Davidson, 1980), 70.

6. Paul-Henri Thiry, Baron d'Holbach, *Essai sur les préjugés,* quoted by Charles Taylor, *Sources of the Self: The Making of Modern Identity* (Cambridge: Harvard University Press, 1989), 353.

7. Antoine-Nicolas de Condorcet, *Sketch for a Historical Picture of the Human Mind,* trans. June Barraclough (New York: Noonday, 1955), 4.

8. Pierre Hadot, *Qu'est que la philosophie antique?* (Paris: Gallimard, 1990), 390.

9. Alexander Nehamas, *The Art of Living: Socratic Reflections from Plato to Foucault* (Berkeley: University of California Press, 1998), 2.

2. THE WILD PHILOSOPHER

1. James Boswell, *The Journals of James Boswell, On the Grand Tour: Germany and Switzerland, 1764,* ed. Frederick A. Pottle (New Haven: Yale University Press, 1928), 215. Unless otherwise noted, all quotations in this section are from this volume of Boswell's journals, 215–66.

2. Peter Martin, *A Life of James Boswell* (New Haven: Yale University Press, 2000), 50.

3. James Boswell, *The Life of Samuel Johnson, L.L.D.* (Oxford: Oxford University Press, 1953), 359.

4. Jean-Jacques Rousseau, *Confessions,* in *The Collected Writings of Rousseau,* Roger D. Masters and Christopher Kelly, gen. eds., 10 vols. to date (Hanover, N.H.: Dartmouth College/University Press of New England, 1990–), 5: 597–98.

5. Boswell, *Germany and Switzerland,* 220.

6. Quoted in Robert Darnton, *The Great Cat Massacre: And Other Episodes in French Cultural History* (New York: Vintage, 1985), 243.

7. Jean-Jacques Rousseau, *Julie; or, the New Heloise,* in *Collected Writings,* 6: 3.

8. Boswell, *Germany and Switzerland,* 235.

9. Rousseau, *Confessions,* 3, 5. For a revealing analysis of the *Confessions,* and especially how Rousseau offers his own life as an alternative exemplar to classical and Christian models, see Christopher Kelly, *Rousseau's Exemplary Life: The "Confessions" as Political Philosophy* (Ithaca: Cornell University Press, 1987). For an extended analysis of Rousseau's *Confessions* in relation to Augustine, see Ann Hartle, *The Modern Self in Rousseau's Confessions: A Reply to St. Augustine* (Notre Dame, Ind.: University of Notre Dame Press, 1983).

10. Rousseau to Guillaume-Chrétien de Lamoignon de Malesherbes, January 12, 1762, in *Confessions*, 574–75. For a comprehensive account of Rousseau's early life, see Maurice Cranston, *Jean-Jacques: The Early Life and Work of Jean-Jacques Rousseau, 1712–1754* (New York: Norton, 1982). The other two volumes of Cranston's biography, to be cited below, are similarly useful. See also Raymond Trousson's helpful two-volume treatment of Rousseau's life, *Jean-Jacques Rousseau* (Paris: Tallandier, 1988, 1989), and, most recently, Leo Damrosch, *Jean-Jacques Rousseau: Restless Genius* (New York: Houghton Mifflin, 2005).

11. Jean Starobinski was the first to underscore the importance of Rousseau's experience at Bossey for understanding his life and thought. See *Jean-Jacques Rousseau: Transparence and Obstruction*, trans. Arthur Goldhammer (Chicago: University of Chicago Press, 1988), 7–9.

12. Maurice Cranston *The Solitary Self: Jean-Jacques Rousseau in Exile and Adversity* (Chicago: University of Chicago Press, 1997), 87.

13. Rousseau, *Confessions*, 17.

14. Ibid.

15. Ibid., 37.

16. Ibid., 40.

17. Ibid., 40–41.

18. Ibid., 69–71.

19. Starobinski, *Rousseau*, 122.

20. Rousseau, *Confessions*, 103, 124–25.

21. Ibid., 162, 202–3.

22. Ibid., 146.

23. Ibid., 280; advertisement to Rousseau, *Les Muses galantes* (The gallant muses), in *Collected Writings*, 10: 181.

24. See Rousseau, *Confessions*, 242.

25. See Robert Darnton, *The Literary Underground of the Old Regime* (Cambridge: Harvard University Press, 1982).

26. Damrosch, *Rousseau*, 160–61.

27. Rousseau, *Confessions*, 110.

28. Arthur M. Wilson, *Diderot* (New York: Oxford University Press, 1972), 68.

29. Damrosch, *Rousseau*, 207.

30. Rousseau, *Confessions*, 291.

31. Damrosch, *Rousseau*, 206.

32. See Rousseau to Mme de Warens, *CC*, 2: 112–13.

33. Damrosch, *Rousseau*, 208.

34. Rousseau, *Confessions*, 341.

35. Ibid., 342.

36. Rousseau to Malesherbes, January 12, 1762, in *Confessions*, 575.

37. Jean-Jacques Rousseau, *Emile; or, On Education*, trans. and ed. Allan Bloom (New York: Basic, 1979), 34. Later in the work, Rousseau writes: "I will be told that I, too, dream. I agree, but I give my dreams as dreams, which others are not careful to do, leaving it to the reader to find out whether they contain something useful for people who are awake" (112n).

38. See Damrosch, *Rousseau*, 213.

39. Rousseau, *Confessions*, 342.

40. See Rousseau to Malesherbes, January 12, 1762, in *Confessions*, 575; Jean-Jacques Rousseau, *Letter to Christophe de Beaumont*, in *Collected Writings*, 9: 26; Jean-Jacques Rousseau, *Rousseau Judge of Jean-Jacques: Dialogues*, in *Collected Writings*, 1: 23.

41. Jean-Jacques Rousseau, *Discourse on the Sciences and the Arts*, in *First and Second Discourses*, trans. Roger D. Masters and Judith R. Masters (New York: St. Martin's, 1964), 32.

42. See Sally Howard Campbell and John T. Scott, "The Politic Argument of Rousseau's *Discourse on the Sciences and the Arts*," *American Journal of Political Science* 49 (October 2005): 819–29.

43. Rousseau, *Discourse on the Sciences and the Arts*, 34, 63.

44. Quoted in Wilson, *Diderot*, 120.

45. Jean-Jacques Rousseau, *Letter on French Music*, in *Collected Writings*, 7: 174. For a discussion of Rousseau's contribution to the Quarrel of Bouffons and his career as a musician and musical theorist more generally, see the Introduction to *Collected Writings*, vol. 7.

46. Jean-Jacques Rousseau, *Discourse on the Origin and Foundations of Inequality Among Men*, in *First and Second Discourses*, 91–92.

47. Rousseau, *Confessions*, 326.

48. Rousseau, *Julie*, 453.

49. Rousseau, *Discourse on Inequality*, 126.

50. Ibid., 149.

51. Rousseau, *Letter to Christophe de Beaumont*, 31. For an interpretation of Rousseau's thought that emphasizes the principle of the "natural goodness of man," see Arthur M. Melzer, *The Natural Goodness of Man: On the System of Rousseau's Thought* (Chicago: University of Chicago Press, 1990).

52. Rousseau, *Discourse on Inequality*, 151, 141.

53. Ibid., 181.

54. Voltaire to Rousseau, August 30, 1755, *CC*, 3: 317.

55. Rousseau, *Discourse on Inequality*, 201–3.

56. See Jean-Jacques Rousseau, *Reveries of the Solitary Walker*, Third Walk, in *Collected Writings*, vol. 8.

57. Damrosch, *Rousseau*, 289.

58. Quoted ibid., 293.

59. Jean-Jacques Rousseau, *Letter to d'Alembert on the Theater,* in *Collected Writings,* 10: 352n.

60. For Rousseau's statement concerning his adoption of "Citizen of Geneva," see *Julie,* 20.

61. Rousseau, *Emile,* 37.

62. Rousseau, *Letter to Christophe de Beaumont,* 9: 46–47.

63. Rousseau to the Marquise de Créqui, June 7, 1762, *CC,* 11: 38–39.

64. Rousseau, *Confessions,* 485–89.

65. Rousseau to Alexandre Delyre, December 20, 1764, *CC,* 22: 252.

66. Rousseau to James Boswell, December 3, 1764, *CC,* 22: 159.

67. Boswell, *Germany and Switzerland,* 220. Unless otherwise noted, all quotations in this section are from this volume of Boswell's journals, 220–66.

68. Cranston, *Solitary Self,* 14–17, 25–26. See appendixes 415–16 in *CC,* 26: 378–82.

69. Joseph Teleki had remarked on these odd shoes after visiting Rousseau at Montmorency in 1761. See Maurice Cranston, *The Noble Savage: Jean-Jacques Rousseau, 1754–1762* (Chicago: University of Chicago Press, 1991), 272.

70. Quoted in Ernest Campbell Mossner, *The Forgotten Hume* (New York: Columbia University Press, 1942), 136.

71. See Cranston, *Solitary Self,* 16.

72. Quoted in Jean Guéhenno, *Jean-Jacques Rousseau,* 2 vols. (London: Routledge and Kegan Paul, 1966; Paris: Gallimard, 1962), 2: 151.

73. Rousseau to Delyre, December 20, 1764, *CC,* 22: 252.

74. Rousseau, *Confessions,* 502–3.

75. Boswell, *Germany and Switzerland,* 150.

76. See Rousseau, *Julie,* 44.

3 . THE GREAT SCOT

1. Quoted in Peter Martin, *A Life of James Boswell* (New Haven: Yale University Press, 2000), 60.

2. Quoted ibid.

3. Quoted in Ernest Campbell Mossner, *The Life of David Hume,* 2nd ed. (Oxford: Oxford University Press, 1980), 394.

4. David Hume, "My Own Life," in *Essays Moral, Political, and Literary,* ed. Eugene Miller (Indianapolis: Liberty, 1985), xxxiii.

5. Mossner, *Life of David Hume,* 51.

6. Hume to Dr. George Cheyne, March or April 1734, *LDH,* 1: 12–18. There has been scholarly debate over the intended recipient of the letter, from which all the subsequent passages concerning Hume's self-diagnosis are taken. Mossner argues that it was meant for Dr. John Arbuthnot, a man of varied interests including the study of melancholy (*Life of David Hume,* 83–85). Hume to Michael Ramsay, July 4, 1727, *LDH,* 1: 10.

7. Hume to Cheyne, March or April 1734, *LDH*, 1: 12–18.

8. Hume, "My Own Life," xxxiii.

9. Mossner, *Life of David Hume*, 204.

10. David Hume, "Of Civil Liberty," in *Essays*, 91.

11. David Hume, *A Treatise of Human Nature*, ed. L. A. Selby-Bigge (Oxford: Oxford University Press, 1975), xvi.

12. Ibid., 649 (abstract).

13. Ibid., 88, 165.

14. Ibid., 77.

15. Ibid., 252, 253.

16. Ibid., 260.

17. Ibid., 264.

18. Ibid., 269.

19. Hume, "My Own Life," xxxiv.

20. Hume to Henry Home, December 2, 1737, *NLDH*, 2.

21. Hume, "My Own Life," xxxv.

22. Quoted in Mossner, *Life of David Hume*, 119.

23. David Hume, "On Essay Writing," in *Essays*, 534–35. Hume's distinction between the "learned" and "conversible" worlds appears to derive from Shaftesbury's similar distinction in his *Characteristisks*.

24. David Hume, "The Sceptic," in *Essays*, 169, 180.

25. David Hume, "Of the Origin of Government," *Essays*, 38.

26. Hume also made several revisions in the edition of 1753–54 to a related essay published earlier, "Of the Rise and Progress of the Arts and Sciences," that also seem to reply to the arguments of Rousseau's *Discourse on the Sciences and Arts*. See David Hume, "Of the Rise and Progress of the Arts and Sciences," in *Essays*, 130–31.

27. David Hume, "Of Refinement in the Arts," in *Essays*, 280.

28. Jean-Jacques Rousseau, *On the Social Contract*, ed. Roger D. Masters and trans. Judith R. Masters (New York: St. Martin's, 1978), 99.

29. David Hume, *An Enquiry Concerning Human Understanding*, ed. L. A. Selby-Bigge, 3rd ed. (Oxford: Oxford University Press, 1975), 83–84.

30. Jean-Jacques Rousseau, *Discourse on the Origin and Foundations of Inequality Among Men*, in *First and Second Discourses*, trans. Roger D. Masters and Judith R. Masters (New York: St. Martin's, 1964), 102.

31. Hume, "My Own Life," xxxvi.

32. Hume to Ramsay, April or May 1755, *LDH*, 1: 220.

33. James Boswell, *The Life of Samuel Johnson, L.L.D.* (Oxford: Oxford University Press, 1953), 405.

34. Hume to Ramsay, April or May 1755, *LDH*, 1: 220.

35. For analyses of Smith's debt to Rousseau and conversation with him, see Den-

nis Rasmussen, *The Problems and Promise of Commercial Society: Adam Smith's Response to Rousseau* (State College: Penn State University Press, 2008); Ryan Patrick Hanley, "Commerce and Corruption: Rousseau's Diagnosis and Adam Smith's Cure," *European Journal of Political Theory* 7 (2008): 137–58.

36. Mossner, *Life of David Hume*, 301.

37. David Edmonds and John Eidenow, *Rousseau's Dog: Two Great Thinkers at War in the Age of Enlightenment* (New York: HarperCollins, 2006), 21.

38. Hume, "My Own Life," xxxvi–xxxvii.

39. David Hume, "Of the Study of History," in *Essays*, 563, 567.

40. Tellingly, in the British Library's catalogue, David Hume is identified as "the historian," not "the philosopher." See David Wootton, "Hume, 'the historian'" in *The Cambridge Companion to Hume*, ed. David Fate Norton (Cambridge: Cambridge University Press, 1993), 307.

41. Hume to William Strahan, May 3, 1755, *LDH*, 1: 221–22.

42. Donald Livingston, *Hume's Philosophy of Common Life* (Chicago: University of Chicago Press, 1984), 317.

43. James Boswell, *Boswell's London Journal, 1762–1763*, ed. Frederick A. Pottle (New Haven: Yale University Press, 1950), 206, 197.

44. Rules and Orders of the Select Society, quoted in *LDH*, 1: 219, ed. n. 2.

45. James Buchan, *Crowded with Genius: The Scottish Enlightenment, Edinburgh's Moment of the Mind* (New York: HarperCollins, 2003), 57.

46. Hume, *Enquiry Concerning Human Understanding*, 2.

47. David Wootton, "Of Miracles: Probability and Irreligion" in *Studies in the Scottish Enlightenment*, ed. M. A. Stewart (Oxford: Oxford University Press, 1990).

48. Hume to Edward Gibbon, March 18, 1776, *LDH*, 2: 311.

49. See Mossner, *Life of David Hume*, 340.

50. Hume to Ramsay, June 1755, *LDH*, 1: 224.

51. Quoted in Mossner, *Life of David Hume*, 248.

52. Hume to Hugh Blair, 1761, *LDH*, 1, 348–51.

53. Quoted in Mossner, *Life of David Hume*, 223.

54. Hume to David Mallet, November 8, 1762, *LDH*, 1: 369.

55. Quoted in Mossner, *Life of David Hume*, 421.

56. Hume to Robert Clerk, December 12, 1761, *NLDH*, 65.

57. Quoted in Mossner, *Life of David Hume*, 494.

58. Hume to Gilbert Elliot, March 27, 1764, *LDH*, 1: 429.

4. THE LORD OF FERNEY

1. For a useful analysis of the relationship between Rousseau and Voltaire, see Henri Gouhier, *Rousseau et Voltaire: Portraits dans deux miroirs* (Paris: Vrin, 1983).

2. Rousseau to Voltaire, December 11, 1745, *CC*, 2: 92.

3. Voltaire to Jean Le Rond d'Alembert, January 9, 1765, *CC*, 23: 73–74.

4. Quoted in Maurice Cranston, *The Noble Savage: Jean-Jacques Rousseau, 1754–1762* (Chicago: University of Chicago Press, 1991), 208.

5. Rousseau to Voltaire, June 17, 1760, *CC*, 7: 136.

6. Cranston, *Noble Savage*, 263.

7. Voltaire to d'Alembert, March 19, 1761, *CC*, 8: 272.

8. See Theodore Besterman, *Voltaire* (Oxford: Oxford University Press, 1976), 66–77.

9. Jean Goldzink, *Voltaire: La Légende de Saint Arouet* (Paris: Gallimard, 1989), 46.

10. Voltaire to Jean Frédéric Phélypeaux, c. April 20, 1726, *Correspondence*, ed. Theodore Besterman, 51 vols. (Geneva: Voltaire Foundation, 1968–), 2: 287 (D271).

11. In fact, Voltaire had for some time planned to go to England, and Rohan's assault and the ensuing controversy actually delayed his departure. See Nicholas Cronk's introduction to Voltaire, *Letters Concerning the English Nation* (Oxford: Oxford University Press, 1999).

12. Jean Orieux, *Voltaire* (Paris: Flammarion, 1966), 210.

13. Roger Pearson, *Voltaire Almighty: A Life in Pursuit of Freedom* (London: Bloomsbury, 2005), 97.

14. Voltaire, *Lettres philosophiques* (Paris: Gallimard, 1986), 97, 99.

15. Ibid., 60–61.

16. Besterman, *Voltaire*, 177.

17. See Pearson, *Voltaire Almighty*, 117.

18. Quoted in Besterman, *Voltaire*, 189.

19. On *Zaïre*, ibid., 174.

20. Ibid., 163.

21. For Diderot's remark on Catherine, see Arthur M. Wilson, *Diderot* (New York: Oxford University Press, 1972), 645.

22. Frederick the Great to Voltaire, February 24, 1751, in Voltaire, *Correspondence*, 12: 136 (D 4401).

23. Voltaire to Marie Louise Denis, December 18, 1752, *Correspondence*, 13: 283 (D5114).

24. Besterman, *Voltaire*, 344.

25. Quoted ibid., 383.

26. Quoted in Peter Gay, *The Enlightenment*, vol. 1, *The Rise of Modern Paganism* (New York: Norton, 1966), 435.

27. Quoted ibid., 1: 436.

28. Gavin de Beer and André-Michel Rousseau, "Voltaire's British Visitors," *Studies in Voltaire and the Eighteenth Century* 49 (1967): 11.

29. Orieux, *Voltaire*, 635.

30. De Beer and Rousseau, "Voltaire's British Visitors," 99–100, 11.

31. Ibid., 74.

32. Quoted ibid., 86.

33. James Boswell, *The Journals of James Boswell, On the Grand Tour: Germany and Switzerland, 1764*, ed. Frederick A. Pottle (New Haven: Yale University Press, 1928), 285, which includes Voltaire to James Boswell, February 11, 1765.

34. Ibid., 307–8.

35. Ibid.

36. Friedrich Melchior Baron von Grimm, *Correspondance littéraire*, ed. Jean Maurice Tourneux, 16 vols. (Paris: Garnier, 1877–82), January 1, 1766, 6: 457–58.

37. Jean-Jacques Rousseau, *Letters Written from the Mountain*, letter 5, in *The Collected Writings of Rousseau*, Roger D. Masters and Christopher Kelly, gen. eds., 10 vols. to date (Hanover, N.H.: Dartmouth College/University Press of New England, 1990–), 9: 224–25.

38. See Robert Darnton, *The Literary Underground of the Old Regime* (Cambridge: Harvard University Press, 1982).

39. See Christopher Kelly, *Rousseau as Author: Consecrating One's Life to the Truth* (Chicago: University of Chicago Press, 2003).

40. Lester G. Crocker, *Jean-Jacques Rousseau: The Prophetic Voice, 1758–1778* (New York 1974), 242–43.

41. For "philosophical sect" see especially Jean-Jacques Rousseau, *Rousseau Judge of Jean-Jacques: Dialogues*, in *Collected Writings*, 1: 238.

42. Jean-Jacques Rousseau, *Reveries of the Solitary Walker*, in *Collected Writings*, 8: 21.

43. Quoted in Wilson, *Diderot*, 285.

44. Voltaire to Pierre Robert Le Cornier de Ciderville, March 2, 1731, *Correspondence*, 2: 63 (D404).

45. Voltaire to Étienne Noël Damilaville, December 26, 1764, *CC*, 23: 293.

46. Théodore Tronchin to Mme Necker, February 18, 1765, *CC*, 24: 41.

47. Voltaire to Charles Bordes, March 4, 1765, *CC*, 24: 138.

48. Quoted in Cranston, *Noble Savage*, 278.

5. LE BON DAVID

1. David Hume to Gilbert Elliot, July 5, 1762, *LDH*, 1: 336–37.

2. *Année Littéraire* 3 (1763): 39–40, quoted in Harvey Chisick, "The Representation of Adam Smith and David Hume in the *Année Littéraire* and the *Journal Encyclopédique*," in *Scotland and France in the Enlightenment*, ed. Deirdre Dawson and Pierre Morère (Lewisburg, Pa.: Bucknell University Press, 2004), 253. Some contemporaries, like Horace Walpole, believed that Hume had intentionally imitated the style of Voltaire's history, but Hume himself makes clear that the Frenchman's "agreeable" book appeared in England after he had written the lion's share of his own first volume. See Hume's letter to the Abbé le Blanc, November 5, 1755, *LDH*, 1: 226. Hume re-

fers here to Voltaire's *Age of Louis XIV,* but he may have read his earlier *History of Charles XII.*

3. Quoted in Ernest Campbell Mossner, *Life of David Hume,* 2nd ed. (Oxford: Oxford University Press, 1980), 457.

4. Horace Walpole to Thomas Gray, January 25, 1766, *Letters of Horace Walpole,* 2 vols. (New York: Putnam, 1890), 1: 42.

5. Marie-Charlotte Hippolyte de Campet de Saujon, Comtesse de Boufflers, to Hume, March 13, 1761, in Hume, *LDH,* 2: 366–67.

6. Hume to Boufflers, May 15, 1761, *LDH,* 1: 345.

7. Boufflers to Hume, March 13, 1761, *LDH,* 2: 366.

8. Mossner, *Life of David Hume,* 432.

9. Quoted in ed. n. 2 to Hume to Boufflers, July 3, 1763, *LDH,* 1: 387.

10. Ibid., 1: 388.

11. Quoted in Mossner, *Life of David Hume,* 211.

12. Quoted ibid., 436.

13. Hume to Baron Mure of Caldwell, September 1, 1763, *LDH,* 1: 392–94; Hume to Adam Smith, September 13, 1763, *LDH,* 1: 395.

14. Hume to Alexander Carlyle, September 15, 1763, *LDH,* 1: 398.

15. Hume to Boufflers, September 22, 1763, *LDH,* 1: 402; David Hume, "My Own Life," in *Essays Moral, Political, and Literary,* ed. Eugene Miller (Indianapolis: Liberty, 1985), xxxiv.

16. Boufflers to Hume, October 19, 1763, *LDH,* 1: 406.

17. Ibid.

18. Quoted in David P. Jordan, *Transforming Paris: The Life and Times of Baron Haussmann* (New York: Free Press, 1995), 15.

19. Jean-Jacques Rousseau, *Emile; or, On Education,* trans. and ed. Allan Bloom (New York: Basic, 1979), 355.

20. Hume to Alexander Wedderburn, November 23, 1763, *LDH,* 1: 414.

21. Ibid., 1: 415.

22. Horace Walpole to the Countess of Suffolk, September 20, 1765, *Letters of Horace Walpole,* ed. Paget Toynbee, 16 vols. (Oxford: Oxford University Press, 1924), 6: 1052.

23. *Mémoires et correspondance de Mme d'Épinay,* 3 vols. (Paris: Badouin, 1818), 3: 284, quoted in Mossner, *Life of David Hume,* 444.

24. Hume to Hugh Blair, April 26, 1764, *LDH,* 1: 436.

25. Quoted in Mossner, *Life of David Hume,* 446.

26. Hume to William Robertson, December 1, 1763, LDH, 1: 416.

27. John Jardine to Hume, August 1764, *LDH,* 2: 353.

28. See Dena Goodman, *The Republic of Letters: A Cultural History of the French Enlightenment* (Ithaca: Cornell University Press, 1994), esp. chap. 3.

29. See ibid.; see also Benedetta Craveri, *Madame du Deffand and Her World*, trans. Teresa Waugh (London: Orion, 2002), 63.

30. Quoted in Benedetta Craveri, *The Age of Conversation*, trans. Teresa Waugh (New York: New York Review of Books, 2005), 358.

31. Jean-Jacques Rousseau, *Julie; or, the New Heloise*, in *Collected Writings*, 6: 191 (part 2, letter 14).

32. Hume to Blair, December 1763, *LDH*, 1: 420.

33. Craveri, *Madame du Deffand and Her World*, 38.

34. Mossner, *Life of David Hume*, 452, 451.

35. Goodman, *Republic of Letters*, 100.

36. Hume to Eliot, September 22, 1764, *LDH*, 1: 470.

37. Hume to Blair, April 6, 1765, *LDH*, 1: 496.

38. See Alan Kors, *D'Holbach's Coterie: An Enlightenment in Paris* (Princeton: Princeton University Press: 1976), 94–96.

39. Denis Diderot, *Lettres à Sophie Volland*, ed. André Babelon, 2 vols. (Paris: Gallimard, 1930), 2: 298.

40. Compare David Berman, "David Hume and the Suppression of 'Theism,'" *Journal of the History of Philosophy* 21 (1983): 375–87, and *A History of Atheism in Britain from Hobbes to Russell* (London: Routledge and Kegan Paul, 1988), who argues that the discussion between Holbach, Hume, and the others was a highly coded exchange meant to gauge the precise brand of "atheism" to which each individual subscribed.

41. Edward Gibbon, *Memoirs of My Life* (Hammondsworth: Penguin, 1984), 136.

42. Scholars like J. C. A. Gaskin have argued that, for Hume, belief in the divine does not have the same status as our beliefs in the uninterrupted existence of an external world or the expectation that past regularities will be repeated in the future ("Hume on Religion," in *The Cambridge Companion to Hume*, ed. David Fate Norton [Cambridge: Cambridge University Press, 1993], 313–44). Yet even though Hume relegated religious belief among the "secondary passions," it seems sufficiently deep-seated and resilient to make a skeptic wonder whether this is a distinction without a difference.

43. David Hume, *Natural History of Religion*, ed. H. E. Root (Stanford: Stanford University Press, 1956), 27.

44. David Hume, *An Enquiry Concerning Human Understanding*, ed. L. A. Selby-Bigge, 3rd ed. (Oxford: Oxford University Press, 1975), 162.

45. Sterne's *Letters*, quoted in Mossner, *Life of David Hume*, 502.

46. Hume to Boufflers, July 6, 1764, *LDH*, 1: 448–50.

47. Boufflers to Hume, July 6, 1764, *LDH*, 2: 370. The probable reason that the letter bears the same date as Hume's is that Boufflers had already begun her letter, devoted to a critique of John Home's *Douglas*, when Hume's missive arrived.

48. Hume to Boufflers, July 14, 1764, *LDH*, 1: 451.

49. Boufflers to Hume, July 21, 1764, *LDH*, 2: 372.

50. See *CC*, 15: 187.

51. Hume to Boufflers, July 29, 1764, *LDH*, 1: 456.

52. Boufflers to Hume, July 30, 1764, *LDH*, 2: 373.

53. Hume to Boufflers, August 3, 4, or 5, 1764, *LDH*, 1: 458.

54. Elliot to Hume, September 22, 1764, *LDH*, 1: 469, n. 3.

55. David Hume, *A Treatise of Human Nature*, ed. L. A. Selby-Bigge (Oxford: Oxford University Press, 1975), 413, 414.

56. Hume to Elliot, September 30, 1764, *LDH*, 1: 473.

57. Hume to Boufflers, August 18, 1764, *LDH*, 1: 462.

58. Hume to Boufflers, October 31, 1764, *LDH*, 1: 476.

59. Ibid.

60. Hume to Boufflers, December 10, 1764, *LDH*, 1: 486.

61. Undated note by Boufflers, quoted in *LDH*, 1: 486, n. 1.

6. A STONE'S THROW FROM PARIS

1. The account is based on Rousseau's version of events in the *Confessions*, book 12, in *The Collected Writings of Rousseau*, Roger D. Masters and Christopher Kelly, gen. eds., 10 vols. to date (Hanover, N.H.: Dartmouth College/University Press of New England, 1990–), 5: 621–22.

2. Quoted in Lester G. Crocker, *Jean-Jacques Rousseau: The Prophetic Voice, 1758–1778* (New York 1974), 244.

3. Hume to Marie-Charlotte Hippolyte de Campet de Saujon, Comtesse de Boufflers, January or February 1765, *LDH*, 1: 493.

4. Hume to Boufflers, January 26, 1765, *LDH*, 1: 493.

5. Rousseau, *Confessions*, 611.

6. See Maurice Cranston, *The Solitary Self: Jean-Jacques Rousseau in Exile and Adversity* (Chicago: University of Chicago Press, 1997), 18–20; James Boswell, *Boswell in Holland, 1763–1764*, ed. Frederick A. Pottle (New Haven: Yale University Press, 1952), 277.

7. Quoted in David Edmonds and John Eidenow, *Rousseau's Dog: Two Great Thinkers at War in the Age of Enlightenment* (New York: HarperCollins, 2006), 33.

8. Rousseau, *Confessions*, 592.

9. Cranston, *Solitary Self*, 104.

10. Rousseau, *Confessions*, 614.

11. Friedrich Melchior Baron von Grimm, *Correspondance littéraire*, ed. Jean Maurice Tourneux, 16 vols. (Paris: Garnier, 1877–82), October 1, 1765, 6: 381–82.

12. Jean-Jacques Rousseau, *The Reveries of the Solitary Walker*, in *Collected Writings*, 8: 42.

13. Rousseau, *Confessions*, 625.

14. Rousseau, *Reveries*, 64, 43.

15. Rousseau, *Confessions*, 630, 628–29.

16. Rousseau, *Reveries*, 44.

17. Ibid., 46.

18. Rousseau, *Confessions*, 631.

19. François-Joseph de Conzié to Rousseau, March 15, 1764, *CC*, 24: 225; Prince de Würtemberg to Rousseau, March 18, 1764, *CC*, 24: 247–48. For Rousseau on Conzié, see *Confessions*, 179.

20. Rousseau to Lord Marischal Keith, January 26, 1765, *CC*, 28: 194.

21. Jean-Jacques Rousseau, *Julie; or, the New Heloise* (part 2, letter 3), in *Collected Writings*, 6: 162–63.

22. Rousseau to Keith, January 26, 1765, *CC*, 28: 194.

23. Marquise de Verdelin to Rousseau, October 10, 1765, *CC*, 27: 99–100.

24. Keith to Hume, October 2, 1762, *LDH*, 1: 364.

25. Boufflers to Hume, June 14, 1762, *LDH*, 2: 367–68.

26. Hume to Boufflers, July 1, 1762, *LDH*, 1: 363.

27. Hume to Rousseau, July 2, 1762, *LDH*, 1: 364–65.

28. Rousseau to Hume, February 19, 1763, *LDH*, 2: 382.

29. Hume to Boufflers, January 22, 1763, *LDH*, 1: 371–75.

30. Keith to Hume, March 22, 1765, *CC*, 24: 281–82; Keith to Rousseau, March 27, 1765, *CC*, 24: 316–17. See also Keith to Rousseau, April 20, 1765, *CC*, 25: 144–45.

31. Rousseau to Verdelin, October 18, 1765, *CC*, 27: 137.

32. Rousseau to Karl Emmanuel von Graffenreid, October 20, 1765, *CC*, 27: 147.

33. Quoted in Cranston, *Solitary Self*, 75.

34. Rousseau to Graffenried, October 17, 1765, *CC*, 27: 131.

35. Rousseau to Thérèse Le Vasseur, October, 30, 1765, *CC*, 27: 197–98.

36. Rousseau to Le Vasseur, November 4, 1765, *CC*, 27: 217.

37. Rousseau to Abraham Pury, November 8, 1765, *CC*, 27: 235.

38. Keith to Rousseau, November 19, 1765, *CC*, 27: 284.

39. Hume to Rousseau, October 22, 1765, *LDH*, 1: 525–27.

40. Pierre-Alexandre Du Peyrou to Rousseau, November 25, 1765, *CC*, 27: 304–5.

41. Rousseau to Verdelin, November 14, 1765, *CC*, 27: 262.

42. Rousseau to Hume, December 4, 1765, *CC*, 28: 17.

7. FIRST IMPRESSIONS

1. Rousseau to Pierre Guy, December 7, 1765, *CC*, 28: 21–22.

2. Rousseau to Alexis-Claude Clairaut, March 3, 1765, *CC*, 24: 126.

3. Hume to Clairaut, ed. n., Rousseau to Clairaut, March 3, 1765, *CC*, 24: 126.

4. Rousseau to Jean-Jacques de Luze, December 16, 1765, *CC*, 28: 48.

5. Rousseau to the Marquise de Verdelin, December 17, 1765, *CC*, 28: 51.

6. Friedrich Melchior Baron von Grimm, *Correspondance littéraire,* ed. Jean Maurice Tourneux, 16 vols. (Paris: Garnier, 1877–82), January 1, 1766, 6: 457–58.

7. Rousseau to Marianne de la Tour, December 24, 1765, *CC*, 28: 87.

8. Denis Diderot to Sophie Volland, December 20, 1765, *CC*, 28: 73.

9. Lester G. Crocker, *Jean-Jacques Rousseau: The Prophetic Voice, 1758–1778* (New York 1974), 49.

10. Jean-Jacques Rousseau, *Confessions,* in *The Collected Writings of Rousseau,* Roger D. Masters and Christopher Kelly, gen. eds., 10 vols. to date (Hanover, N.H.: Dartmouth College/University Press of New England, 1990–), 5: 454–55.

11. Jean-Batptiste Tollot to Gabriel Seigneux de Correvon, August 1745, *CC*, 3: 341, cited by Leo Damrosch, *Jean-Jacques Rousseau: Restless Genius* (New York: Houghton Mifflin, 2005), 264. For the amount of Rousseau's bill to Conti, Marie-Charlotte Hippolyte de Campet de Saujon, Comtesse de Boufflers, to Rousseau, July 12, 1761, *CC*, 9: 59.

12. For details on the Temple, see Thirza Vallois, *Around and About Paris: From the Dawn of Time to the Eiffel Tower* (Paris: Iliad, 1995), 77–97.

13. Maurice Cranston, *The Solitary Self: Jean-Jacques Rousseau in Exile and Adversity* (Chicago: University of Chicago Press, 1997), 153.

14. Although unable on the earlier occasion to witness the child's feats on the violin, Rousseau remarked on them in a note he added to *Emile,* the work whose publication led to his flight from the city. See Jean-Jacques Rousseau, *Emile; or, On Education,* trans. and ed. Allan Bloom (New York: Basic, 1979), 147n.

15. Rousseau to Alexandre Du Peyrou, January 1, 1766, *CC*, 28: 146.

16. Hume to Hugh Blair, December 28, 1765, *LDH*, 1: 527–29.

17. Ibid., 529.

18. Ibid., 530–31.

19. Jean le Rond d'Alembert to Rousseau, June 15, 1762, *CC*, 11: 82–83; André Morellet to Hume, December 31, 1765, *CC*, 28: 142.

20. See Jean Starobinski, *Jean-Jacques Rousseau: Transparence and Obstruction,* trans. Arthur Goldhammer (Chicago: University of Chicago Press, 1988), 84–90. See also Christopher Kelly, "Rousseau's Philosophic Dream," *Interpretation* 23, no. 3 (1996): 417–44.

21. Hume to Blair, December 28, 1765, *LDH*, 1: 530.

22. Ibid.

23. Ibid.

24. Hume to Blair, February 11, 1766, *LDH*, 2: 13.

25. Hume to Boufflers January 19, 1766, *LDH*, 2: 2.

26. André Morellet, *Mémoires,* quoted in ed. n. to Rousseau, *CC*, 28: 143.

27. Robert Liston to Henrietta Ramage, January 13, 1766, *CC*, 28: 187–88.

28. Hume to Blair, December 28, 1765, *LDH*, 1: 527–31.

29. Rousseau to de Luze, December 26, 1765, *CC*, 28: 107.

30. Rousseau to Du Peyrou, January 1, 1766, *CC*, 28: 145.

31. Verdelin to Rousseau, January 3, 1766, *CC*, 28: 154–55.

32. Quoted in Cranston, *Solitary Self*, 159.

33. Hume to Boufflers, January 19, 1766, *LDH*, 2: 2.

8. A PUBLIC SPECTACLE

1. William Rouet to William Mure, January 10, 1766, *CC*, 28: 171.

2. Quoted in Maurice Cranston, *The Solitary Self: Jean-Jacques Rousseau in Exile and Adversity* (Chicago: University of Chicago Press, 1997), 161.

3. *Gazette d'Utrecht*, January 21, 1766, rpt. in *CC*, 28: 189.

4. Voltaire to Etienne Noël Damilaville, January 15, 1766, *CC*, 28: 193.

5. Hume to the Marquise de Barbentane, February 16, 1766, *LDH*, 2: 15.

6. See Ian R. Christie, *Wars and Revolutions: Britain, 1700–1815* (Cambridge: Harvard University Press, 1982), chap. 3.

7. Cranston, *Solitary Self*, 161.

8. Charles-Geneviève-Louis-Auguste-André-Timothée Éon de Beaumont to Rousseau, February 20, 1766, *CC*, 28: 313–17. This letter is only partly quoted and translated by Gary Kates, who omits d'Eon's postscript dealing with "our common friend M. Hume." See Kates, *Monsieur d'Eon Is a Woman: A Tale of Political Intrigue and Sexual Masquerade* (Baltimore: Johns Hopkins University Press, 2001). A year before d'Eon's letter to Rousseau, Hume had been pulled into the diplomatic vortex created by the chevalier's machinations when d'Eon's accusation against the newly appointed French ambassador for plotting against his life had gone to court and Louis XV's foreign minister asked Hume why George III had not intervened.

9. In *Monsieur d'Eon Is a Woman*, Kates argues persuasively that d'Eon was neither a transsexual nor a transvestite but instead made a deliberate intellectual decision to demonstrate his alienation from French political life. Oddly, while Kates mined Rousseau's writings on gender to explain d'Eon's decision, he omits any mention of Rousseau's own decision, no less deliberate, to don his caftan.

10. Quoted in Cranston, *Solitary Self*, 33–34.

11. Rousseau to Marie-Charlotte Hippolyte de Campet de Saujon, Comtesse de Boufflers, January 18, 1766, *CC*, 28: 198.

12. Hume to John Home, February 24, 1766, *LDH*, 2: 7.

13. Hume to Barbentane, February 16, 1766, *LDH*, 2: 16.

14. John Stewart to Hume, November 15, 1765, *CC*, 26: 267.

15. Hume to Boufflers, January 19, 1766, *LDH*, 2: 3.

16. Jean-Jacques Rousseau, *Essay on the Origin of Languages*, in *The Collected Writings of Rousseau*, Roger D. Masters and Christopher Kelly, gen. eds., 10 vols. to date (Hanover, N.H.: Dartmouth College/University Press of New England, 1990–), 7:

304. For a discussion of the drafting of the *Essay*, see the editor's introduction to this volume, xxvii.

17. Hume to Hugh Blair, March 25, 1766, *LDH*, 2: 31.

18. Ian Macintyre, *Garrick: A Life* (London: Allen Lane, 1999), 140.

19. Quoted in Harry William Pedicord, *The Theatrical Public in the Time of Garrick* (New York: Columbia University Press, 1954), 44–45.

20. Quoted in Cranston, *Solitary Self*, 162.

21. Hume to Barbentane, February 16, 1766, *LDH*, 2: 15.

22. Christopher Hibbert, *George III: A Personal History* (New York: Penguin, 1998), 47.

23. David Garrick, *Zara*, in *The Plays of David Garrick*, 7 vols. (Carbondale: Southern Illinois University Press, 1980), 6: 146. The Prologue, written by Colley Cibber for Aaron Hill's version, was often used by Garrick, including on the evening of January 23, 1765.

24. Dougald MacMillan, *Drury Lane Calendar, 1747–1776* (Oxford: Oxford University Press, 1938), 117.

25. Jean-Jacques Rousseau, *Letter to d'Alembert on the Theater*, in *Collected Writings*, 10: 291.

26. Cranston, *Solitary Self*, 80.

27. Rousseau, *Letter to d'Alembert*, 300.

28. Garrick, *Zara*, 182.

29. David Garrick, *Lethe*, in *Plays*, 1: 14–15.

30. Hume to Home, February 2, 1766, *LDH*, 2: 8. See also Hume to Barbentane, February 16, 1766, *LDH*, 2: 15.

31. Joseph Cradock, *Literary and Miscellaneous Memoirs*, 4 vols. (London: J. B. Nichols, 1828), 1: 205–6.

32. Ibid., 1: 206.

33. Denis Diderot, *The Paradox of Acting*, trans. Walter Herries Pollock (New York: Hill and Wang, 1957), 33, 19.

34. Quoted in Macintyre, *Garrick*, 117, 345.

35. Sarah Lennox Bunbury to Sarah O'Brien, February 5, 1766, *CC*, 28: 273.

36. Stépahnie-Félicité de Genlis, *Mémoires*, 2 vols. (Paris: Firmin-Didot, 1928), 1: 101–5.

37. Paul-Henri Thiry, Baron d'Holbach to David Garrick, February 9, 1766, *CC*, 28: 289.

38. Rousseau to the Marquis and Marquise de Ars, January 22, 1766, *CC*, 28: 218.

39. Hume to Boufflers, January 19, 1766, *LDH*, 2: 2.

40. Hume to Barbentane, February 16, 1766, *LDH*, 2: 14.

41. Hume to Blair, March 25, 1766, *LDH*, 2: 29.

42. Rousseau, *Essay on the Origin of Languages,* 322.

43. Quoted in Lester G. Crocker, *Jean-Jacques Rousseau: The Prophetic Voice, 1758–1778* (New York 1974), 223.

9. POSES AND IMPOSTURES

1. Maurice Cranston, *The Noble Savage: Jean-Jacques Rousseau, 1754–1762* (Chicago: University of Chicago Press, 1991), 315.

2. In the published version of the correspondence with Rousseau, Hume claims that it was Ramsay who first proposed to draw Rousseau's portrait and then make a present of it to Hume, a claim that differs from other accounts in the question of whose initiative the portrait was. See *A Concise and Genuine Account of the Dispute Between Mr. Hume and Mr. Rousseau,* in *Philosophical Works of David Hume,* 4 vols. (London: Black and Tate, 1826), Hume's note to 1: lxviii.

3. Ramsay quoted in Edgar Wind, *Hume and the Heroic Portrait* (Oxford: Oxford University Press, 1986), 3.

4. Alistair Smart, *The Life and Art of Allan Ramsay* (London: Routledge Kegan Paul, 1952), 124.

5. Alistair Smart, *Allan Ramsay: Painter, Essayist and Man of the Enlightenment* (New Haven: Yale University Press, 1992), 208.

6. See Robert Mankin's insightful article, "Authority, Success, and the Philosopher: Hume vs. Rousseau," in *"Better in France?": The Circulation of Ideas Across the Channel in the Eighteenth Century,* ed. Frédéric Ogée (Lewisburg, Pa.: Bucknell University Press, 2005), 177–200.

7. Here, too, reigns some confusion: the gold-embossed print on the binding is now too dull to be read, but most scholars concur that it originally carried Tacitus's name.

8. Rousseau gave these details in his last work, *Rousseau Judge of Jean-Jacques,* written several years after the fact and colored by Rousseau's emotional instability. See *Rousseau Judge of Jean-Jacques: Dialogues,* in *The Collected Writings of Rousseau,* Roger D. Masters and Christopher Kelly, gen. eds., 10 vols. to date (Hanover, N.H.: Dartmouth College/University Press of New England, 1990–), 1: 91–94.

9. Hume to John Home, March 22, 1766, *LDH,* 2: 27.

10. See Rousseau to Pierre-Alexandre Du Peyrou, December 24, 1765, *CC,* 28: 88–89; Du Peyrou to Rousseau, October 28, 1765, *CC,* 27: 193.

11. James Boswell, *Boswell on the Grand Tour: Italy, Corsica, and France, 1755–1766,* ed. Frank Brady and Frederick Pottle (New Haven: Yale University Press, 1955), particularly entries for January 27–30, 1766, pp. 272–79.

12. Hume to Marie-Charlotte Hippolyte de Campet de Saujon, Comtesse de Boufflers, January 12, 1766, *LDH,* 2: 11.

13. Boswell, *Italy, Corsica, and France,* 279. Boswell's account of his dalliance with

Thérèse (covering the period from February 1–11, 1766) is the only portion of his journals that was torn out by Boswell's heirs, but the original editor and publisher of the journals, Colonel Isham, wrote down a summary of the episode.

14. Ibid., 277–79.

15. Ibid.

16. Ibid., 280–83.

17. Hume to the Marquise de Barbentane, February 16, 1766, *LDH*, 2: 15–16.

18. Hume to William Fitzherbert, February 25, 1766, *CC*, 28: 328.

19. Daniel Malthus to Rousseau, January 16, 1766, *CC*, 28: 194–95; Malthus to Rousseau, February 24, 1766, *CC*, 28: 324–25.

20. Louis Courtois, *Le Séjour de Jean-Jacques Rousseau* (Geneva: Slatkine Reprints, 1970), 29–32.

21. Hume to Hugh Blair, March 25, 1766, *LDH*, 2: 29–30.

22. Hume to Home, March 22, 1766, *LDH*, 2 26; Hume to Fitzherbert, March 4, 1766, *NLDH*, 132–33.

23. Hume gives two largely similar accounts of this episode in letters to Blair (March 25, 1766, *LDH*, 2: 29–30) and Boufflers (April 3, 1766, *LDH*, 2: 36).

24. Smart, *Allan Ramsay*, 206. Smart does not offer any references, however, for this meeting—one which, moreover, conflicts with the dating of Hume's March 4 letter to Fitzherbert.

25. Hume to Rousseau, March 10 or 17, 1766, *LDH*, 2: 25.

26. Paul-Henri Thiry, Baron d'Holbach to Hume, March 16, 1766, *CC*, 29: 39–40.

27. Hume to Boufflers, April 3, 1766, *LDH*, 2: 36.

28. Hume to Blair, March 25, 1766, *LDH*, 2: 28–29.

29. Hume to Boufflers, January 19, 1766, *LDH*, 2: 1–2.

30. Hume to Blair, March 25, 1766, *LDH*, 2: 29.

31. David Hume, *A Treatise of Human Nature*, ed. L. A. Selby-Bigge (Oxford: Oxford University Press, 1975), 264.

32. Hume to Rousseau, March 22, 1766, *LDH*, 2: 27.

33. Hume to Rousseau, March 27, 1766, *LDH*, 2: 33.

34. See Courtois, *Le Séjour de Jean-Jacques Rousseau*, 35–36.

35. Rousseau to Richard Davenport, March 22, 1766, *CC*, 29: 47–48.

36. Rousseau to Hume, March 22, 1766, *CC*, 29: 49.

37. Rousseau to Davenport, March 22, 1766, *CC*, 29: 48.

38. Rousseau to Hume, March 22, 1766, *CC*, 29: 49.

39. Hume to Rousseau, March 30, 1766, *LDH*, 2: 33.

40. Rousseau to Hume, March 29, 1766, *CC*, 29: 66–67.

41. See Courtois, *Le Séjour de Jean-Jacques Rousseau*, 39; Rousseau to Marianne-Françoise de Luze, May 10, 1766, *CC*, 29: 198–99.

42. Rousseau to Du Peyrou, March 29, 1766, *CC*, 29: 72–73.

43. Rousseau to Du Peyrou, June 21, 1766, *CC*, 29: 266.

44. Reproduced in *CC*, 30: 3.

45. Rousseau to de Luze, May 10, 1766, *CC*, 29: 198–99.

46. See Jean-Jacques Rousseau, Letters to the Duchess of Portland, in *Collected Writings*, 8: 314 (ed. n. 178).

47. For these and the following anecdotes, see William Howitt, *Visits to Remarkable Places* (London: Longmans, 1840), 503–16. Another valuable source is J. H. Broome's article "Jean-Jacques Rousseau in Staffordshire, 1766–1767," in *University of Keele Occasional Papers* (1966), 3–24. Our thanks to Professor Malcolm Crook at the University of Keele for this reference.

48. Charles Darwin, *The Life of Erasmus Darwin*, ed. Desmond King-Hele (Cambridge: Cambridge University Press, 2003), 47. No such correspondence exists between Erasmus Darwin and Rousseau, and so the story of their meeting cannot be verified. A slightly different version of the story is related by Howitt, *Visits to Remarkable Places*, 515. For more on the Lunar Society, see Jenny Uglow, *The Lunar Men: The Friends Who Made the Future, 1730–1810* (London: Faber and Faber, 2002). For more on the literary and intellectual blossoming centered in Lichfield, see John Brewer, *The Pleasures of the Imagination: English Culture in the Eighteenth Century* (Chicago: University of Chicago Press, 1997), chap. 15.

49. Mary Dewes to Rousseau, November 29, 1766, *CC*, 31: 224.

50. Rousseau to Dewes, December 9, 1766, *CC*, 31: 247.

51. See Dewes to Rousseau, November 29, 1766, *CC*, 31: 224.

52. Davenport to Hume, May 14, 1766, *CC*, 29: 212.

53. Courtois, *Le Séjour de Jean-Jacques Rousseau*, 50–53.

54. Rousseau to Du Peyrou, June 14, 1766, *CC*, 29: 260–61.

55. Davenport to Hume, June 23, 1766, *CC*, 29: 276–77.

56. Maurice Cranston, *The Solitary Self: Jean-Jacques Rousseau in Exile and Adversity* (Chicago: University of Chicago Press, 1997), 18–19, 38–39.

57. Hume to Boufflers, January 19, 1766, *LDH*, 2: 3.

58. Hume to Boufflers, January 12, 1766, *LDH*, 2: 8–9. As the editorial notes indicate, this letter is almost certainly incorrectly dated, and was probably written in the beginning of February.

59. Hume to Boufflers, January 19, 1766, *LDH*, 2: 3.

60. Lord Marischal Keith to Rousseau, c. March 3, 1766, *CC*, 29: 13.

61. See Hume to Boufflers, April 3, 1766, *LDH*, 2: 37.

62. Hume to Henry Seymour Conway, April 5, 1766, *LDH*, 2: 38.

63. Hume to Rousseau, May 3, 1766, *LDH*, 2: 40–41.

64. [Horace Walpole,] "Letter from the King of Prussia to Rousseau," rpt. in *CC*, 28: 345 (appendix 431).

65. Horace Walpole to Thomas Gray, January 25, 1766, *Letters of Horace Walpole*,

2 vols. (New York: Putnam, 1890), 1: 42; David Edmonds and John Eidenow, *Rousseau's Dog: Two Great Thinkers at War in the Age of Enlightenment* (New York: HarperCollins, 2006), 160.

66. Horace Walpole to Conway, January 12, 1766, *CC*, 28: 178. For the role of Walpole in the quarrel between Rousseau and Hume, see Frederick A. Pottle, "The Part Played by Horace Walpole and James Boswell in the Quarrel Between Rousseau and Hume: A Reconsideration," in *Horace Walpole: Writer, Politician, and Connoisseur*, ed. Warren Hasting Smith (New Haven: Yale University Press), 255–342. Our thanks to James J. Caudle for bringing this essay to our attention.

67. Edmonds and Eidenow, *Rousseau's Dog*, chap. 13.

68. Hume to Barbentane, February 16, 1766, *LDH*, 2: 16.

69. Hume to Boufflers, January 12, 1766, *LDH*, 2: 10.

70. Rousseau to Du Peyrou, March 14, 1766, *CC*, 29: 29.

71. Hume to Boufflers, May 16, 1766, *LDH*, 2: 46.

72. See Rousseau to Guillaume-Chrétien de Lamoignon de Malesherbes, May 10, 1766, *CC*, 29: 191.

73. See *CC*, 29: 299–305 (appendix 437).

74. Hume to Boufflers, May 16, 1766, *LDH*, 2: 46.

75. See *CC*, 29: 305–6 (appendix 438).

76. Hume to Rousseau, May 17, 1766, *LDH*, 2: 49.

77. See Theodore Besterman, *Voltaire* (Oxford: Oxford University Press, 1976), 500–501.

78. Voltaire, *Lettre au Docteur Pansophe*, in Voltaire, *Oeuvres complètes*, ed. Louis Moland, 51 vols. (Paris: Garnier, 1879), 26: 19–27.

79. Hume to Rousseau, May 3, 1766, *LDH*, 2: 41–42.

80. Rousseau to Conway, May 21, 1766, *CC*, 29: 205–6.

81. Hume to Boufflers, May 16, 1766, *LDH*, 2: 45–46.

82. Hume to Rousseau, May 17, 1766, *LDH*, 2: 48–49.

83. Hume to Davenport, June 19, 1766, *LDH*, 2: 51; Hume to Davenport, June 1766, *LDH*, 2: 52–53.

84. Hume to Rousseau, June 19, 1766, *LDH*, 2: 51–52.

85. See Hume to Lord Hertford, February 27, 1766, and May 8, 1766, *LDH*, 2: 18–23, 42–44.

86. Hume to Rousseau, May 19, 1766, *LDH*, 2: 53–54.

10. HUME, JUDGE OF LE BON DAVID

1. Rousseau to James Boswell, August 4, 1766, *CC*, 30: 203.

2. Rousseau to Hume, June 23, 1766, *CC*, 29: 274–75.

3. Ibid.

4. Hume to Hugh Blair, March 25, 1766, *LDH*, 2: 30; Hume to Marie-Charlotte Hippolyte de Campet de Saujon, Comtesse de Boufflers, April 3, 1766, *LDH*, 2: 36.

5. Rousseau to Hume, June 23, 1766, *CC*, 29: 275.

6. Hume to Rousseau, June 26, 1766, *LDH*, 2: 55–56.

7. Ibid., 56.

8. Ibid.

9. See Maurice Cranston, *The Solitary Self: Jean-Jacques Rousseau in Exile and Adversity* (Chicago: University of Chicago Press, 1997), 100.

10. Rousseau to François Henri d'Ivernois, March 31, 1766, *CC*, 29: 79.

11. Rousseau to the Marquise de Verdelin, April 9, 1766, *CC*, 29: 99–101. See also Rousseau to Verdelin, May 25, 1766, *CC*, 29: 221–23.

12. Rousseau to Guillaume-Chrétien de Lamoignon de Malesherbes, May 10, 1766, *CC*, 29: 188–94.

13. Lord Marischal Keith to Rousseau, April 26, 1766, *CC*, 29: 152. See also de Verdelin to Rousseau, April 23, 1766, *CC*, 29: 134–35.

14. Rousseau to Pierre-Alexandre Du Peyrou, May 31, 1766, *CC*, 29: 237.

15. Hume to Richard Davenport, June 26, 1766, *LDH*, 2: 54.

16. Rousseau to Hume, July 10, 1766, *CC*, 30: 29. The entire letter comprises pp. 29–46. We will dispense with specific page citations for the passages we quote throughout this chapter.

17. For the drafts of Rousseau's letter to Hume of July 10, 1766, see *CC*, vol. 30.

18. See Dena Goodman, "The Hume-Rousseau Affair: From Private Querelle to Public Procès," in *Eighteenth-Century Studies* 25 (Winter 1991–92): 171–201.

19. Note a to Rousseau to Hume, July 10, 1766, *CC*, 30: 47.

20. Jean-Jacques Rousseau, *Rousseau Judge of Jean-Jacques: Dialogues*, in *The Collected Writings of Rousseau*, Roger D. Masters and Christopher Kelly, gen. eds., 10 vols. to date (Hanover, N.H.: Dartmouth College/University Press of New England, 1990–), 1: 5.

21. Rousseau to Hume, July 10, 1766, *CC*, 30: 30.

22. Jean-Jacques Rousseau, *Essay on the Origin of Languages*, in *Collected Writings*, 7: 290.

23. Allan Bloom, Introduction to Jean-Jacques Rousseau, *Emile; or, On Education*, trans. and ed. Bloom (New York: Basic, 1979), 5.

24. Quoted in Hume, *A Concise and Genuine Account*, lxxii. The entire work comprises xxxvii–cviii of the volume of Hume's philosophical writings from which it is drawn, with Rousseau's letter to Hume of July 10, 1766, covering lxv–c.

25. Quoted ibid., lxxiv.

26. Notes i, k, n, and q to Rousseau to Hume, July 10, 1766, *CC*, 30: 48–51.

27. Hume, *A Concise and Genuine Account*, note to lxxvii.

28. Note r to Rousseau to Hume, July 10, 1766, *CC*, 30: 51.

29. Note t ibid.

30. Notes x and y to Rousseau to Hume, July 10, 1766, *CC*, 30: 51–52.

31. Notes aaa and bbb ibid., 54.

32. According to Louis A. Sass, the "reality of everything the patient notices can seem heightened, as if each object were, somehow, being hyperbolically so. . . . The mood is such that no object or occurrence can seem accidental; everything is 'just so.'" See his *Madness and Modernism: Insanity in the Light of Modern Art, Literature, and Thought* (Cambridge: Harvard University Press: 1998), 52.

33. Hume to Mme la Présidente de Meinières, July 25, 1766, *LDH*, 2: 152.

34. Hume to Rousseau, July 22, 1766, *LDH*, 2: 66–67.

35. Ibid., 67.

36. Ibid.

37. Ibid., 68.

38. Ibid.

39. See Clifford Geertz's elaboration of Gilbert Ryle's notion of "thick description" in *The Interpretation of Cultures* (New York: Basic, 1973), 3–30.

40. David Hume, *An Enquiry Concerning Human Understanding*, ed. L. A. Selby-Bigge, 3rd ed. (Oxford: Oxford University Press, 1975), 162.

41. Arthur M. Melzer provides several important insights in his article "Rousseau and the Modern Cult of Sincerity," in *The Legacy of Rousseau*, ed. Clifford Orwin and Nathan Tarcov (Chicago: University of Chicago Press, 1997), 274–95.

42. Rousseau, *Emile*, 280. See Arthur M. Melzer, "The Origin of the Counter-Enlightenment: Rousseau and the New Religion of Sincerity," *American Political Science Review* 90 (June 1996): 344–60.

43. As Melzer has argued, from "the standpoint of Rousseauian selfhood it is less important to be true to reality than to be true to oneself" ("Rousseau and the Modern Cult of Sincerity," 289).

44. David Hume, *A Treatise of Human Nature*, ed. L. A. Selby-Bigge (Oxford: Oxford University Press, 1975), 261–62.

11. AN ENLIGHTENMENT TRAGEDY

1. David Hume, *A Treatise of Human Nature*, ed. L. A. Selby-Bigge (Oxford: Oxford University Press, 1975), 265.

2. Hume to Hugh Blair, July 1, 1766, *LDH*, 2: 57.

3. Ibid., 58.

4. Hume to Richard Davenport, July 3, 1766, *LDH*, 2: 58.

5. Hume to Marie-Charlotte Hippolyte de Campet de Saujon, Comtesse de Boufflers, July 15, 1766, *LDH*, 2: 59–61.

6. Hume to Davenport July 15, 1766, *LDH*, 2: 64–65.

7. Ibid.

8. Ernest Campbell Mossner, *Life of David Hume*, 2nd ed. (Oxford: Oxford University Press, 1980), 217.

9. David Hume, *An Enquiry Concerning Human Understanding*, ed. L. A. Selby-Bigge, 3rd ed. (Oxford: Oxford University Press, 1975), 91.

10. Hume to Davenport, July 15, 1766, *LDH*, 2: 64–65.

11. Blair to Hume, July 10, 1766, *CC*, 30: 82.

12. Adam Smith to Hume, July 6, 1766, *CC*, 30: 16–17.

13. Paul-Henri Thiry, Baron d'Holbach to Hume, July 7, 1766, *LDH*, 2: 409–11.

14. David Edmonds and John Eidenow, *Rousseau's Dog: Two Great Thinkers at War in the Age of Enlightenment* (New York: HarperCollins, 2006), 184.

15. Mossner, *Life of David Hume*, 526. The sources for these passages in Hume's lost letter are the Encyclopedist Jean-François Marmontel's *Mémoires* and a letter of July 7, 1766, from Mme la Présidente de Meinières to Hume, rpt. in *LDH*, 2: 411–23. For Hume's reply to this letter, see *LDH*, 2: 68–72.

16. Julie de Lespinasse and Jean Le Rond d'Alembert to Hume, July 6, 1766, *LDH*, 2: 408.

17. Boufflers to Hume, July 22 and 25, 1766, *LDH*, 2: 415–19.

18. Hume to Boufflers, August 12, 1766, *LDH*, 2: 77.

19. Hume to d'Alembert, July 15, 1766, *NLDH*, 136–42.

20. D'Alembert to Hume, August 5, 1766, *CC*, 30: 207.

21. Ibid.

22. D'Alembert to Hume, July 21, 1766, *CC*, 30: 130–32.

23. Hume to Horace Walpole, July 26, 1766, *LDH*, 2: 71; Walpole to Hume, July 26, 1766, *CC*, 30: 172–73.

24. Anne-Robert-Jacques Turgot to Hume, July 23, 1766, *CC*, 30: 147–50.

25. Hume to Turgot, August 5, 1766, *LDH*, 2: 75; ellipsis in original. For examples of his friends' view of Rousseau's actions, see Lord Marischal Keith to Hume, August 15, 1766, *CC*, 30: 244–45; Boufflers to Hume, September 6, 1766, *CC*, 30: 327.

26. Boufflers to Rousseau, July 27, 1766, *CC*, 30: 174–75.

27. Rousseau to Boufflers, August 30, 1766, *CC*, 30: 291–93. Rousseau explains the delay in answering Boufflers's letter of July 27 by saying that it had reached him only a few days earlier.

28. Rousseau to Pierre Guy, August 1, 1766, *CC*, 30: 196–97.

29. Hume to Boufflers, July 15, 1766, *LDH*, 2: 62.

30. Hume to Davenport, September 2, 1766, *LDH*, 2: 86–87.

31. Holbach to Hume, September 1, 1766, *CC*, 30: 308–9.

32. Hume to Davenport, September 2, 1766, *LDH*, 2: 86–87.

33. Hume to William Strahan, October 1766, *LDH*, 2: 95.

34. Hume to Walpole, November 20, 1766, *LDH*, vol. 2, 108. See also Hume to Walpole, October 30, 1766, *LDH*, 2: 98.

35. David Hume, *A Concise and Genuine Account of the Dispute Between Mr. Hume and Mr. Rousseau*, in *Philosophical Works of David Hume*, 4 vols. (London: Black and Tate, 1826), 1: cvi.

36. In the diplomatic letter she eventually wrote to Hume, the imperious salonnière reserved her scorn uniquely for Rousseau; Mme du Deffand to Hume, August 13, 1766, *LDH*, 2: 433–34.

37. Meinières to Hume, July 7, 1766, *LDH*, 2: 411–12.

38. Hume to Boufflers, August 12, 1766, *LDH*, 2: 77.

39. Hume to Walpole, November 20, 1766, *LDH*, 2: 108.

40. Hume to d'Alembert, July 15, 1766, *NLDH*, 141.

41. Edmonds and Eidenow tend in *Rousseau's Dog* to assume a contemporary understanding of what is public versus private, and therefore tend to indict Hume for making the affair public.

42. Dena Goodman, "The Hume-Rousseau Affair: From Private Querelle to Public Procès," in *Eighteenth-Century Studies* 25 (Winter 1991–92): 143.

43. Dena Goodman, *The Republic of Letters: A Cultural History of the French Enlightenment* (Ithaca: Cornell University Press, 1994), 237, 235. See also Keith Baker, *Inventing the French Revolution* (Cambridge: Cambridge University Press, 1990), 167–99.

44. Mona Ozouf, "Public Spirit," in *A Critical Dictionary of the French Revolution*, trans. Arthur Goldhammer (Cambridge: Cambridge University Press, 1989), 772.

45. Robert Darnton, *The Great Cat Massacre: And Other Episodes in French Cultural History* (New York: Vintage, 1985), 228, 248.

46. Meinières to Hume, July 7, 1766, *LDH*, 2: 412.

47. Holbach to Hume, July 7, 1766, *LDH*, 2: 410.

48. D'Alembert to Hume, July 21, 1766, *LDH*, 2: 414.

49. Hume to Jean-Jacques Trudaine de Montigny, August 12, 1766, *LDH*, 2: 81.

50. Hume to Turgot, August 5, 1766, *LDH*, 2: 75.

51. Quoted in Donald W. Livingston, *Philosophical Melancholy and Delirium: Hume's Pathology of Philosophy* (Chicago: University of Chicago Press, 1998), 40.

52. Hume to Turgot, September 1766, *LDH*, 2: 88.

12. SO GREAT A NOISE

1. See Mme du Deffand to Horace Walpole, October 21, 1766, *CC*, 31: 48–51.

2. David Hume, *A Concise and Genuine Account of the Dispute Between Mr. Hume and Mr. Rousseau*, in *Philosophical Works of David Hume*, 4 vols. (London: Black and Tate, 1826), 1: viii.

3. See Robert Darnton, "The High Enlightenment and the Low-Life of Literature," in *The Literary Underground of the Old Regime* (Cambridge: Harvard University Press, 1982), 1–40. According to Darnton, Suard "wrote little and had little to say — nothing, it need hardly be added, that would offend the regime. He toed the party line of

the philosophes and collected his reward" (7). Dena Goodman is less critical of Suard's career, describing him as an editor who sought to "shape a citizenry for the Republic of Letters" ("The Hume-Rousseau Affair: From Private Querelle to Public Procès," in *Eighteenth-Century Studies* 25 [Winter 1991–92]: 171–201, quotation at 167).

4. Jean-Baptiste-Antoine Suard to Hume, November 2, 1766, *CC*, 31: 106.

5. Hume to Suard, November 5, 1766, *LDH*, 2: 102.

6. Jean Le Rond d'Alembert to Voltaire, July 16, 1766, *CC*, 30: 108.

7. Voltaire to Etienne-Noël Damilaville, July 30, 1766, *CC*, 30: 188.

8. For one among the many letters sent by Voltaire, see Voltaire to Damilaville, August 11, 1766, *CC*, 30: 232. See Rousseau to Voltaire, May 31, 1765, *CC*, 25: 357.

9. Voltaire to Théodore Tronchin, September 16, 1766, *CC*, 30: 372.

10. Rpt. as Voltaire to Hume, October 24, 1766, *CC*, 31: 55–59. Voltaire made the same pronouncement in a half-dozen private letters to a half-dozen of his regular correspondents on a single day, October 31 (see Voltaire to Elie Bertrand, October 31, 1766, *CC*, 31: 100, including the editorial notes and remark to this letter).

11. Voltaire to James Marriott, February 26, 1766, *CC*, 32: 181.

12. Voltaire to Charles Borde, November 29, 1766, *CC*, 31: 227–28.

13. Friedrich Melchior Baron von Grimm, *Correspondance littéraire*, ed. Jean Maurice Tourneux, 16 vols. (Paris: Garnier, 1877–82), October 15, 1766, 7: 139–46.

14. T. Verax, "Le Rapporteur de bonnefoi," quoted in Goodman, "Hume-Rousseau Affair," 192–93.

15. "Remarques d'un anonyme," quoted ibid., 196.

16. Grimm, *Correspondance littéraire*, October 15, 1766.

17. *Saint James Chronicle*, November 27–29, 1766, rpt. in *CC*, 31: 340 (appendix 465).

18. *Saint James Chronicle*, December 11–13, 1766, rpt. in *CC*, 31: 345 (appendix 469).

19. *Saint James Chronicle*, December 16–18, 1766, rpt. in *CC*, 31: 348 (appendix 471).

20. *Saint James Chronicle*, December 9–11, 1766, rpt. in *CC*, 31: 343 (appendix 467).

21. *Saint James Chronicle*, December 16–18, 1766, rpt. in *CC*, 31: 343–44 (appendix 468).

22. Rpt. in *CC*, 32: 299–300 (appendix 518).

23. Hume to Marie-Charlotte Hippolyte de Campet de Saujon, Comtesse de Boufflers, February 2, 1767, *LDH*, 2: 120. For Boswell's poems and the print, see Frederick A. Pottle, "The Part Played by Horace Walpole and James Boswell in the Quarrel Between Rousseau and Hume: A Reconsideration," in *Horace Walpole: Writer, Politician, and Connoisseur*, ed. Warren Hasting Smith (New Haven: Yale University Press), 285–91.

24. *Saint James Chronicle*, January 13–15, 1767, rpt. in *LDH*, 2: 447.

25. *Gentleman's Magazine*, November 1766, rpt. in *CC*, 31: 336–37 (appendix 461).

26. Jean-Jacques Rousseau, *Letter to d'Alembert on the Theater*, in *The Collected Writings of Rousseau*, Roger D. Masters and Christopher Kelly, gen. eds., 10 vols. to date (Hanover, N.H.: Dartmouth College/University Press of New England, 1990–), 10: 277.

27. *Courrier d'Avignon,* October 4 and November 7, 1766, rpt. in *CC* 31: 327–28 (appendix 459).

28. *Journal Encylopédique,* April 1, 1767, rpt. in *CC,* 33: 300–301 (appendix 544).

29. Goodman, "Hume-Rousseau Affair," 199.

30. Toussaint-Pierre Lenieps to Rousseau, October 30, 1766, *CC,* 31: 96–97; Pierre-Alexandre Du Peyrou to Rousseau, *CC,* 31: 131–32.

31. Hume to Richard Davenport, November 23, 1766, *LDH,* 2: 112–13. For the explanation of the letter, see Hume to John Crawford, December 20, 1766, *NLDH,* 156–57.

32. Rousseau to Davenport, November 27, 1766, *CC,* 31: 214–15.

33. Lord Marischal Keith to Rousseau, September 5, 1766, *CC,* 30: 320.

34. Rousseau to Keith, December 11, 1766, *CC,* 31: 254–55.

35. Keith to Du Peyrou, December 24, 1766, *CC,* 31: 307.

36. Rousseau to Keith, March 19, 1767, *CC,* 32: 224.

37. Rousseau to Du Peyrou, January 8, 1767, *CC,* 32: 27–31.

38. Du Peyrou to Paul Moultou, December 5, 1778, *CC,* 31: 327.

39. Rousseau to the Duchess of Portland, February 12, 1767, in Jean-Jacques Rousseau, *Reveries of the Solitary Walker,* in *Collected Writings,* 8: 177.

40. Davenport to Rousseau, January 27, 1767, *CC,* 32: 75.

41. Rousseau to Davenport, January 31, 1767, *CC,* 32: 76–77.

42. Hume to Hugh Blair, February 24, 1767, *LDH,* 2: 121.

43. Henry Seymour Conway to Davenport, March 18, 1767, *CC,* 32: 222.

44. Hume to William Robertson, March 19, 1767, *LDH,* 2: 131.

45. Rousseau to Conway, March 26, 1767, *CC,* 32: 246–47.

46. Rousseau to Davenport, December 22, 1766, *CC,* 31: 295–96.

47. Rousseau to Davenport, March 2, 1767, *CC,* 32: 196.

48. Rousseau to Du Peyrou, March 2, 1767, *CC,* 32: 199.

49. Rousseau to Davenport, March 21, 1767, *CC,* 32: 230–32.

50. Davenport to Rousseau, March 28, 1767, *CC,* 32: 236.

51. Davenport to Hume, May 4, 1767, *NLDH,* 217.

52. Rousseau to Davenport, April 30, 1767, *CC,* 33: 37.

53. See Du Peyrou to Rousseau, January 27, 1766, *CC,* 28: 234; Rousseau to Jean-François-Maximilien Cerjat, January 18, 1767, *CC,* 32: 53–54.

54. Rousseau to Charles Pratt, Baron Camden, May 5, 1767, *CC,* 33: 44.

55. Hume to Davenport, May 16, 1767, *NLDH,* 163–64.

56. Rousseau to Davenport, May 18, 1767, *CC,* 33: 69.

57. Hume to Davenport, May 9, 1767, *NLDH,* 162.

58. David Edmonds and John Eidenow, *Rousseau's Dog: Two Great Thinkers at War in the Age of Enlightenment* (New York: HarperCollins, 2006), 258.

59. Rousseau to Conway, May 18, 1767, *CC,* 33: 63–67.

60. Hume to Anne-Robert-Jacques Turgot, May 22, 1767, *LDH,* 2: 138–39. See

also Hume to Blair, May 27, 1767, *NLDH*, 168–70, where Hume also remarks on Rousseau's use of the third person in the letter; and Hume to Boufflers, May 22, 1767, *NLDH*, 165–67.

61. See Leo Damrosch, *Jean-Jacques Rousseau: Restless Genius* (New York: Houghton Mifflin, 2005), 432–33.

13. HOW PHILOSOPHERS DIE

1. Hume to Gilbert Elliot, October 16, 1769, *LDH*, 2: 208.

2. Hume to Adam Smith, February 8, 1776, *LDH*, 2: 308.

3. Hume to William Strahan, June 12, 1776, *LDH*, 2: 326.

4. Hume to John Home, June 10, 1776, *LDH*, 2: 325.

5. All quotations in this section are taken from Boswell's sketch, "An Account of My Last Interview with David Hume, ESQ.," in *Boswell in Extremes, 1776–1778*, ed. Charles Weis and Frederick Pottle (New York: McGraw-Hill, 1986), 11–15.

6. Smith to Strahan, November 9, 1776, *LDH*, 2: 450–52.

7. Ibid., 452.

8. David Hume, "The Sceptic," in *Essays Moral, Political, and Literary*, ed. Eugene Miller (Indianapolis: Liberty, 1985), 180.

9. Quoted in Jean Guéhenno, *Jean-Jacques Rousseau*, 2 vols. (London: Routledge and Kegan Paul, 1966; Paris: Gallimard, 1962), 2: 249.

10. Jean-Jacques Rousseau, *Reveries of the Solitary Walker*, in *The Collected Writings of Rousseau*, Roger D. Masters and Christopher Kelly, gen. eds., 10 vols. to date (Hanover, N.H.: Dartmouth College/University Press of New England, 1990–), 8: 10.

11. Ibid., 10–11.

12. This, at least, is Métra's claim in his *Correspondence secrète*, quoted in *Les Rêveries du promeneur solitaire*, ed. S. de Sacy (Paris: Gallimard, 1972), 254.

13. Quoted in Rousseau, *Reveries*, 281 n. 16.

14. Ibid., 11–12.

15. "Knowledge of death and its terrors is one of the first acquisitions that man has made in moving away from the animal condition" (Jean-Jacques Rousseau, *Discourse on the Origin and Foundations of Inequality Among Men*, in *First and Second Discourses*, trans. Roger D. Masters and Judith R. Masters [New York: St. Martin's, 1964], 116).

16. Allan Bloom, Introduction, to Jean-Jacques Rousseau, *Emile; or, On Education*, trans. and ed. Bloom (New York: Basic, 1979), 10.

17. Rousseau, *Emile*, 55.

18. Two contemporary scholars who have written eloquently on this subject are Alexander Nehamas, in *The Art of Living* (Berkeley: University of California Press, 1998), and Pierre Hadot, in *Philosophy as a Way of Life* (Oxford: Oxford University Press, 1995).

19. Rousseau, *Reveries*, 28, 5–7.

20. Hume to Marie-Charlotte Hippolyte de Campet de Saujon, Comtesse de Bouf-flers, August 20, 1776, *LDH*, 2: 335.

21. Jean-Jacques Rousseau, *Confessions*, in *Collected Writings*, 5: 549.

22. Ibid., 71.

23. Jean-Jacques Rousseau, *Confessions*, in *Oeuvres complètes*, 5 vols. (Paris: Galli-mard, 1959–95), 1: 1272 (note a to p. 85). This passage is discussed by Guéhenno, *Jean-Jacques Rousseau*, 2: 191–92, and briefly noted by Leo Damrosch, *Jean-Jacques Rous-seau: Restless Genius* (New York: Houghton Mifflin, 2005), 425. In his last completed work, *Rousseau Judge of Jean-Jacques*, Rousseau briefly mentions Hume's role in the cre-ation of the portrait by Ramsay that made him look like a "Cyclops." Written after his return to Paris and completed in 1776, Rousseau dwells on the "universal plot" to blacken his name, an obsession that first comes fully to light in his reaction to his quarrel with Hume. The work's dialogic form and especially the way in which Rousseau treats himself in the third person as the innocent accused has its roots in his epistolary trial of Hume in the letter of July 1766. *Rousseau Judge of Jean-Jacques: Dialogues*, in *Collected Writings*, 1: 91–95.

24. David Hume, *A Treatise of Human Nature*, ed. L. A. Selby-Bigge (Oxford: Ox-ford University Press, 1975), 264.

25. Hume, "My Own Life," in *Essays*, xxi, xli–xlii.

26. Hume to Richard Davenport, July 1, 1767, *LDH*, 2: 147–48.

27. Simon Blackburn makes this persuasive argument in the last chapter of *Truth: A Guide* (Oxford: Oxford University Press, 2005).

28. Hume, *Treatise*, 359, 365.

29. Hume to Hugh Blair, March 25, 1766, *LDH*, 2: 1135–36.

30. Hume to Anne-Robert-Jacques Turgot, May 22, 1767, *LDH*, 2: 137.

31. Hume to Boufflers, December 23, 1768, *LDH*, 2: 192.

32. Hume to Turgot, September 1766, *LDH*, 2: 91.

33. Hume to Home, March 22, 1766, *LDH*, 2: 27.

34. Hume to Boufflers, January 22, 1763, *LDH*, 1: 373–74.

35. Hume, *Treatise*, 363.

36. David Gauthier, *Rousseau: The Sentiment of Existence* (Cambridge: Cambridge University Press, 2006), 170.

37. Quoted in Terence Penelhum, *Themes in Hume* (Oxford: Oxford University Press, 2000), 4. Rousseau also seemed to recognize this at the end of his life. In *Rousseau Judge of Jean-Jacques*, the character "Rousseau" makes a stunning admission: "But I also know that absolute solitude is a state that is sad and contrary to nature: affectionate feel-ings nourish the soul, communication of ideas enlivens the mind. Our sweetest existence is relative and collective and our true self is not entirely within us" (118).

38. Penelhum, *Themes in Hume*, 4.

Index

Understanding, 87–88; truth and, 187–88, 192; understanding and, 5, 41, 42–43, 74, 82–83, 136, 152, 168–69; Walpole letter and, 144; Wootton Hall arranged by, 1–2, 134–36
Hume, Katherine, 38
Hutcheson, Francis, 48

insanity, 172–73, 182, 197, 207–8
Irvine, Peggy, 37
Ivernois, François-Henri d', 94, 153

Jardine, John, 79
Johnson, Samuel: Boswell and, 9; Boufflers and, 75; Hume and, 38, 200; on Monboddo, 49; on patriotism, 199; Rousseau and, 123; Voltaire and, 66
Julie; or, the New Heloïse (Rousseau): England in, 98; Hume-Rousseau quarrel and, 154, 158–59, 165, 188; publication of, 10–11, 51; Voltaire on, 57, 70, 186; on women, 80; writing of, 27, 28–29, 45

Kames, Lord, 45, 48, 49
Keith, James Francis Edward, 92n
Keith, Marischal George: Hume-Rousseau quarrel and, 153, 159, 193; pensions and, 142–43, 147; Rousseau, exile of, 33, 35, 92, 94, 98–99, 100, 101, 102, 103
knowledge, 23–24, 41–42. *See also* understanding

Lacy, James, 119–20
language: Hume-Rousseau quarrel and, 154, 157; Rousseau and, 117, 122–23, 125, 126–27, 138, 139, 140
La Rochefoucauld, François de, 89
La Tour, Marianne de, 106
Leibniz, Gottfried Wilhelm, 4
Lenieps, Toussaint-Pierre, 192
Le Pelletier de Fargeau, Louis-Michel, 203
Lespinasse, Julie de, 81–82, 174, 176, 177
Lethe (Garrick), 119, 122–23

Letter on French Music (Rousseau), 22–23
Letter on the Deaf and the Dumb (Diderot), 127n
Letters Written from the Countryside (Tronchin), 69
Letters Written from the Mountain (Rousseau), 67–71, 91, 93–94, 153
Letter to d'Alembert (Rousseau), 28, 57, 121, 209
Le Vasseur, Thérèse: Boswell and, 132–33, 149–50; children of, 69; in Dover, 197; at Lake Bienne, 96; in London, 1, 116; in Montmorency, 27; in Môtiers, 32, 34, 35, 36, 90, 94; in Paris, 132, 204; Rousseau, exile of, 101; Rousseau, relationship with, 116–17, 202; at Wootton Hall, 139, 193, 195
Lévée de Voltaire, La (Huber), 63, 65
life, 5, 6–7, 46
Life of Johnson (Boswell), 9
Lisbon, 3
Liston, Robert, 112
Locke, John, 38, 42, 59
Louis XIV, King of France, 58, 61
Louis XV, King of France: Calas Affair and, 63; Conti and, 73, 107; Hume and, 78, 85; Rousseau and, 23, 142
Louis XVI, King of France, 51, 78, 107n
Lunar Society, 140n
Luxembourg, Charles François Frédéric and Madeleine Angélique, Duc and Duchesse de, 30, 92, 106, 132

Madison, James, 47
Malesherbes, Chrétien-Guillaume de Lamoignon de, 30, 153, 177
Mallet, David, 54
Malthus, Daniel, 134, 140
Malthus, Thomas, 134
Mandeville, Bernard, 47
Maria Theresa, Empress of Austria, 76
Marmontel, Jean-François, 80, 81, 176
Martinet, Jacques-Frédéric, 90–91
Meinières, Octavie Guichard Durey de, 180, 181